Local Authorities and Regional Policy in the UK: Attitudes, Representations and the Local Economy

R.M. BALL

D1330518

P·C·P

Paul Chapman
Publishing Ltd

To
Nuala, Kevin, Catriona and, especially, Kieran
who missed out last time.

Copyright © R M Ball 1995.

Paul Chapman Publishing Ltd
144 Liverpool Road
London
N1 1LA

British Library Cataloguing in Publication Data

Ball, R. M.
  Local Authorities and Regional Policy in
  the UK: Attitudes, Representations and
  the Local Economy
  I. Title
  330.941
  ISBN 1-85396-255-4

Typeset by Dorwyn Ltd, Hampshire
Printed and bound by Athenaeum Press, Gateshead, Tyne & Wear

A B C D E F G H   9 8 7 6 5

CONTENTS

ACKNOWLEDGEMENTS

This book could not have been completed without the support of a large number of people and I gratefully acknowledge their contribution.

Although the final product may not reveal it, the book relies to a great extent on the collection and collation of a major data set – local authority (and other) submissions to the 1992/1993 Assisted Areas map review exercise. The feel for the subject area – and the basic data base for underpinning the discussion – both result from this material. As such, all those who supported the assembly of material must take some credit for the production of what, regardless of the book quality, stands as a novel and usable data base. This involves a number of individuals.

In particular, I must thank the various local government officers – some 250 – who provided copies of their submission documents, and occasionally offered useful comments or suggestions, Paul Hawker and colleagues at the DTI in London who willingly provided support by giving access to those submissions not supplied directly and by offering other valuable advice, and the respondents in the supplementary survey. These were: Ray Garside, Stoke-on-Trent City Council (who first alerted me to the review exercise); Caroline Bull, Thanet District Council (now of Thames Valley TEC); Gerard Godfrey, Dumfries and Galloway Regional Council; Brian Hodge, London Borough of Hackney; Peter Jolley, Swale District Council; Dai Larner, Bradford Metropolitan District Council; Graham McWilliams, Alyn and Deeside District Council; Roger Madge, Dover District Council; Barbara Mothershaw, Chester City Council; Sian Rogers, Ellesmere Port and Neston District Council; Paul Roberts, Clwyd County Council; Ken Welsh, East Kent Initiative.

I also received excellent support on the project from my Research Assistants, Chris Attwood and Kieran Mansfield. Additional help came from undergraduate students reading my final year course in economic geography, colleagues in my department who allowed me time off to complete the manuscript, Owen Tucker, who drew the maps and diagrams so professionally, and Jon Stobart, who provided useful last minute comments on the text.

Alan Townsend kindly commented on the draft proposal for the book.

I must also gratefully acknowledge the academic support of Andy Pratt, who commented on the idea and approach, and Rob Imrie, who read an early draft of some of the text, and generally advised from an early stage. The chance to discuss the material with these younger and wiser heads was invaluable, although they can take no responsibility for any errors or inconsistencies.

The book was written in a three-month blast and I cannot fail to acknowledge various friends scattered throughout the UK and other parts of Europe: their moral support was of great value in helping me to retain a modicum of sanity during the production process.

Rick Ball
December 1994

FIGURE ACKNOWLEDGEMENTS

The following illustrations used in the book were drawn directly from the review submissions and originators indicated:

Pan Publications Ltd, Great Yarmouth; Great Yarmouth Borough Council – Figure 4.2; Figure 8.15; Hastings Borough Council – Figure 4.3, Figure 7.1 and Figure 7.2; Steve Wilson, Aquarius Design, Lincoln; Mansfield District Council – Figure 4.4; Bradford Metropolitan Borough Council – Figure 5.3; East Kent Initiative – Figure 5.4; Allerdale Borough Council – Figure 9.1(a); Copeland Borough Council – Figure 6.1; Figure 9.1(b); Portsmouth City Council – Figure 6.2; Figure 8.10; Weymouth and Portland Borough Council for the South Dorset Economic Partnership – Figure 6.3; Figure 9.3; London Borough of Hackney – Figure 7.3; Coventry City Council – Figure 8.2 (top); Rotherham Metropolitan Borough Council – Figure 8.2 (bottom); Brighton Borough Council – Figure 8.3; Great Grimsby Borough Council – Figure 8.4; St Helens Metropolitan Borough Council; Wigan Metropolitan Borough Council – Figure 8.5; Calderdale Metropolitan Borough Council – Figure 8.6; Sedgefield District Council – Figure 8.7; Central Regional Council – Figure 8.8; Lancaster City Council – Figure 8.9; Figure 9.6; Doncaster Metropolitan Borough Council – Figure 8.11; Sheffield City Council – Figure 8.12; Darlington Borough Council – Figure 8.13; Nottinghamshire County Council – Figure 8.14; Suffolk County Council – Figure 9.2; Isle of Wight Development Board; Isle of Wight County Council – Figure 9.4 and Figure 9.5; Arfon Borough Council – Figure 9.7.

Figure 5.1 (drawn by Dave Follows) and Figure 5.2 (drawn by Andy Lawrence) are both reproduced from a chapter by the author in Phillips, A.D.M. (ed) (1993) The Potteries: Continuity and Change in a Staffordshire Conurbation, Allan Sutton, Stroud.

INTRODUCTION

Local Attitudes and the Changing Assisted Areas Map

This is a book about an aspect of spatial economic policy that is firmly set in uncharted territory. It focuses on local sensitivities, representations and reactions to the 1992/1993 review of the Assisted Areas map, building a discussion and analysis around that event. However, it is not just the story of the review. Although it covers the processes and the outcomes that followed, its central concern is to draw out and develop a stream of analyses. The event is thus seen as merely a basis for the analysis of local sensitivities to centrally administered spatial economic policy. Having said that, some useful insights into perceptions of, and attitudes to, the use of regional policy are afforded by the process.

Falling into the Topic

The germ of the idea for the book dates from 1984 and a previous round of regional policy reviews in Britain. It was one of those ideas that we all have from time to time and that we file away for later use. The 1984 review of regional policy by the Thatcher government provided a useful opportunity to collect together, at the time for teaching purposes, some of the local authority responses to the White Paper (Department of Trade and Industry, 1983). Clearly, these contained up-to-date material on local economic conditions and could be used to gain an idea of local attitudes to development, policy and so on.

Twenty or so of these submissions were collected – including those by active metropolitan authorities such as West Yorkshire, Coventry, Greater Manchester, Cleveland and the Greater London Council (GLC) – and they were immensely revealing for the breadth of views and styles of representation that they contained. In a truly fascinating way, the GLC's response called for, amongst an array of sensible reforms (many of which are incidentally still 'live' issues in the 1990s), the inclusion of the whole of Inner London as Assisted Areas, with Hackney and Tower Hamlets as Special Development Areas, and even Westminster as an Intermediate Area (GLC, 1984, p. 5).

It is ironic to think that in 1993 a Conservative government would actually award Assisted Area status to some of these areas. Needless to say, and despite a strong set of arguments, neither Westminster nor any other London Borough secured Assisted Areas status in 1984. However, for one researcher, and probably for others, there was the germ of an idea, coupled with an awareness of all the possibilities that the material provided.

The story now comes forward eight years to June 1992. The 1992/1993 review of the Assisted Areas map – much less significant as it only covered the map and not the actual policy structures – provided another opportunity to engage with this research area. Once again, local authority and, this time, other representations were obtained, the initial intention being to collect thirty or forty for analysis. Eventually, however, as enthusiasm built, and as the potential that such a set of information had was realised, it was decided to obtain as many as possible. The end result was that the project finally obtained copies of, or access to, all the submissions made during the consultation phase of the review (Department of Trade and Industry, Scottish Office and Welsh Office, 1992). This amounted to some 317 local authority representations and many others from individuals, businesses and other agencies.

This information represents a veritable treasure trove of potential and it is from the stream of insights that the material allows, together with some follow-up survey work at the local level, that this book has emerged.

Building an Analysis

In essence, the book builds an assessment around a number of identifiable strengths of the material, which are that it:

- provides an up-to-date review of the condition and standing of regional policy in Britain;
- assesses aspects of the role of local authorities – individually or in partnership – in 1990s local economic development, in particular in terms of the use of resources;
- facilitates the identification and analysis of local authority attitudes to and perceptions of regional policy;
- surveys and assesses the process of policy formation in selected aspects of local authority economic policy, in particular with regard to central–local links and the quest for external resources;
- investigates the ways in which local authorities and other local agencies represent their local economies to the outside world;
- analyses the ways in which local labour market problems (in particular, dimensions of unemployment) are interpreted, articulated and represented by local authorities;
- assesses the importance of peripherality in the perceptions and representations of local authorities;
- assesses the importance of the changing position of key sectors such as defence and the changing attractions of some geographical locations such as coastal areas in the perceptions of local authorities;

- allows us to discuss the local government dimension to north–south differences in local economic prosperity, in particular by focusing on southern authorities;
- shows how authorities have and, in future, might more effectively engage in the 'bidding process' that is such an important part of spatial economic policy in the mid-1990s;
- offers a critical appraisal of the value of building research around submitted documentation; fuses qualitative and quantitative analysis;
- through the inclusion of activities, suggests ways in which the unique material presented in the book might be used for educational and training purposes – as such, the book can be used as a text in appropriate courses, or as a base document for the use of local economic specialists.

In these ways, then, the submissions are taken as the starting point for a stream of analyses that engage with local attitudes, representations and sensitivities over the whole domain of local economic 'position' and performance.

Filling a Void

Building analyses around a major block of unique empirical material, which potentially covers all parts of the British space economy, adds to the substance of our understanding of local economic development, meeting a major need identified by various writers over the last few years, namely the 'oversupply of hypotheses, relative to the empirical evidence' in local economic development (Bovaird, 1993, p. 31), and the general acceptance that 'comparable information on local authority economic initiatives is virtually non-existent' (Armstrong and Twomey, 1993).

Moreover, the book offers a novel approach, using material and covering an area of policy that is virtually uncharted and unrealised. It is rather different from many books on related topics in that, in part, it builds analysis around empirical material derived from a one-off event – and, even then, something that, while commanding media attention of a degree ('Cartography of distress redrawn', *Financial Times*, 24 July 1993), hardly 'hit the headlines' for any length of time. What it does is to demonstrate the richness of insight that can be derived from such a bank of material that, with the usual resource limitations confronting researchers, could not conceivably be easily assembled in any other way. It thus contrasts dramatically with the more conventional treatments that can be found elsewhere.

Given the material involved, this is a book that is located at the intersection between spatial economic policy generated by central government, and that involving local interests. It is firmly set in the buffer zone between the two levels of intervention, controversy and debate. It is about not only genuinely local economic policies and representations but also regional policy, at least as perceived by local authorities. Moreover, it clearly also confronts the connections between local and central government as regards the regional policy question. In sum, it enables so much to be said about spatial economic policy and from a relatively fresh and uncharted perspective.

The implication here is of a distinct information void in the areas of concern in the book. The example of one of the more comprehensive source texts on the information base for local and regional studies (Healey, 1991) will help to con-firm this contention. Despite its exhaustive coverage of conventional (and some lesser known) sources of data on economic activity and land use, the text offers virtually no guidance on either the sources of information of the kind used in this book, or the uses of conventional data in this type of context. Although perhaps outside its remit, this is a major omission. We have excellent coverage of the basic data, but nothing on how it is used (and abused), when it is used and why it is used – and these are very significant aspects of it all. In these terms, the present book should fill a notable gap in the understanding of spatial economic policy processes.

The Structure of the Book

Part 1 sets the scene for the discussion to follow, offering an assessment of the policy context behind the 1992/1993 review of the Assisted Areas map. It high-lights issues and debates connected to spatial economic policy in the 1990s and identifies research potentials.

Chapter 1 engages with a number of central issues and debates in spatial economic policy – transformations in the types and strength of policy; shifts from welfare policy to place-based competitiveness; the rise of local economic de-velopment; the role of coalitions in local economic policy; local autonomy–dependency issues; and local-regional interrelationships in the space economy. These issues are discussed within the context, concepts and approaches of exist-ing literature and research findings. Part of the chapter includes an assessment of the basis and development of local economic policy in the 1990s and some of the constraints that have ensued. This provides an important foundation for con-sidering ways of looking at, and interpreting, the range of local reactions to the 1992/1993 review.

In discussing the submissions analysis, Chapter 2 sets out expectations about local reactions to the review process. The discussion focuses on motives behind engagement or non-engagement and draws on existing literature to discuss the factors conditioning local authority attitudes and approaches. This includes an evaluation of local problems and needs, policy approaches, experiences of local–central relations, personnel factors, historical policy factors, and policy processes as they operate at the local level. The chapter also goes on to focus on represen-tations and to develop a basis for their assessment later in the book.

Chapter 3 discusses the ways in which submissions to the 1992/1993 review exercise can be used to draw out issues and debates and to develop concepts and ideas. It offers two basic elements. First, it critically assesses the value of such analysis for drawing out policy implications and for highlighting policy issues. Second, and linked to this, it discusses the appropriate methodology for analy-sing local submissions. In essence the argument is that, with some provisos, the analysis of submissions can be used to excellent effect. Moreover, it is suggested that, in the sense of wider application and applicability, the enormous volume of material of this type represents an untapped source for researchers and analysts.

Having established the credentials of the material base and approach used in the book, Part 2 goes on to document and analyse local authority engagement in the review process. Chapter 4 sets out and analyses the broad level and type of

responses (or non-response) made to the 1992/1993 review by all local authorities in Great Britain – in other words, it focuses on the 'who', 'what', 'how' and
'why' elements of the local reactions. The distribution of response and non-
response is discussed and evaluated. For the former, the basic nature of the
submissions are described and there is some analysis of liaisons between authorities and the private sector, together with an evaluation of the quality and approach of the local submissions. This sets up a supporting chapter (Chapter 5)
that investigates the policy process in a number of selected areas. Using survey
data collected for the task, it analyses the processes of engagement in more
detail. The motives, processes and management of representations at the local
level are analysed, and the chapter considers the production of consensus, the
role of key individuals, the relationships between coalitions in the review process, and the lobbying and managing functions that supported the submission
documents.

Part 3 focuses on local authority attitudes and sensitivities to regional policy.
Chapter 6 reviews local attitudes to regional industrial policy, and investigates
and analyses the local authority submissions by focusing on the detail of the
responses. The discussion considers the perceived benefits of Assisted Area
designation from the perspective of the local authority submissions and other
local interests, and endeavours to develop an understanding of such attitudes.
Chapter 7, drawing on one of the debates implicit in the 1992 review exercise,
narrows the analysis down to an assessment of 'southern' attitudes to regional
policy. This provides a useful background to the pressures for change and the
final outcome of the review process when Assisted Area status was granted to a
number of areas in London and the South East.

Part 4 builds on the discussion of needs-led sensitivities and attitudes to regional policy in Part 3, by delving into the issue of the representation of local
economic problems. A conventional local economic submission or statement
would present a set range of figures in a set format for a predetermined range of
areas. But the submissions were very different from that. They were representations of the local economies involved, offering a particular 'fix' on their spaces,
and their analysis is of great interest.

Chapters 8 and 9 therefore present a detailed analysis of local authority submissions as representations. The submissions are analysed in terms of the strategies adopted and arguments put forward; the stress on and representation of
key elements such as unemployment and the local labour market (Chapter 8)
and peripherality (Chapter 9) and the representations made and mechanisms,
icons and images used. An attempt is made to draw out the wider implications of
these representations for the areas involved.

The concluding chapter, Chapter 10, contains three parts. First, it discusses the
outcome of the review exercise and some of the reactions. Second, it draws
together the broad findings of the book. Third, it reflects on some of the findings,
discussing issues linked to local–central relationships, the role of place marketing
in spatial economic policy, the formation and development of coalitions, the
importance of local views on regional policy, and the implications that follow
from alternative approaches to the representation of local economic problems.
The process of Assisted Areas adjustment is also given a critical appraisal.

The structure of the book can thus be summarised as: (*see over*)

There are at least two potential 'learning' spin-offs from the core of the book.
The first is the understanding of the policy areas involved. The second is that the

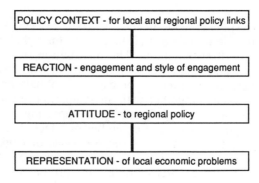

discussion and analysis offers some insights into the ways in which governments may be successfully engaged in the quest for external funding. Appendix 3 contains suggested activities that might be used, either by practitioners in local economic development seeking to professionalise their policy construction activity, or by lecturers and students intent on fostering a greater understanding of such policy arenas. Linked to this learning process, Appendix 2 maps out some implications for the style, approach and success or otherwise of local authority representations to central government.

Fresh Perspectives on Familiar Issues

The book offers a fresh perspective on local authority economic development policy and, at the same time, provides insights into the development of regional policy in Britain. First, the area of local authority attitudes to regional policy has not been explored in the literature so far. The 1984 review of regional policy by the central government did not draw anything more than marginal or localised comment from the academic community (e.g. Ball, 1985). Second, and most significantly, such an investigation generates a whole series of new perspectives on both local authority economic development and regional policy as operated by central government. In particular, in the former case, it offers an opportunity to explore the strategies used by local authorities in their attempts to influence central government policy, the representations that they construct and so on. Third, with the 1993 changes to the regional policy map – and its retention for at least three years according to central government – as well as the build up of a new and more vigorous debate on regional policy (Department of Trade and Industry, 1994), at least part fostered by European Union pressures, this is a very topical and controversial area. The inclusion of parts of London and the South East of England in the revised map has reinforced that feeling. In this respect, the book will not only focus on the processes developed by local authorities in the review exercise; it will also explore and comment on the policy outcomes.

In general then, this book uses the review exercise to draw out a whole range of issues and insights, building its analysis around the themes of *engagement* in the review process, *attitudes* to regional policy, and *representations* of local economic problems. Aimed at students and practitioners in the field of local and regional economic policy, it represents a new and novel way of investigating topics that are basically underexplored simply because it is difficult to generate information on them.

PART 1

Setting the Context

1

ISSUES AND DEBATES IN SPATIAL ECONOMIC POLICY

The ever-increasing array of . . . schemes by which local areas can attract resources . . . places an ever-greater premium on local authority knowledge and capacity to pursue (them).

(Pickvance, 1990a, p. 34)

The relation of local policy to higher spatial levels of intervention has received remarkably little attention . . . (yet) . . . local economic policy . . . depends on higher level policy.

(Eisenschitz and Gough, 1993, pp. 184–6)

The very profound problems encountered in some regions have not been eradicated by the various regional initiatives . . . however, there (has been) a beneficial impact in job creation, industrial movements . . . investment decisions and . . . (regional policy) has prevented the closure of many firms in Assisted Areas. There is a strong need for the continuation of targeted and effective regional policy.

(Association of District Councils, 1991, p. 12)

As a form of state aid, regional policy has become increasingly marginalised.

(Martin, 1993a, p. 272)

Regional policy – 'central government tokenism'

(Fothergill, 1992, p. 62)

In this chapter, we engage with a number of central issues and debates in spatial economic policy, including transformations in the types and strength of policy; shifts from welfare policy to place-based competitiveness; the rise of local economic development and the 'new localism'; local economic policy needs and issues in the 1990s; and the background to the 1992/1993 review of the Assisted Areas.

In particular, we focus on the parallel developments of regional policy on the one hand, and an emergent, yet constrained, local economic policy on the other. Against the background of developments in these strands of policy, we focus on the relationships between them – in other words, on central–local relations. Such an analysis is essential if we are to understand the local and regional context of the Assisted Areas review, i.e. what lay behind the review itself, and what kinds of issues and attractions (if any) were of consequence in influencing the local response or reaction and, in effect, the submissions. Of course, the submissions were much more than simple bid documents, and in Chapter 2 we go on to consider the motives and influences conditioning the fact and the nature of local submissions. This also flags up some unknowns as regards these policy areas and in this way provides a basis for the exploration and examination in later chapters, a foundation for considering ways of looking at, interpreting and drawing insights from the range of local reactions to the 1992/1993 review.

In effect, this chapter serves three purposes within the context of the book. First, it provides a survey of the regional policy and local economic policy fields as they pertain to contemporary debates; second, it offers a contextualisation for the review response analysis that follows; third, it allows us to identify under-covered areas of understanding in the spatial economic policy arena.

1.1 Components and Themes in Spatial Economic Policy

1.1.1 Transformations in the type and strength of spatial economic policy

Given that this is a book at least tacitly about British regional policy, it seems reasonable to ask why are we investigating it, when this is very much seen as the fading face of spatial economic policy? The answer is that while regional policy has dwindled to what appears to be a 'token' level, and has to be defined as a fading element, it is an area of policy that carries some wider and non-immediate importance. It is a long-term survivor; it has strong political and European connotations; and it represents a measure of central recognition of localised problems (Pickvance, 1985; 1990a). Moreover, in terms of the narrative of this book, reactions to changes in regional policy can be used as a surrogate – an indicator of wider attitudes, and a vehicle for teasing out perspectives on policy approach. Finally, given its political significance and the variable political attitude and approach involved (Urry, 1990), it may well make a comeback in the future. It is never entirely 'off the present agenda' but even when it has faded it is never more than a short step away from a return to centre stage.

An important set of questions for this book to consider are what lies behind this tenacity (Armstrong and Taylor, 1987) and, linked to this, what is its significance in the mid to late 1990s UK economy? These are questions that must be addressed.

There are plenty of books about the development of spatial economic policy, and as this rich, if rather stolid, heritage of research on the area can be readily consulted (Parsons, 1988; Armstrong and Taylor, 1987; Prestwich and Taylor, 1990; and so on) no attempt is made in this chapter to present a full, detailed review. That said, it is necessary to chart the broad trends in regional and related spatial economic policy strands in as much as it contextualises contemporary positions. It thus gives context for the Assisted Areas review, helps to comprehend the dwindling level, yet continuity of interest, and to recognise that regional policy is still influential even though it barely exists in the contemporary policy arena. Particularly important for this book, it carries a significance for the 'local' – some have argued that it is locally driven (Pickvance, 1985) and that it always has been a response to local stimulus (Bruce, 1993); others have stressed the established – perhaps even somewhat cosy – complementarity in the past between regional and local economic policy (Begg, 1993; Miller, 1990) and this is a question that we return to in section 1.1.5.

In order to understand contemporary ideas about regional policy we have to briefly consider their historical antecedents. Both regional policy and indeed local economic policy owes its origins to moves in the late 1920s and early 1930s when there were policies designed to shift people (essentially miners) out of the North and Scotland and into the Midlands and South of England (industrial transference) and to encourage manufacturing regeneration and expansion in the former (the various Special Areas Acts – see the excellent reviews in Mc-Crone, 1969; and Parsons, 1988). From 1945, regional policy fluctuated between vigorous and passive operation in response to a combination of regional pressures and government predelictions, but the foundations for a welfare-based policy were firmly laid down. A number of important restructurings took place – a shift from automatic to discretionary assistance, and the introduction of a spatially differentiated tiering in the available incentives. The gradual build-up of action led to some substantial impacts being claimed for the policy (see Parsons, 1988). The coverage of the variously defined assisted areas changed dramatically over the period (see Pickvance, 1990a). Most significantly, by the 1960s, the rationale for regional policy had shifted from social-welfare to growth and demand management.

Into the 1970s and beyond, regional policy has become a different feature. It is incentives only, and applicable to an ever-dwindling array of Assisted Areas, although European Commission agreements allow just over one-third of the UK population to be included within such designated areas. It has gone through rather more radical changes in this recent period with the favouring of greater cost-effectiveness, and greater selectivity in its additional focus on some service industries and small firms (Martin and Townroe, 1992). Regional policy has, in effect, been streamlined with a view to reducing its financial draw on the state (Table 1.1). The ethos of the policy has shifted even more so from welfare to growth and from the quest to reshape the regions with welfare issues in mind to an enterprise-led ideology designed to encourage the market to invest in the regions. With a dwindling financial contribution in real terms (Table 1.1a), regional policy seem firmly 'off the agenda'.

The rolling back of the state in the form of a paring down of regional policy spending was accompanied in the 1980s by a shift towards the urban sphere. The overall policy package has thus been shifted in the direction of urban aid – invoking what Martin and Townroe (1992) refer to as a general trend in 'central government localism' in area assistance. The introduction of Urban Development Corporations, Enterprise Zones and other elements of the urban policy package were examples of this centrally controlled local policy. This has been interpreted as an attack on the local autonomy of local authorities.

Despite this erosion of the role of regional policy as the dominant strand of spatial economic policy, we cannot escape a return to the view that regional policy retains an importance beyond its level of allocated resources and its policy weaponry. Although it has been marginalised (Martin, 1993a) to a level at which it appears to be a token gesture (Fothergill, 1992) it survives tenaciously. Much of the detailed criticism of its operation and impact focuses on the type rather

Table 1.1   Regional industrial assistance in the 1980s and 1990s

(a) Government expenditure on regional financial assistance to industry in the UK at 1978–79 prices for selected years (£ million)

1978–79	714
1979–80	560
1980–81	629
1981–82	651
1982–83	662
1983–84	450
1984–85	437
1985–86	395
1986–87	460
1987–88	334
1988–89	338
1989–90	284
1990–91	248
1991–92	213

Note: Figures include all regional policy elements and payments through Development Agencies and to nationalised industries.

(b) Regional financial assistance for selected years (£ million)

1984–85	518
1987–88	422
1990–91	330
1991–92	264
1993–94	253
1995–96	268

Note: Figures include Regional Selective Assistance, Regional Enterprise Grants, and Regional Development Grants; note that they are not indexed.
Sources: Hansard, Written answers, CW9, 5 June 1992, pp. 676–7; DTI, 1993 (unpublished data).

than the principle of regional intervention. Moreover, it could, quite conceivably, and in a different political climate from that operating in Britain in the mid-1990s, make a return to greater eminence (see Association of District Councils, 1991). That aside, and looking to the local scale, it seems that regional policy holds a position in the consciousness of spatial economic problems and policies that transcends the reality of its resource allocation. There have been distinct 'southern' pressures for its curtailment or, more often, its extension into the south (see Balchin and Bull, 1987; and Chapter 7) and, more generally, it seems to be typified by an enduring tension between regional needs and the pressure to curtail spending. It could be said that it tends to generate more controversy than its resources and powers would indicate. However, access to it, or a denial of it, can, as we shall chart in Part 3, make a substantial difference to the fortunes of localities (Economic Development panel of the Royal Town Planning Institute, 1993).

In essence, a more focused, more constrained and more competitive style of regional policy remains in the UK of the mid-1990s. It is weaker than ever before but still significant. This book concentrates on regional policy as it remains an area of sensitivity and contention. More important, it is the essential 'golden egg' that, even if they were not necessarily really bidding for status alone (see Chapter 2), precipitated the local submissions forming the core material for the book.

1.1.2 The regional policy package in the mid-1990s

Regional industrial policy lives on in a muted version of its former self.
(Damesick and Wood, 1987, p. 260)

Since the mid-1980s, regional policy has dwindled to modest proportions. There has been a withdrawal of resources, a cutback in the areas of coverage and in the strengths of the policy tools. Yet, we would argue that it retains a relevance that transcends its total spend. That said, it is necessary to set out the policy package as it applied at the time of the 1992/1993 Assisted Areas review exercise.

The Assisted Areas map defines those areas of Great Britain where regional industrial incentives operated by the Department of Trade and Industry/Scottish Office/Welsh Office are available. As it stood in late 1992, the policy package had been in place since the late 1980s. It involved a number of components, available in a two-tier system of designated Development Areas and Intermediate Areas:

Regional Selective Assistance

This comprises the bulk of the available regional industrial assistance. Available in all Development and Intermediate Areas, it is a discretionary and negotiable grant which is potentially available to assist capital investment projects which create and/or safeguard employment in the areas and which would not otherwise proceed. Awards of assistance are the minimum considered necessary and are not available for revenue costs (such as rent, rates and labour costs).

Assistance levels are negotiable – with the Department of Trade and Industry assessing the needs of companies against total capital spend and the number of jobs involved. Eligible costs include fixed assets, usually over three years. Fixed capital costs include expenditure on land, site preparation, buildings, plant and machinery – both new and second-hand.

This form of grant can thus be made available for start-ups (including inward investment); expansion plans; modernisation; rationalisation plans where jobs are preserved; relocations where there is a net increase in jobs; and asset purchase from a doomed business.

Regional Enterprise Grant

These are of two types:

Investment Grants: to encourage investment projects in manufacturing and some service sectors. These are available to companies employing less than 25 people and can provide 15 per cent of fixed asset expenditure up to a £15,000 maximum. They cannot be granted along with a Regional Selective Assistance award and are available only in Development Areas or a European Commission RECHAR programme area.

Innovation Grants: to encourage innovation projects leading to the development and introduction of new or improved products and processes.

Applicable in both Development and Intermediate Areas, the grants are available to companies employing less than 50 people and are up to 50 per cent of eligible costs (maximum of £25,000).

Exchange Risk Guarantee Scheme

Applicable to both Development and Intermediate Areas, this enables companies to take advantage of foreign currency loans from the ECSC (European Coal and Steel Community) up to £500,000. The borrower accepts a sterling liability and the government takes on the exchange risk.

Other elements

The Enterprise Initiative: involves preferential rates for consultancy under the national scheme. Under this scheme, financial support is available to most companies in Britain employing fewer than 500 people. This takes the form of an award of 50 per cent of the cost of between 5 and 15 consultant days covering key management functions. Companies operating in Assisted Areas qualify for an award of half of the costs of this consultancy.

European Coal and Steel Community Conversion Loans are available within former coalfield areas to companies in the public sector for project capital expenditure.

European Investment Bank loans are available for private or public projects which are deemed to help regional development.

Provision or improvement of basic services: Assisted Areas that are also designated as Objective 2 areas under the European Commission Structural Funds are also eligible for specific grants providing infrastructure for industrial estates. These involve road schemes and improvements; water, sewage and sewage treatment; and electricity/gas installations – involving up to 30 per cent of eligible expenditure on road schemes, land schemes, or installation costs, more for infrastructure.

The stated aims

To reduce regional imbalances in employment opportunities and to encourage the development of indigenous potential within the Assisted Areas on a stable long-term basis (DTI, Scottish Office and Welsh Office, 1992, p. 2). In effect, the policy as it existed in July 1992, and as read by one major local authority, had two aims:

- to direct inward investment to Assisted Areas by use of discretionary grant awards; and
- to stimulate the growth of indigenous firms by mainly focusing upon small to medium-sized organisations, and on increasing the rate of new business start-

up (Strathclyde Regional Council, Economic and Industrial Development Committee report, September 1992).

It is worth noting that many authorities are sensitive to the two surviving tiers of regional industrial assistance, Intermediate Areas and Development Areas, and the varying support that is available. Thus, 'it is difficult to attract inward investment to areas which do not have full Development Area status, though Intermediate Area status brings some benefits' (Stirling District Council, Briefing, 20 November 1992).

We will discuss the benefits and constraints of regional policy later in the book. For now, it is worth noting that many authorities viewed the acquisition of Assisted Area status as bringing 'considerable benefits to the local economy' (quoted from a Kent County Council briefing note on Assisted Area status in East Kent following the revision to the map in August 1993).

The limitations and the attractions

Clearly, the regional policy package available at the time of the review in 1992 was a shadow of that existing throughout much of the post-war period. Honed down to modest levels of demand on state resources, constrained to a small number of high unemployment areas in the regions outside the South East, generally given a relatively low priority in government circles, policy was low on the agenda of government and able to generate little interest – or so it seemed until the 1992/1993 Assisted Areas review.

However, we have already noted in the introduction to the book that, despite its much maligned image and its poor press, the chance to secure status was grabbed by many authorities and viewed as a real coup if awarded. There does seem to be a gap between considered opinion on the overall value of regional policy and the interpretation of value which it is given at the level of receipt – at the sharp end! That makes the study of attitudes to regional policy in Part 3 of the book a particularly pertinent angle on the whole issue.

Regardless of past glories or future question marks against its survival, regional policy does also have a political influence that extends beyond the resources at its disposal and the effects that it can have. The very term 'regional policy' evokes feelings of support for parts of an economy – it is a (potentially cheap) way for governments to show their concern for places that have been left behind by waves of investment, which brings political benefits to the instigators. More perplexing for those involved, and for the political value that might accrue to central government, there has been an enduring tension between central and local government over regional policy. To central government in the 1980s, regional policy was costly, ineffective and out of step with the ideas of market-led growth. For local authorities, with similar concerns over effectiveness, there was added the criticisms of the insensitivity of blanket aid, lack of co-ordination with local authority policies, and underfunding (Damesick and Wood, 1987). Yet access to the resources involved was seen as extremely important. In this sense, the tension remains intact.

From a broader, critical perspective, it is clear that it is the array of indirect regional policies (Martin, 1993a) that have greatest economic and social impact across areas. Yet the overt opportunity to access resources via regional industrial grants and linked policies, perhaps to gain a foothold in the quest to tap into other sources of funds (European Commission, for example), seems to be an important motivating element.

The key point from the perspective of this book is that regional policy holds some attraction for local groups, even if it is a shadow of its former self. Whether that attraction is confined only to the resources on offer is a matter we return to in Chapter 2 when addressing the motives and approaches of local authorities in the Assisted Areas review. For the time being, we might view the regional policy package as the regional 'benefit' that just might entice a reaction from local authorities.

1.1.3 The rise of the local

Although its antecedents are also set firmly in the 1930s, local economic policy is much more a product of the post-1970 period than is regional policy (Pickvance, 1990a). According to Pickvance, its origins lie firmly rooted in nineteenth-century developments in civic improvement, municipal enterprise and municipal socialism, together with the spread of Keynesian ideas about state regulation of the economy. However, its period of real growth came after the mid-1960s, spurred on by the increase in unemployment and the reaction of Labour councils, after 1979 in particular, to Conservative governments. There was a movement towards the generation of alternative policies at the local authority level to counteract the shift towards market-led growth at the national scale. According to Syrett (1994), the combination of changes in state apparatus and the differentiated impacts of economic restructuring have precipitated a more proactive stance from local authorities. There is a consensus over the role of local economic policy but not over its precise form and it is here that local authority approaches tend to be differentiated. This reflects differing ideological and political positions over the most appropriate goals and forms of local economic development, and the seriousness with which such approaches are followed.

As a result of differing approaches, the tools developed and deployed by local authorities in economic policy range widely between facilitative elements (infrastructure development; political lobbying; promotion), interventionist elements (advice; investment; Science Parks), and directive elements (planning agreements; liaisons with local businesses over development plans) (Syrett, 1994). The range of political positions fuse with particular combinations of tools and policy approaches – from those on the left seeking to intervene directly in the local development process and to stress jobs over profits, to those on the right seeking merely to facilitate local enterprise within an ideological stance that favours market solutions. More directly, approaches may range from direct, deliberate involvement of some dimension, to a virtual non-involvement in the local economic development process. In reality, though, consensus shows itself at the local level with liaisons of support for feasible middle ground policies that draw on a variety of policy weapons. Of course, one of the factors that both plays off these considerations and influences policy potential is access to central government support, one of which is Assisted Area status, in which authorities may show either little interest or major concern, according to their policy position.

There are emergent strengths in a local authority involvement in the space economy. Local authorities and their partner agencies have a feel for the needs and potentials of their local economic spaces – a resonance with the 'local' – and the executant nature of their role and political legitimacy enables any commitment to be politically supported (Pickvance, 1990; Urry, 1990).

Local variations in economic policy approaches might be seen as reflecting the positions of an authority in the scale of activeness. As Novy argues, local economic policy has developed through a variety of states, from inactive or preactive to reactive and finally to proactive. Local variations reflect the position of an authority in this policy development path, linking to the length and scale of the local experience of involvement. In addition, though, there are opportunities to use and constraints to contend with. The conditions for a more active involvement in local economic policy for an authority are when its area of jurisdiction coincides with the local economic space (Urry, 1990; what Bennett and McCoshan, 1993 refer to as 'bounded'), or when the opportunities for local liaison are particularly fluid (Harloe, Pickvance and Urry, 1990; Bennett and McCoshan, 1993).

The constraints on local 'activity' link to the limited effective powers available, local parochialism working in a negative, inward-looking fashion (Bennett and McCoshan, 1993) and the non-availability of resources. Local authorities that are 'stretched' for resources are less likely to be active participants in local economic policy, although there are, of course, various policies that while low in cost may be high in value (e.g. business advice). In these terms, the powers available and the general approach to local authority involvement in substantial part reflects the degree of local initiative (Pickvance, 1990a) and that brings us to the role of key individuals (politicians or, more often, officers), coalitions and liaisons between various local 'interests', and involvement traditions (see Chapter 2).

A concern for issues of local economic development is a central feature of virtually all local authorities in the UK of the 1990s. As such, matters of resource distribution (via, for example, regional policy) and image (via, designation or non-designation) cause great concern amongst local officers and politicians. Conflicts and tensions abound, especially in the ongoing debates centring on autonomy and control or dependency and subservience of the 'local' relative to central government involvement in the space economy. The changing complexion of local economic policy both reflects and is reflective of such issues.

1.1.4 Transformations in the complexion of local economic policy

Addressing the changing complexion of local authority economic policy brings us to some contemporary issues in this area. The most recent legislation at the time of the 1992 review was the 1989 Local Government and Housing Act. This simultaneously gave a range of powers to local authorities but restricted their activities and retained a central control over them (for a fuller analysis, see Eisenschitz and Gough, 1993, Chapter 1). A central question in local economic policy is what authorities and the partner agencies can and have done themselves – autonomous changes – and what is imposed on them from outside.

The local autonomy–central dependency debate

According to Bruce (1993), the common dilemma for many practitioners engaged in local economic development is the need to press the case for greater government recognition while fighting to sustain local autonomy. Although it may be rather too simple to structure a discussion around the themes of autonomy and dependency as if they were some kind of alternatives, it does present an important perspective on the whole area of local authority economic policy and approach and on the tensions that pervade it in central–local relations. It is clear that the powers and level of control of local authorities have been eroded by the 'assault' of central government localism via urban initiatives, and the curtailing and constraining of local authority executive powers in the local economy (Eisenschitz and Gough, 1993). Local authorities desire control over their local economic destinies but are clearly tied by legislation and purse strings. That said, the notion that local autonomy is severely restricted is arguably an illusory claim.

For a start, there is evidence of central government toleration of centrist local economic policies (Eisenschitz and Gough, 1993, p. 117). Moreover, it is not clear to what extent central controls on local authority economic policy actually hinder autonomy in the reality of ways and means that local authorities can harness in forwarding local economic policy objectives. The debate is clearly synthesised by Miller (1994). As Miller records, some theorists would argue that, within limits, local state policies have a real flexibility; others would suggest that the local is subservient and dependent. To some, local autonomy and local politics is of questionable significance – there is a feeling that, in an increasingly global economy, local authorities have been virtually forced to adopt pro-growth strategies, 'sidelining' local politics. The reality is somewhere in between – local autonomy is not complete by any means, but local authorities do have powers, and can circumvent control in various ways (Cochrane, 1990). Perhaps the key question is one posed by Cox, that the issue at stake is not the autonomy – that is accepted – but the effectiveness of the policies pursued (Cox, 1993). This allows us to bring back into play the idea that some local authorities might seek to develop local economic initiatives through a vibrant, autonomous approach and not quite such a dependent, subservient mode as some would argue. This, of course, has a bearing on the sensitivities of authorities to policy changes, or at least the extent to which they are willing to publically pronounce on them.

That said, there is clearly a certain level of central imposition and control, and this reveals itself most clearly in the shift of central government spatial economic policy from an emphasis on welfare to place-based competitiveness. Along with the shift towards enterprise that has typified regional policy, there has been a shift towards competition in the pursuit of area policy resources. This is apparent in at least two respects; 'special treatment area' designations (Pickvance, 1985) – in the conditions under which a variety of urban policies have been developed; and in the distribution of resources – in the survival of the largely discretionary elements in regional policy.

In the arena of urban policy, Stewart has documented the changing face of central state urban policy and the so-called 'new localism'. From the introduction of Enterprise Zones to 'City Challenge' many contemporary schemes have required active local authority involvement in a competitive, zero sum game for acquisition. Under this latest stage of urban policy, inter-area competition and place marketing has a more distinct presence under the Single Regeneration Budget (SRB) with a locally driven bidding process and what Stewart describes as 'competitive localism' (Stewart, 1994).

As a consequence of all these trends, the whole style and approach of spatial economic policy has been altered. Local authorities, for example, have always consulted with central government over policy designations and suchlike (Department of Trade and Industry, 1983) but matters have changed substantially. We can now speak of the 'bidding process', whereby much aid must be bid for, sought out under competitive conditions. Under this kind of regime, representations about local economic problems, policy needs at the local level and so on, take on a more competitive guise. Indeed, the representations made by local authorities on the subject of the 1992 Assisted Areas can be firmly interpreted in this context. It may be oversimplifying a complex array of motives and considerations (see Chapter 2), but this brings us back to the question of local autonomy. Success in this 'bidding game' may be interpreted as providing a vehicle for enhancing and expanding local autonomy via the introduction of new investment, new economic activities and, over the long term, potentially less reliance on the public purse.

Two developments are part and parcel of the new competitiveness that pervades spatial economic policy: one is the growth of local authority place marketing, and the other the emergence of coalitions and partnerships.

From place marketing to representations

Whether it is seen as marginal or central, there are some substantial implications for place marketing. Indeed, for many authorities, the matter has gone beyond simple marketing and towards the reshaping of place. This is part of the emergent competitiveness which pervades the arena of spatial economic policy in the 1990s and requires a fuller assessment. However, in addressing the issue of representations as regards regional (or other spatial) policy support, we come up against tensions between what might potentially prove to be conflicting constructions or images of the locality. In the language of image construction, contrast the signs in promotional literature that are used to convey messages of growth and prosperity, with those likely to appear in the submissions discourse. How these kinds of tensions are resolved – if indeed they are – is an important question for local authorities seeking to create or preserve consensus in the local economic policy arena.

Place marketing

Many of the recent developments in spatial economic policy have contributed to the consolidation of place marketing, and the industry that has grown up around it. There is an enhanced competitive feel to spatial economic development in the 1990s. This stems from a number of developments in the policy arena that have served to sharpen inter-area competition. We have already charted most of them – the shifts in the powers and possibilities for local authorities to engage in the economic development process has sharpened up the awareness of a 'winners and losers' zero sum game. There is also what might be labelled a counter-circumvention that has occurred through central government localism in the area of urban policy (the Urban Development Corporations, for example). As we have noted, for years, local authorities have struggled to circumvent threats to local autonomy (Cochrane, 1995). With the UDCs and other centrally controlled, but essentially local, policies they have been countered. Place competition has undoubtedly been stimulated by much post-1980s urban policy that has required local authorities to 'bid' for support through various schemes (Stewart, 1994). Added to all this, there is the matter of the conditions under which regional policy is organised and structured. The shift from state to market regulation gives a new relevance, a fresh impetus to successful place marketing. The acquisition of Assisted Area status, derogated as 'marginal' by many writers – and in financial terms that is so – can turn the fortunes of a local economy if it leads to some prestigious new inward investment. Or, so the argument goes!

Regardless of the efficacy of policy, developments such as these have sharpened competive edges and generated a scenario under which there is, at times, a feeling of a local scrambling for resources. In the terms of this book – and the review of the Assisted Areas map – the whole gambit of bidding and representing relates closely to the notion of place marketing.

The rise of a place marketing industry and the great growth in local authority promotional activities can be traced back to the mid-1970s when economic recession started to hit the traditionally successful manufacturing and mining areas of the Midlands, the North and South Wales (Fretter, 1993). Place marketing conventionally involves presenting positive images to boost private sector confidence and the direct selling of relocation and development opportunities. However, there is a debate over the ability of local authorities to market themselves in ways which will facilitate local economic development (Cochrane, 1995). In the new competitive environment, place marketing has extended beyond simple promotion to boost confidence in an area, and towards the reshaping and refashioning of places. The involvement of local authorities and key groups works to ensure that the refashioning suits locally defined priorities. However, to some, there may be limited room for action (Cox and Mair, 1991) because local authority political agendas are tied to others (e.g. businesses, etc.). Is this, asks Cochrane, local political success or is it the result of outside forces, or some combination of them (Cochrane, 1995)? What is certain is that some places are capable of successfully marketing themselves – playing the game – while others are not, and, as we have already argued, there is a premium for those authorities able successfully to promote themselves in the 'bidding game'.

There is no doubt that many local authorities do engage in active 'place marketing', which links with ideologies of the local economy and the images that might be generated alongside them. Hinting at a 'growth via reindustrialisation' ideology in parts of the North East of England, Sadler cites the varying emphases and common themes in a movement in place marketing that glosses over problems. There is a suggestion that place marketing has selectively appropriated particular aspects of a locality's culture to further a series of predetermined (national) political goals (Sadler, 1993).

The contemporary 'bidding game' requires a different perspective on the marketing of a place. This is not so much 'gilding the smokestacks', the creation of new forms of identity for old industrial regions via symbolic representations (Watson, 1991), as projecting an image of its problems and, perhaps, its potentials. The 'marketing' of places in terms of their problems presents a contrasting picture. The major differences in the submissions as representations of place are that they must construct a case for 'winning' spatial policy funding. Although the representations constructed may well 'leak' into the outside world, and the very fact of engagement in a review of any 'special treatment areas' indicates compliance and leads authorities sometimes to think carefully about whether to 'reveal' their local economic weaknesses, they are place marketing for government public consumption rather than for the private sector. In this respect, they are likely to present the counter position; to some degree at least, the negative side of things.

This presents a real dilemma – there are tensions between the perceived need to project a case for greater central government recognition (perhaps as an Assisted Area) while endeavouring to retain local autonomy (Bruce, 1993). Engagement with urban policy initiatives that required local authority compliance, i.e. central government localism, works through the ceding of local autonomy. The quest for regional industrial grants is less problematical, but it still generates a short-term reliance on the centre.

Similar to the appropriation of cultural fixes, the marketing of problems takes local economic aspects to project an image. Here, and despite the more closely confined 'rules of engagement' that are set with review exercises (see DTI, Scottish Office and Welsh Office, 1992), the tendency is to 'talk down' rather than to 'talk up'. However, there is a likely premium on moderating the 'talk down' in favour of a strategy that recognises and projects the potentials of a locality.

Bound up with issues of imagery, there has been work on the representation of landscape or of urban space (see Kearns and Philo, 1993). However, the question of representations of local economic problems – potentially a rewarding pursuit, and certainly for this book – has not been addressed.

The fact of representation, and the style in which it is done, is important because there is a link between successful promotion/image construction and investment growth (see Watson, 1991). Obviously, this is connected to local economic status, and the ideological base around which any local economic development is pursued. Clearly, in dealing with submissions, we are focusing on representations that contain selectively created images. These images include signs containing codes which structure the messages about a particular scenario – they seek to construct an impression (Sadler, 1993).

The question is what vehicles and methods are used? Even if a controlled presentation of basic data is required, there is always scope for flexibility (Pickvance, 1990a), and in any case there are ongoing arguments about the efficacy of local economic indicators (see Chapter 8). What construction of visual images might be attempted through, for example, submission logos? More will be said on this in discussing representations in Chapter 2.

Finally, what difficulties are created by the inevitable tensions that emerge between a promotion of 'all is rosy' and a 'bid' for assistance that projects local economic problems? These are all tensions generated by the shifts in policy towards more competitiveness.

Armed with the basic analysis of representational approaches and explanations which is set out in Chapter 2, in Part 4 of the book we will focus on two key aspects of local economic change and, using the submissions material, assess the character of local authority representations in terms of:

- how local authorities represent their economic problems?
- what actually conditions the ways that they do it and with what significance?

This will enable us to develop an entirely fresh perspective on the vagaries of the 'bidding game' and the quest for 'special treatment'.

Safety in numbers – local coalitions and liaisons

The second element of change that connects with the shift towards a more competitive policy profile is the emergence and growth of local coalitions and liaisons. This development, very much part of local action in some areas and certainly important in moulding the kinds of representations projected through place marketing, can be viewed as an attempt to move towards quasi-autonomy. Just as the new competitive environment of (urban and) regional policy has given rise to a more concerted and widespread endeavour to market places, so it has functioned – via the bid process – as a stimulus to collaboration (Stewart, 1994; Beynon and Hudson, 1993).

There are various ways of approaching the idea of coalitions and collusion. To some, it extends to the intricate networks that typify some localities (and not others) (Bennett and McCoshan, 1993; Axford and Pinch, 1994). In their quest to engage with local economic issues in a meaningful way, local authorities in some areas have actively entered into such coalitions, to the extent that full part-nership and networking prevails. For others, the idea of coalition involves a more subtle blend of local actors and agencies (Pickvance, 1985), not just place-dependent elements of capital. We might even envisage the notion of 'defensive' coalitions – not so much with 'economic growth' in mind, but with local econ-omic survival to the forefront (see Lawless, 1994). The chance to secure some special status – the 'opportunity structure' of something like potential Assisted Area status – could itself act as a catalyst for the formation of coalitions, either on a permanent or on a temporary basis. Whatever the scale and type of coali-tion and collusion, the local authority must itself be viewed as a coalition of competing and conflicting interests. How it resolves any internal conflicts and reaches consensus – and whether it enters into any initially less permanent liaisons in spatial economic policy – is of great interest and importance.

The role of local coalitions, especially when centred on local authorities (in isolation as coalitions or in collusion with others), is important in the context of review exercises such as the 1992 Assisted Areas example. If, following Pick-vance (1985), we interpret regional policy as a response to 'bottom-up' pressures, then the role of coalitions in the process becomes more clear-cut. Spatial coali-tions may or may not press for the inclusion of an area within a special treatment area, but regardless of that engagement decision (Chapter 4), the important point is that pressures are exerted through this vehicle. That, according to Pick-vance, more forcefully connects the idea and existence of coalitions to territorial politics. Central control over local authority activity is tight, but there is still scope for territorial politics to come into play. There is often discretion and flexibility in the use of central government funds, their distribution often has a bargaining element (as does regional policy), and, most significantly, central government spatial policy is a method of distributing resources that actually occurs via territorial politics (Pickvance, 1985).

Despite 'sea-changes' in the rules and conventions of local economic policy – many imposed from 'above' – there is an enduring feeling of the important links between the 'local' and the 'regional'. As Pickvance argues, regional policy has to be, in effect, locally driven, and is retained partly for the purposes of appeasing the 'local'. Approaches to the study of spatial policy have tended to be 'top-down', driven by central government definitions of problems and priorities for their solution. This has led to a neglect of 'bottom-up' pressures from localities and regions, and that is important because, as we have already argued, regional policy can, perhaps must, be interpreted as a response to 'bottom-up' pressures more than as a large-scale subsidy to industrial capital. Why else would it have survived? (Pickvance, 1985) (This, of course, offers a rationale for focusing on 'local' attitudes and representations in the context of this book.)

More than this, central government-led policies, such as those involving regional industrial grants and suchlike, very much condition what the local authorities can do. Urry, in explaining local economic and related policy variations, draws on the three key elements of conditions, resources and strategies (Urry, 1990). We can interpret the quest for Assisted Area status at least partly as a search for resources that can assist a local authority in upgrading its local economic policy effort. As we show in the following section, central–local links are very important in this respect.

1.1.5 Local–central connections in spatial economic policy

Success in the arena of local economic development is partly attributable to local authority dynamism in securing resources and in representing the needs and potentials of its area (Pickvance, 1990a). In this respect, the relationships and connections between the local and the central take on great importance.

As such, having investigated themes in both the centrally administered urban and regional policies in Britain and the locally motivated action by local authorities and their array of 1990s partners, we need to move on to a consideration of the relationships between these two contrasting scales of involvement. In as much as we can do this, it should provide an essential basis to the evaluation of responses to the Assisted Areas review exercise.

Clearly, the relationships between central government and local authorities in spatial economic policy are vitally important. The latter is very much a controller of 'purse strings' and, as various writers have noted, local action is to some degree dependent on what the centre allows in terms of resources (Johnson and Cochrane, 1981). But there is rather more to it than that – an engagement with the 'bidding process' that reflects dependence on the central state may be done with the intention of, over the longer term, achieving a more autonomous position for the local authority (see Chapter 2).

A key point here is that relationships between central and local – certainly as regards regional policy and local authorities (Eisenschitz and Gough, 1993) – are important but relatively undocumented and virtually unexplored. There are exceptions in the arena of land-use planning (see Tye and Williams, 1994) and we can draw some ideas from such work. Yet, it is difficult to isolate evidence on the specifics – the channels, strengths, direct/indirect nature, and degree of influence of connections and policy interchanges.

At the same time, there is much comment in the literature on the past failings of relationships between central and local government. For example, in the formative local economic policy years of the 1980s, there was an apparent indifference on the part of central government to engaging with a willingness on the part of local authorities across the UK to increase their economic development involvement. The opportunity to create a more locally responsive regional policy with the shift to selective, discretionary assistance in 1984 – a policy that could usefully lock in to local authority knowledge and understanding of local conditions – was passed up in a generally continuing remote-controlled system (Damesick and Wood, 1987).

While the question of the relationships between central government spatial economic policy and local authorities has not been given anything more than tentative treatment in the literature, we can rectify that position to some degree in this book. Our starting point can be some of the few examples of relevant research. For example, some writers have at least touched on the existence of relationships. Miller notes the past complementarity of local authority economic roles as regards regional policy (Miller, 1990) although, more recently, Bovaird (1993) suggests that the regional policy framework operates (problematically and) independently of government local economic development initiatives.

Prestwich and Taylor (1990) discuss local reactions to Assisted Area changes such as the descheduling of Mid-Wales from 1984, noting the replacement of the assistance with a virtually identical local package. Moreover, they suggest, there are occasional tensions between 'national' and 'local' policy. Especially during periods of 'passive' regional policy, local authorities can act to the detriment of effective national regional policy. These interesting issues are, however, left unexplored, presumably because there was either no 'mileage' in it or, more likely, an absence of fuller material or data.

In one of the few instances of research directly targeted at the effects of Assisted Area regrading, Begg investigates the consequences of the withdrawal of regional incentives on the (local) investment behaviour of firms, concluding that over the long term the impact of withdrawal is substantial (Begg, 1993). In a different vein, Pickvance has noted an important, if not vital, role of central–local interactions that gives, in itself, a clear rationale for investigating the areas covered in this book. Not confined to the argument that regional policy is locally driven (Pickvance, 1985), this is that paralleling the growing competitive strand in spatial economic policy, there is a real premium on local abilities to influence policy and designations (Pickvance, 1990a). According to Pickvance, and this is something that is confirmed by later analysis in the book, there is sufficient flexibility in the system of granting support and designation to make it important for local authorities to acquire the capacity to pursue resources. This occurs in the opportunity to influence the creation of schemes, and in acquiring special status. In one of the few cases in which the subject of this book has been addressed, Pickvance suggests that local initiatives can be influential, and that it is always worth while submitting. Evidence from the West Midlands, where resistance to status delayed designation, is offered in support of this contention. In the increasingly competitive environment of the 1990s, the pressure is very much on local authorities – in wider coalitions or not – to pursue resources in order to avoid falling behind in the race.

We know that this is important, but we don't know much about the detail. This has either been mentioned by commentators as a gap, or ignored in the obliviousness of authors intent on offering the standard, conventional analysis of policy. Typically, Chisholm, in discussing central (regional) and local policy separately, offers a rather uncritical assessment. There is a conclusion that local authorities cannot easily 'go it alone' and a faint mention of problems such as dereliction being 'helped by national regional policy' (Chisholm, 1990, p. 181). However, there is nothing more. In effect, this little corner of the spatial economic policy arena has simply not generated interest and exploration – but it is important! (See Armstrong and Twomey, 1993.)

Besides underexploration in research, many assessments of local economic policy in the past have either failed even to recognise or at least underplayed the important activity or role of lobbying for resources (e.g. see Chandler and Lawless, 1985; a notable exception is Bruce, 1993 – an article written from the practitioner viewpoint). The focus has been much more firmly on hard policies such as factory construction or soft policies such as small firms advice. Less tangible elements of policy involvement – such as the quest for resources from central government – have not been addressed. However, lobbying and cajoling for support is an activity that takes place, it may generate resources, it may replace other policy elements – it will certainly have an opportunity cost – and it is thus important. As such, there is a clearly vital role for local authorities in leveraging, not just for local liaisons (Roberts, Collis and Noone, 1990), but also for external resources, and there is also the significant question – increasingly entering into debates – about the cost-effectiveness of participation in the competitive environment of spatial economic policy (the 'bidding process') (Oatley, 1994). If the chances of successful acquisition are modest, then there may be a case for holding back participation, an issue that has a particular relevance for the smaller, less-resourced local authorities.

If we consider this situation against a background of the shifting emphasis in much local authority economic policy – what Novy (1990) considers to be a jump from preactivity to proactivity – then the absence of material becomes more serious. In the past there has been only minimal analysis of some of the ways in which this has occurred (representations, etc.). We often read about local officers/councillors making representations to government, but little or no documentation or analysis is available (an exception is Bennett and McCoshan, 1993).

Of course, it is interesting to note that the lack of access to resources may suit certain factions within local authorities. For example, as one researcher discovered, it is sometimes apparent that local politicians use the absence of efficient regional policy to justify their own initiatives far beyond their formal mandate (Johannisson, 1990).

Although we can marshall relatively little of great substance on local–central connections *vis-à-vis* regional policy, the research findings reported in Parts 2, 3 and 4 of the book (especially Chapter 6 on attitudes to regional policy) reveal the importance with which local authorities view regional policy and the funding opportunities that in appropriate cases have accrued. The pot may have shrunk and the areas of designation may have receded, but the chance to acquire aid is, for many (but not all), an intoxicating one.

In conclusion, we can usefully view spatial economic policy in terms of parallel strands which sometimes converge and overlap and which have been increasingly intertwined, but about which we have, so far, relatively limited knowledge. The major parts of this book focus on local–central relations as manifest in reactions to the Assisted Areas review exercise and we will be exploring this less charted territory throughout much of Parts 2, 3 and 4. In particular, we will be locking on to the processes of engagement in the review, the attitudes to regional policy, and the representations of local economic problems. Each of these will offer a fresh and hitherto unexplored perspective of the review exercise and local–central relations. For now, and having briefly reviewed the development of the two strands of spatial economic policy, and discussed the issue of local–central relations, we can set out the bases of the 1992/1993 review of the Assisted Areas. Why did it occur and what is its significance for spatial economic policy?

1.2 The 1992 Review – Motives and Criteria

In June 1992 the government announced that it would be undertaking a review of the Assisted Areas map that had been in place since 1984. Local authorities and other organisations wishing to make representations were invited to submit these within a period of three months. Clearly, given the conventional processes involved in local authority policy formation – the Committee system, for example – this represented a rather tight schedule. That said, many submissions were of a very high quality. Moreover, since most submissions either did not go to Committee because of time limits, or were nodded through, we have a collection of submissions that is very much officer-led (although framed in terms which local officers would expect to be politically acceptable in their authorities).

1.2.1 Motives

Against the background to spatial economic policy development outlined and assessed in this chapter so far, we can, controversially, interpret the review exercise in the following ways:

- as a vehicle for a genuine sharpening of regional policy applications;
- as a mechanism for securing a partial withdrawal from such intervention.

Cutting back the number of Assisted Areas is one way of reducing the demands on any regional policy budget. As we have already argued, since the late 1970s, the British government has been looking critically at regional policy as an artificial construct and constraint that runs counter to the philosophy of generating a competitive environment and rolling back the direct influence of the state. It was, of course, curtailed in its designs by at least two factors – the political sensitivity of regional issues, and the European dimension (Damesick and Wood, 1987).

1.2.2 Criteria

Clearly, measures of unemployment were viewed as major components in the review. The content of the submissions was channelled with the request that they focus on the following elements:

- persistence of unemployment rates above the national average over recent years
- proportion of long-term unemployment in the local workforce
- likely future demand for jobs in terms of local economic and demographic structures

- activity rates
- inner city and urban problems
- peripherality
- the occurrence of 'pipeline' closures or rundowns

All this was subject to the directive that submissions should consider whether, realistically, the localities involved fell into the worst third of the country in terms of employment opportunities and structural factors (DTI, Scottish Office and Welsh Office, 1992, p. 2).

In general, this means that we have a unique array of materials in the form of local submissions that can be analysed as engagements, attitudes and representations. Moreover, by inference, this gives us a direct route to the thinking on spatial economic criteria by central government in the early to mid-1990s. In essence, as we set out in Figure 1.1, the review offers a great potential for teasing out a whole variety of policy angles and aspects.

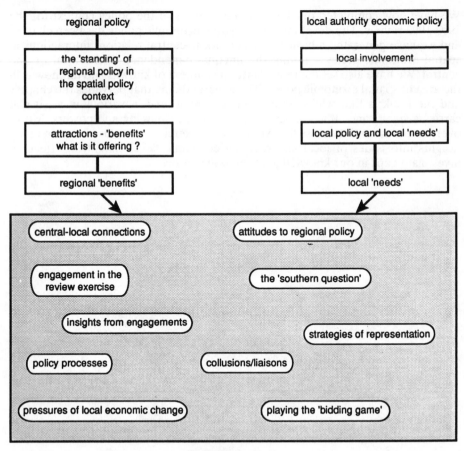

The book content

Figure 1.1 Local 'needs' and regional 'benefits': a scenario for the exploration of issues from the 1992/1993 Assisted Areas review.

Given the remit of the review exercise, and in the context of Figure 1.1, we can use the various local submissions to explore some of the gaps in our knowledge of local–central relations in spatial economic policy. These include issues related to: first, conventional local economic analysis – the development of local economies, the perception of problems from within, and their style and method of representation; second, a consideration of processes – local policy formation and strategies of representation, the role of local government officers in policy formation, the significance of representations, and local–central connections; and third, local attitudes to wider policy issues – adding a local view or attitude to the conventional critique of regional policy.

In essence, much can be gleaned from the review exercise on these important questions.

1.3 Concluding Comments

We have now completed our background analysis of the policy context for the 1992/1993 review. The development of spatial economic policy has been charted and we have generated a basic analysis of local–central relations/interactions in spatial economic policy – noting the unequal dependency of the local on the central. We have also set the review into the context of knowns and unknowns in the area of spatial economic policy. The general theme that pervades the chapter and the book is that while regional policy has waned in various ways, it still carries a significance that transcends its level of resourcing and powers. Moreover, events around the Assisted Areas review exercise can be used to gain many insights into issues of local and regional economic development, in effect, to investigate gaps in our knowledge of the policy process.

2

SUBMISSIONS ANALYSIS: LOCAL AUTHORITY ENGAGEMENT, ATTITUDE AND REPRESENTATION

Chapter 1 described the policy context of the 1992/1993 review of the Assisted Areas and established the value of analysing a range of issues which it raised. In this chapter, we set out expectations about the local reaction, assessing the factors conditioning the occurrence and nature of local submissions, and providing a foundation for the analyses that follow in later parts of the book.

The chapter discusses the factors likely to be significant in accounting for the level and style of engagement of some local authorities and not others, and in conditioning attitudes to regional policy, and representations of the local economy. This necessarily builds on the discussion in Chapter 1, but explores some of the finer detail of motives of engagement, factors conditioning the response (or lack of engagement) and, in general, the whole approach to the review exercise. Finally, the chapter underpins the book in two respects, not only establishing a context for understanding the local authority responses and reactions to the review, but also setting a basis for, later, offering some evaluative comment on the quality and approach of the submissions and some prescriptions for success or otherwise in the 'bidding game'.

2.1 Exploring the Submissions

In attempting to generate some expectations about local authority reactions to the review exercise, we can begin with a discussion about initial motives.

2.1.1 Local motives

The initial question that needs to be addressed is what motivates local authorities to engage in the review process? In this respect, we can hypothesise a number of ways of interpreting submissions. Although we are developing our discussion and analysis around submissions that were made in response to a central government consultation paper about the Assisted Areas map, it is clear that the motives for responding are likely to be much more complex than simply the quest for immediate success in securing Assisted Area status. Indeed, in some cases, generally as a secondary aim, submissions may be stimulated by an endeavour to project an image to other parts of an authority. It would thus be somewhat myopic to read only a bid for 'special treatment' into the submissions. There are two sets of reasons behind such a claim:

- Some submissions were obviously defending their existing status, while others were seeking to gain status for the first time or to regain status lost in an earlier round of policy changes (most notably, the refined map introduced in 1984). As such, it is difficult to generalise, even if we assume that the only motive is to secure status and the access to resources that accompanies it. However, there are wider complications.
- Clearly, there was likely to be a much wider array of motives than simply getting 'on the map'.

As such, we need to recognise the range of motives that are likely to be involved in the decision to engage in the review process. Submissions can be interpreted in a variety of ways that are not mutually exclusive. Thus, we might anticipate:

1. Submissions as bid documents, actually seeking to retain or acquire Assisted Area status and thus to secure potential access to 'special treatment' (Pickvance, 1985) – in this case, regional policy resources.

As we have argued in Chapter 1, the endeavour and ability to draw in external resources is a vital element of local authority activity in the 1990s. The quest for resources is bound to be an important consideration for any authority seeking to develop its local economic policy – resources are one of the central conditioning factors in local economic policy variations (Urry, 1990). Of course, there are more complex, related motives linked to bidding. This is a way in which the 'local' may loosen the shackles of subservience to the 'central' during the course of development. The chance to draw in additional development – inward investment, for example – that would not have ordinarily arrived, offers localities an opportunity to build greater long-term prosperity and thus, in principle, and ironically, to reduce the reliance on central government economic support – whether regional, urban or simply reactive (unemployment; training; etc.). This may reimpose the strength of the local authority – and heighten business interest and power.

Submissions as 'bids' for resources is the obvious motive, but there are others. Alternatively or in addition, we might view:

2. Submissions as vehicles for getting on the assistance agenda – setting out 'problems' before central government. Showing that there is a concern for and desire to ameliorate unemployment, industrial demise, etc. at the local level, may be seen as providing a basis for gaining access to future resource opportunities and applications; in other words, setting out problems with a view to accessing resources at some future time – perhaps via European Commission regional policy designation.

In a related sense, we might interpret:

3. Submissions as more widely construed image constructions – seeking to project a particular image to central government and, perhaps, to the outside world.

Under these circumstances, a submission could be interpreted in a number of ways. If direct and deliberate, it could be seen as a defensive device, designed to appease local interests, members of a coalition in the local economy, in an attempt to demonstrate that the local authority (or some groups, such as officers, within it) is seriously intent on engaging with local economic issues. Often it seems, local economic strategies are aimed as much at groups within the confines of the Council itself, as they are at outside influences (Fenton, 1992). A submission could even be seen as the internal (authority) protestations of a single officer or councillor about the lack of commitment to local regeneration. Alternatively, this 'projection' may not be a deliberate strategy; it may simply be a spin-off effect in combination with the quest for resources motive.

4. Submissions might also be viewed as statements of viewpoint, offering attitudes about, in this case, the value and character of regional policy *per se.*

This is the case of the 'local' attempting to influence the course of central government policy development, generally for the benefit of the local economy involved. In some cases, it is likely that submissions were aimed at altering policy access in other places. For example, by arguing for a denial of policy benefits to other areas, a local authority may improve its competitive position overall.

Finally, and perhaps less obviously,

5. Submissions could be interpreted as representations of the local economies and the specific local economic problems involved.

This could also be seen as motivated by indirect factors, perhaps to project an image to specific groups within or outside a local coalition in order to specify resource needs, or to engage and win over others as regards particular local strategies. While there may be an overall recognition of local economic problems in many authorities, there is not always a full recognition of the origins, extent or prescriptive needs, and such a submission may rectify that position. As with (3) above, the motivating force may involve local political purposes in being seen to be defending the local economic territory.

In most cases it is likely that the motives behind the submissions were conditioned by some combination of these considerations. As such, understanding the level of engagement is somewhat complex. Of course, regardless of whether they were directly and deliberately motivated by a desire to project an image or to make a statement, the submissions would have had that potential impact.

Even though an explanation is likely to be difficult to tease out, there is much to be gained in moving towards an understanding. The relevance of these motives lies in the insights they offer for local–central relations.

2.1.2 Factors conditioning the local reactions and responses

Given the motives discussed in section 2.1.1, it is likely that some local authorities will be more inclined to engage in the review process than others. This not only assists us to assess the place-based reaction and to draw insights from that; it is important because it can reveal local attitudes to economic development and so on. Although restrictions of space preclude a full, detailed analysis here, it is important briefly to review the factors and influences involved.

In order to provide a base for evaluating various aspects of the local submissions, we can usefully assess their expected distribution and rationale. In general, various core factors condition local attitudes and approaches to local economic development and we might reasonably expect them to influence and inform reactions to the review process (see Urry, 1990; Bennett and McCoshan, 1993). However, unlike local economic development in general, the topic of regional policy designation is likely to trigger reactions linked more specifically to policy-related factors. These involve a number of key elements and are identified below. Where appropriate, those elements expected to be key to local reactions to the Assisted Areas review are highlighted.

Problems and needs

- *Local 'needs'* as reflected in problems such as unemployment and wider notions of local prosperity – these can be measured with standard variables such as unemployment rates. We would expect engagement behaviour to be influenced by shifts in the level of unemployment and by the incidence of problems – long-term unemployment, low wage rates and so on – linked to labour market inadequacies. As a central variable that contains economic, social and political connotations and that is the universally accepted barometer of area economic inadequacy, unemployment is the key indicator.
- *Local economic status* within a changing economy – local prosperity, perhaps as measured by some multivariate approach. Particularly appropriate would be the 'booming towns' classification which fuses a range of 'prosperity' variables, including unemployment levels, house prices and car ownership (Champion and Green, 1990). Perceived limitations in local prosperity would be expected to motivate an authority to seek support via spatial economic policies.

Policy approaches

- *The established local authority attitude* and approach to local economic development. Engagement in and attitude towards the review is expected to be related to the degree to which the local authority has engaged in local economic policy and the complexion of its engagement; the style of the approach to local economic policy – whether it is aggressive or conservative, reactive or more proactive (Harloe, Pickvance and Urry (eds.), 1990; Novy, 1990); and where the policy position 'fits' into notions of local political attitudes to local economic development (Eisenschitz and Gough, 1993). This will itself be linked to policy positions and local ideologies of local economic development. There are many identifiable positions, whether the broadly constructed – for example, interventionist or not, pro or anti-privatisation (Thanet, see Pickvance, 1990b), or environmentally/preservationist-led (Axford and Pinch, 1994) – or the specifically constructed – for example, growth via renewal and the reconstruction of local economic history (Bassett, 1986), growth via the influx of inward investment, or consolidation around a small firm, local enterprise-led position.

Policy approaches are also necessarily influenced by the operation of opportunities for and constraints on local action (Bennett and McCoshan, 1993).

Opportunities might include strong local partnerships in an area, and traditions of co-operation between elements within a local authority and between the authority and local interests such as the Chambers of Commerce and so on. Constraints might include the disparate and fragmented nature of some local authority areas, the 'negative parochialism' and a go-it-alone approach typified by infighting within an authority, and the lack of significant, innovative business leaders willing and able to engage in local economic development matters. These are all important elements in conditioning central–local relations as reflected in the fact and the style of engagement in the review process.

The experiences of local–central relations

- *The past history and fluidity of local–central relations*; including access to other strands of spatial economic policy. A familiarity with other sources of 'special treatment' such as urban aid is likely – via issues of need and of experience – to lead to involvement in the review process.

Personnel factors

- *The involvement of innovative local officers and/or local politicians* (for example, see the various locality examples in Harloe, Pickvance and Urry, 1990).

The role of key individuals and local coalitions is also vital in central–local engagements. A number of commentators have identified the key influence of individuals in local economic development, whether as leading the drive for development via the implementation of local political ideologies, or interpreting and predicting central government policy shifts (Urry, 1990, p. 190; Bennett and McCoshan, 1993, p. 258). In some cases, the ideological position behind local policy developments has reflected local officer attitudes, although these have normally been framed against a background of political agreement. That said, there is at least a potential for officers to have been instigators and to have moulded policy positions themselves – and this is an issue that has not gained much attention in the past.

Historical policy factors

- *A past history of access to regional policy* and the present status.

Clearly, amongst the list of local influences, the previous status of the areas involved as regards regional policy has a substantial bearing on their engagement in the review, their attitude to regional policy, and in all probability their style of representations of local economic problems. We might envisage 'defenders' aiming to retain their status, and 'seekers' endeavouring to get on to the Assisted Areas map for the first time, or to win back status lost at some previous review.

Policy processes at the local level

- *The functioning of processes involved in forming a policy position* – alliances of support in the locality, local political structures, perhaps a local consensus and liaisons of support (Boddy, Lovering and Bassett, 1986) on local economic needs and on an economic strategy approach; the strength of local spatial coalition – and the depth of private sector involvement (see Bennett and McCoshan, 1993).

An important point here is the degree to which a local authority is subject to the views and constraints of other local agencies. It does seem that this factor – manifest through traditions of co-operation (Birmingham) and the political will to forge agreement on approaches to local policy (Sheffield), for example – has some bearing on policy positioning (see Bennett and McCoshan, 1993, p. 245; Boddy, Lovering and Bassett, 1986).

Summary

It will be some combination of these factors that conditions local–central relations in spatial economic policy and hence the fact and the style of engagement of local authorities in review events such as that involving the 1992 Assisted Areas. Local actions and attitudes are a function of the local economy; local political structures; past histories; the existence of key individuals – officers, local councillors or local business representatives; and so on. Amongst these, the status of the local economy in terms of its job-creating past and potential, its link to past and present spatial economic policy assistance, and the presence of key local officers with a taste for resource-seeking, are probably paramount. Key debates here centre on the motives of the local authorities and the key individuals or groups who condition policy, the degree of influence of local authorities, and the policies and strategies pursued by them. These are questions that we will address later in the book when we come to investigate the degree of engagement in the Assisted Areas review process and other features of the event that generate insight into local authority economic policy actions.

At this stage, we might simply state that local authority economic policy and related sensitivity to central government spatial economic policy contains elements of both local autonomy and external dependency, and the two are intertwined in any actions. We have set up this issue already in the book by stressing the tensions between the drive for independent control over policy and the need for development resources from central government funding (Chapter 1). At a local autonomous level we might interpret submissions as reflecting representations of place through local economic problems – a kind of drive to establish the particularities of a local economic profile – perhaps even as defending the territory against economic decline and dislocation. At a dependency level, the submissions link to local–central relations, subservience, entry to the 'bidding game', and representations about the value of and need for regional policy support. This is a lobbying and counselling function of the submissions that connects to dependence on external resources, although it may, over the longer term, provide a foundation for a stronger local economy and a potential for enhanced local autonomy. That is a matter for debate concerning the effects of policy support and the way in which 'prosperity' corresponds to local autonomy. It may well simply transfer the dependency function to dominant local business leaders.

Finally, although we are initially focusing on the act or degree of engagement, we will also be covering the style of engagement in our exploration. That may be just as important and revealing – perhaps more so – than the simple act of engagement itself.

2.2 Representations of Local Economic Problems

A central feature of the 'bidding game' concerns the ways that local authorities represent their economies to the 'outside'. Representations of local economic problems and profiles open up a whole area of insight – but also require a supporting conceptual underpinning. What conditions the representations made, the strategies involved, the images created and so on? Writers have not addressed this perspective on the local economy before, but we can draw some ideas from related work on representing place through marketing (Kearns and Philo, 1993) (and see Chapter 1). For example, Woodward has addressed the debate over the Spitalfields redevelopment in east London. With different agendas for the local future from developers and anti-redevelopment campaigners, two different representations or images of the area were 'constructed'. Spitalfields was portrayed as either derelict and problematic and in need of radical redevelopment or a community with character that needed to be preserved (Woodward, 1993). Work such as this can inform our analysis of representations of local economic problems.

2.2.1 The importance of local representations of economic problems

It is well known that representations of place are important in policy terms. In the discussion about place marketing in Chapter 1, we argued that the image of a place is important in conditioning its chances of 'success' in the economic development stakes. More than that, the way in which the local economy and its problems is 'packaged' and presented sends signals to developers, influences the way that development is viewed from within the area and so on. Representations are also indicative of the objectives of those doing the packaging (Sadler, 1993). In this way, representations 'project and reflect'.

Representations of the kinds of local economic problems discussed in this book are obviously important if they generate resources for enhancing local economic prospects. On the negative side, within the context of a growth-led local strategy, a poor image might connect with a lack of speculative development and constraints on local economic regeneration (Goodwin, 1993).

2.2.2 Promoting a place's problems and potentials – tensions in the dual representations

In Chapter 1 we also discussed the contrasts between the marketing of a place for promotion as an industrial location, and the representations of a place for the purposes of accessing support policies. There are important similarities and differences that inform our understanding of the latter. In contrast to the place marketing for promotion discussed in Chapter 1, the version of marketing that involves representations of local economic problems is much more fraught with potential (perceived) pitfalls. It just might obviate any 'good works' achieved by place promotion of the positive kind – representations might cancel each other out, and they probably do in some instances. There are thus representational tensions in the selling of a place through its 'problems' and through its 'potentials'. Is it possible to do both at the same time? Representations for support often include references to, and become tangential with, regeneration or growth-led place marketing that eschews the growth virtues of a place. Manchester, in its combined submission to the review, adopted this approach, spelling out problems – although not overstressing them – but also focusing on the potential of specific areas – for example, the Trafford Park industrial estate as a growth centre. In this way, the potential tensions may be turned to good effect through a particular strategy of representation.

Marketing for support is not only more 'dangerous' in the negative images that it could project and the local conflicts that it might generate (see Sadler, 1993 on the conflicts between analyses of North East problems, and how the local business community would prefer the area to be represented). Given pre-specified 'rules of engagement', it also has less room for manouevre, less flexibility in the images and ideas that it can project. That said, we might argue that an important area of flexibility here concerns the technical use and portayal of information. This will be discussed a little later.

There are also similarities between promotion for boosting the local economy and for accessing support from central government or elsewhere. The principles that have evolved in the latter may well be applicable in the former. Both construct images for a specific (sometimes targeted) objective. Both utilise the same processes of selectivity in the material projected and strategy in the method of portrayal. The results of both can, in theory, be tested against specified criteria. As such, established approaches for the promotion of a place can be analysed and adapted to the promotion of its problems.

2.2.3 An analytical base for assessing representations of local economic problems

There is, however, little in the literature on representations of local economic problems and so we must construct a fresh analytical base (and one that serves the needs of assessment, understanding and prescription for practitioners). In this regard, it seems that representations of local economic problems can be usefully assessed and interpreted at two levels. At a primary level, representations are guided by local economic policy position and approach. This sets the parameters and bounds of the representational base.

Representational base

The representational base reflects the principles of local economic policy and approach (section 2.1.2) and thus the consensus that has evolved within the confines of local political approaches and any coalition strategy as regards the local economy. It is therefore reflective of the style of involvement – whether the local authority is aggressive or complacent, reactive or more proactive, keen to enter into inter-area competition, the condition of the local economy, and all of the factors that lead to such a policy position. The fact and style of representation as regards a review of the Assisted Areas will derive from the degree of engagement with facilitative support and the role that lobbying for resources is assigned. The representational base conditions whether local authorities will make representations in the first place and, if they are to do so, what the structure and style of the submissions will be. For example, will there be a particular stress on local economic features that have been prioritised as of central concern, or will a broad-brush approach be adopted?

Each representation by each authority is unique. A question that must be raised at this point is whose views are being represented. It may well be that a coalition expresses a viewpoint, but it may equally be an individual officer who is given or takes on the initiative to represent. This has two implications. First, representations may be reflective of a single view. Second, they will vary over time in line with changing personnel, as much as with changing economic circumstances and ideological shifts on the part of local politicians. That said, once established, ideological positions *vis-à-vis* growth strategies become firmly entrenched. As Pickvance argues, local politicians' ideologies regarding economic development show a certain stability, even in the face of changes that, in reality, dislodge the foundations of such approaches. For example, the attraction of firms into a local economy has been justified in the increased fiscal base that it provided. However, in practice, increased rates income led to lower central grants. Yet, the belief in the fiscal advantages of growth prevailed (Pickvance, 1991). As such, representations are time-specific and, potentially, group or individual-specific.

Representational detail

Within and against the baseline position, representations are the product of individual and technical factors. Representational detail refers to the precise strategy and approach adopted in making a representation. It will reflect the use or deployment of key local problems and attitudes to solving them. There are various technical alternatives in representing particular local economic problems and the approach adopted will reflect the decisions and expertise of local officers, and possibly councillors, and the availability of suitable resources for funding a representation. It is at this stage in the process that considerations of the financial costs (and wider benefits) of submissions and the representations made will be assessed. Just as Burgess (1982) questioned the efficacy of allocating resources to potentially ineffective marketing and associated documentation, so the same is beginning to occur in this area of representation.

In these ways, we can interpret local authority representations of local economic problems on two levels: first, at a policy and strategy level – in terms of the representational base; and second, at a linked and complementary technical and resource-based level – in terms of representational detail. Any particular set of representations of, say, local labour market problems can be usefully assessed in these terms.

Representational methods and image construction

Having set the scene with a discussion of the basis of any representations, we can move on to consider representational methods and image construction. In any sphere of activity, representations are typified by their selective use of information and by how they actually project and portray that material. In representing problems in particular ways, local authorities are fashioning a spatial identity whose impact may extend well beyond the confines of the one-off event. Clearly, the whole idea of representations links to place marketing and inter-area competition. In zero sum game terms, and especially given European Commission restrictions on the population that can be included in the Assisted Areas, the award of, say, Assisted Area status to one area will be at the expense of somewhere else. There is thus a potential tendency for representations to be used as competitive devices – to project an image that the area is worse off than neighbours, the average, or whatever. In the quest to differentiate, there may be a search for an alternative angle on a particular problem. There is the possibility of using basic statistical data, diagrams or other images to get the message across.

The question of what to include and how to include it in the Assisted Areas review exercise was partly conditioned by the 'rules of engagement' (section 1.2). However, the degree of flexibility officially allowed gave authorities an opportunity to develop their techniques of representation and, where possible and feasible, to go beyond conventional representations of issues such as unemployment (Chapter 8) or peripherality (Chapter 9); in short, flexibility was permitted by the initial specification (DTI, Scottish Office and Welsh Office, 1992). The approach adopted in fashioning representations, in particular, the degree to which the emphasis is on problems, potentials, or both, will also connect to local economic status.

A focus on representations of local economic problems in the course of the Assisted Areas map review therefore offers some important insights into the policy process. The approaches adopted reflect the nature of the local economy and the particular viewpoint about the use of external support in ameliorating any problems. It is thus related to ideology and policy position, with interventionist authorities expected to be amongst the strongest protagonists or campaigners. For some authorities, constrained by a fear of revealing their local economic limitations, a more defensive posture may prevail. That said, the tendency for local economic policy generally to align to a growth-led approach means that the quest for external resources may be important in many cases and that the great majority of authorities will be keen to enter the 'bidding game'. Whatever the approach, there is a wide range of choice in the data and technique and the method of portrayal. In Part 4 of the book, we will go on to investigate this uncharted territory of the spatial economic policy arena.

2.3 The Background to the Review Response

This chapter has provided an explanatory context for assessing responses to the 1992/1993 review of the Assisted Areas. Building on the policy context set out in Chapter 1, we have used ideas about the motives behind any submission together with evidence from previous research on local economic policy to suggest expected reactions and levels of engagement. We have gone on to discuss the influences affecting local authority representations of their local economic problems, projections of the 'local' that transcend the Assisted Areas review exercise by carrying ideas and images about the places involved, and which may have wider connotations over time.

At this stage it is important to draw and link together two general observations from the debate. First, the majority of local authorities are actively engaged in advancing their local economies, and second, the specific circumstances of the involvement of any single authority or agency is unique. We cannot, as Duncan and Goodwin (1988) have noted, simply read-off policy variations from problem situations. We need to delve into the specificities of any local situation, in terms of both economic status, and local policy profile – the types of employment, the unemployment profile, the role of coalitions and so on.

While there may be a consensus in terms of local economic policy, its enactment varies in as many ways as there are enacters. This is well illustrated in the literature. For example, Urry, in assessing local policy in Swindon, shows how the complexion of the policy position was largely moulded by a growth coalition based around local officers and local councillors. Their expertise, and taste for experimentation in local economic policy, together with the requisite financial and organisational skills to be able to develop a virtually autonomous form of local development policy, was crucial and, in its detailed make-up, unique. However, even this story becomes more complex, because the success of Swindon in local economic terms also meshed with factors such as its geographical location and its relatively low-cost development sites and the ability of local actors to make the most effective use of that local situation over time (Urry, 1990).

There are many examples of the specific nuances of local economic policy in the detailed work of Bennett and McCoshan. For example, the case of Dundee is used to demonstrate the wide range of local factors that combine to produce a policy position. In Dundee, policy has been moulded by traditional rivalries and tensions with other parts of Tayside, infighting within, for example, the District Council, complacency in some of its key businesses, a resistance to innovative policy on the part of the local Chamber of Commerce, and a reticence on the part of many local actors to external policy potentials. This situation, together with a complex relationship with the Scottish Development Agency and, latterly, the Local Enterprise Council, has generated a complex and unique set of local circumstances (Bennett and McCoshan, 1993, pp. 280–4).

Just focusing on one feature of local economic policy generates a feeling for the specificities of each authority. As Eisenschitz and Gough show, the nuances of local politics are sufficient on their own to generate as many different policy complexions as there are authorities. For example, the 'good environment' planning traditions of many Conservative-controlled Home Counties authorities contrast with the centrist traditions developed in Labour strongholds in central Scotland, south Wales and north east England (Eisenschitz and Gough, 1993, p. 271). In addition, each authority has its own local conventions and traditions, its own history of intervention and its own particular economic and social setting, so that no two authorities, even in political heartlands, ever enact the same local economic policy approach, or nurture the same local economic ideals. This uniqueness means that the cameos discussed in Chapter 5, Part 2 take on a real importance within the sweep of this book.

However, there is of course a certain commonality to an understanding of any local situation. As Urry (1990) suggests, policy variations can be addressed using the key factors of conditions (external circumstances involving economic, politi-cal or cultural trends) and resources (legacies of labour force character or built environment, locational attributes, financial resources, organisational abilities within a locality, and legitimacy framed by public support for local policy). Local economic policy approaches and local prognostications on policy change are bound to follow some broadly common influences. The availability of resources, the need for local economic development as perceived by the local authority, the nature of certain types of local conditions, are the key. All this, together with the substantial evidence of consensus in the rationale for local economic policy, renders the assessment and understanding of local policy positions feasible. Moreover, as we have shown earlier in this chapter, there are certain key factors that help us to comprehend the policy position. We have a picture of consensus in local authority economic policies and approaches, with the style and detailed content varying according to a variety of local issues and factors. It is within this context that viewpoints, sensitivities, reactions and representations over cen-trally allocated spatial economic policy resources can be most effectively placed.

The conclusion is that submissions are likely to be motivated by a range of considerations and that, against this background, factors such as relative econ-omic position, past history of status and local aspirations for prosperity combine in potentially complex ways to condition any reaction. Such considerations also influence attitudes to regional policy and the ways in which local economic problems are represented to outsiders. The detailed assessment and interpreta-tion of these features of the local submissions will be completed in Parts 3 and 4.

The review response information allows us to document and analyse the responses/submissions, to move towards an understanding of why there was a response and the nature of those submissions, to comment on various aspects of local–central connections, and, ultimately, even to offer prescriptive suggestions on playing the 'bidding game'. In Part 2, we will investigate the level and nature of the reaction to the review process and attempt an explanation of the degree and style of engagement in terms of the factors set out in this chapter.

2.4 Conclusion:
Reaction (Engagement) – Attitude – Representation

There are various ways in which we can interpret local submissions to the As-sisted Areas review. They can be viewed as straightforward bids for status that lock on to the regional policy issue, as image constructions, and as vehicles for the representation of local economic problems. Each can be developed as a perspective on local authority economic policy. While the chapter has endeav-oured to be scene-setter, it has become just as much a question-raiser. There is so much that we do not know about local–central connections over spatial econ-omic, and especially regional, policy and little or no comparative work across authorities. That leaves an important gap in the interpretation and understand-ing of the policy arena but it is one that can be rectified to a degree using the responses to the Assisted Areas review. This offers a rich source of valuable information and it is towards an evaluation of the material that we turn in Chapter 3.

3

BUILDING AN ANALYSIS FROM RESPONSES TO THE REVIEW

In this chapter we complete two necessary preliminary tasks before the detailed analysis of local engagement with the review. First, we take a harder, more critical look at just what the local responses to both the consultation phase of the review event and its outcome can offer in the way of insights into spatial economic policy. Second, having considered the pros and cons of building analysis around what amounts to a set of representations, we examine the appropriate methods than might be used actually to analyse it. That involves a discussion of the technical, methodological factors and a brief debate about approaches and methods in content analysis – the simple approach that forms part of the analysis in later chapters.

3.1 Submissions Analysis – What it Can and Cannot Tell Us

Standard treatments of the various strands of spatial economic policy, whether focusing on an individual element such as regional policy (Armstrong and Taylor, 1987) or covering the full array of policy approaches (Prestwich and Taylor, 1990), tend to offer a tried and tested formula for analysis and evaluation: a statement of the sphere of influence of each policy element; a critical assessment of its power and influence in the space economy; and an evaluation of its impact. Such an approach – useful in its own domain and context – tends to give a rather superficial and restricted coverage of policy. For example, they often say little or nothing about the degree of engagement of local authorities and others in spatial economic policy, the process of policy/strategy formation on the part of the 'local', compromises and conflicts, or the attitudes and activities of those actors and agencies most heavily involved and implicated. The importance of local economic development has been recognised (Miller, 1990), but the projection of the 'local' into the realms of the 'regional' and the 'national' has certainly not been given much, if any, recognition and attention. The importance of central–local relationships has, of course, been recognised by many researchers (Tye and Williams, 1994; Pickvance, 1990b). More recently, with the shift towards competitive bidding for geographically sensitive policy support, the attention of commentators has been drawn to some of the issues involved. These cover the full width of changing relations between the local and central levels of intervention. Not least of all, the cost-effectiveness of bid document production has become a practical concern (see Oatley, 1994). In this way, the whole arena of the 'bidding game' and the ways in which a local authority or partnership projects and represents itself is likely to come up for much greater scrutiny by practitioners and academics alike.

Against this background, what is the potential of the Assisted Areas review exercise as a basis for analysing spatial economic policy? What can it offer that goes beyond the so-called standard treatments discussed above?

3.1.1 The basic potential of the review exercise

Clearly, the review provides a common reference point around which to document and judge local authority responses. Where else can we obtain:

1. a comparable representation for a wide array of local authorities and local partnerships;
2. detail on participants and non-participants in this aspect of the development process as revealed by responses or otherwise to the review?

The value of the approach becomes even clearer when we start to detail the range of insights that are possible. First, however, we should briefly detail the nature of what we will refer to as the 'review response data base'.

The 317 submissions to the Assisted Areas review varied considerably in their documentation. A small number provided only a letter setting out the local position over local economic change, Assisted Area status and so on. At the other extreme, some authorities – more often those working in partnership with other authorities, agencies (such as TECs), and private sector interests – submitted detailed analyses, sometimes expensively produced. Most commonly, substantial documents were submitted. The review response data base contains transcribed details of each submission providing great potential for comparative analysis and scope for detailed investigation of key issues, areas or policy angles (liaisons, strategies adopted and so on).

3.1.2 The value of the review response data base

The data base has the following potentials:

To assess the submissions in terms of who has made them, what factors and approaches are being used and how the submission/representation is formulated

The data source provides a unique opportunity to develop a full comparative assessment of local attitudes to spatial economic policy. Some recent work has begun to focus on the complexities of local economic policy (for example, Bennett and McCoshan, 1993) but they tend, understandably given resource constraints, to lock on to selected local authorities and other agents covering a range of sample area types. The data source used here enables a comparative analysis to be completed across all localities.

In addition, we really know very little about the detail of local representations – to what extent were central issues or problems such as peripherality, local labour market status, the character of the local industrial base used in the various representations, and in what ways? The review exercise data provides a 'way in' to these issues, constituting a genuinely untapped area of understanding and one which has a great importance within the context of local economic development. How places represent themselves both tells us much about their make-up and influences how they are seen by outsiders.

Finally, a related benefit is that we are able to consider what motives actually lay behind the submissions made. Were they actually seeking Assisted Area status or simply seeking to raise the profile of the locality – or both? Were there other considerations, of the type discussed in Chapter 2, in the submission decision? By using supplementary survey data for a few selected areas (in Part 2, Chapter 5), we are able to investigate this dimension of the review response.

To build on what is a modest array of previous work on local perceptions of policy potential and local representations

Previous research has established the importance of regional policy benefits for those local economies so designated (Begg, 1993; Sheehan, 1993). Elsewhere, there are a whole array of studies that have recognised the catalytic role that policy benefits can have (Chapter 6 covers this aspect of attitudes to and perceptions of regional benefits by local authorities in much more detail). However, rarely have questions of local attitudes to and perceptions of regional policy – or indeed other policy – benefits been posed. Exactly what do local authorities and other local actors think about regional policy; what factors fashion their viewpoints; and so on? Previous research has largely ignored the consideration of these potentially important questions. As Eisenschitz and Gough (1993, p. 184) exclaim, 'the relation of local policy to higher spatial levels of intervention has received remarkably little attention'. The data set offers a unique opportunity to evaluate the viewpoint of local economic practitioners from a wide range of local economic environments on the efficacy of regional policy. In effect, it provides what is a comprehensive data base on this unresearched aspect of spatial economic policy.

To generate an appraisal of local economic position as reflected in the protestations of local interests – most of which are entirely 'officer-led'

Clearly, a key potential with the review exercise data set is that it allows us to build an understanding of local economic geographies at the time of the review. This offers a unique basis around which to assess, essentially officer-based, analyses of local position. As part of this, the submissions often contain research data and/or the findings of research on the local economy as produced by themselves or private consultants. Unless local authorities have a policy of publishing their background research findings – and many do not – such material would not be readily, if at all, available for research analysis. Their inclusion in the submissions offers an added bonus for research and analysis based on the material.

To explore a range of issues that can be generated within the data source – for example, what variations are apparent between localities and local authorities; what strategies have been used and why

As we will find with the analysis of local responses in Chapter 4, there is great variation in, for example, the nature of the submissions and representations made, or in the degree of collusion or liaison between local authorities and other agencies or groups in the area. Detailing exactly what kinds of liaisons have taken place and seeking to understand the substance of such joint representations offers insights into the functioning of coalitions.

In addition of course, by closely analysing the submissions and the processes involved in formulating them, much can be gleaned about the thinking behind local economic policy in any particular area. To take just three examples: which areas did and which areas did not respond to the DTI consultation paper? What coalitions, if any, were formed and do the representations reflect a narrow (single local authority) or a wider locality that pulls together one or more local authorities plus other local interests such as the Training and Enterprise Councils, local businesses and so on? How were the representations framed – did they tend to stress certain strategic ideas that thus reflect the local economic policy approach in the area?

To generate new insights into the processes of spatial economic policy-making at the local level

Throughout the book, and in particular in Chapter 5, we will be seeking to generate fresh theoretical insights into policy. This will involve the construction of theoretical approaches which seek to 'place' local authority submissions and representations into the context of policy formation.

Finally, from a wider perspective, a consideration of the value of the static data source offers an opportunity to evaluate the pros and cons of such data sources with a view to offering guidance on their use in a variety of contexts. In this chapter, we are in the process of such an evaluation.

3.2 Methods of Approach

In the chapter so far we have charted the pros and cons of using local submission documents in the analysis of *local perceptions of need* as evoked through attitudes to regional policy, and *local perceptions of economic problems* as manifested through representations of the local economy. We have concluded that, with suitable reservations, such documents can be an immensely valuable, and are, in effect, a hitherto untapped resource in the study of local authority economic policy. Moreover, we have argued that the representations themselves – their content, style, approach and so on – enable us to delve into local attitudes in a way that is not possible using conventional approaches in local and regional economic studies. The question that remains, however, concerns the methods to be used in analysing the submissions and the advantages and disadvantages that they might have.

3.2.1 Analysing the submissions

Clearly, submissions such as those made by local authorities can be simply read and interpreted in an individual way. The basic arguments can be extracted and so on. Indeed, this qualitative approach is used later in the book. However, there is also much to be gained in standardising the material in some way. The desire to render submissions comparable across localities creates problems similar to those confronting political analysts and others in their work on the content of speeches and documents in the media studies field (Krippendorf, 1980). In analysing statements, speeches and documents there is often a need to analyse the detailed nuances, comments, and so on in an endeavour to tease out, for example, changes in policy and in attitudes. Content analysis is a common method for such a task, and a simple form of this would seem to be a useful approach to adopt and adapt for the purposes of the submissions analysis.

Content analysis normally refers to the systematic analysis of speeches, newspaper reports or other writings in an attempt to describe and classify their content. This is designed to produce classifications that are testable using some objective criteria. While a typical use of the approach would be the analysis of political speeches to elicit changing attitudes or expectations via the subtleties of language, it can be adapted and simplified to analyse documents such as those discussed in this book. That said, a full discourse analysis is not, given the nature of the task, an appropriate approach for the submissions investigation.

While content analysis can be usefully adapted for the purposes of the book, the form used is minimalist, and not subject to the stringency of formal methods. The approach is simply deployed systematically to extract pre-specified elements from the various submissions. In effect, it involves a limited range of angles, being used to:

- summarise submission documents by extracting key pre-specified elements – the Assisted Areas review criteria guidelines; viewpoints about regional policy, etc.;
- compare the actual content of submissions with prescribed guidelines in order to draw out exaggerations;
- compare the proportion of documents ascribed to particular submission features (for example, the space alloted to unemployment analysis);
- analyse documents to draw out the private sector contribution;

and, in a more general way, to:

- assess the quality of a document using objective criteria;
- search for language and visual image themes;
- identify methods used to represent key local economic problems;
- identify strategies implicit in the documentation.

This approach to submissions analysis provides a common comparative basis for evaluating local responses, teasing out strategies and approaches that are initially implicit in the documentation. It cannot, however, explain the attitudes involved in the documents or the type and style of representations made. That needs a rather more direct approach – a survey that can supplement the submissions analysis with fuller inside evidence on the pressures and processes involved in formulating the document, and in this way really open up the processes for scrutiny.

3.2.2 *The supplementary survey*

The submissions stand as statements of attitude, strategy, representation and much more. They are immensely valuable as documentary sources and much can be gleaned from their dissection and analysis. However, the written material cannot reveal the precise thinking behind its formation and production. That requires some supporting follow-up work. A survey was therefore designed to elicit information on responses to the review exercise that could not be discerned from the actual submissions. This sought to generate material on the following:

Forming the submission: the motives behind the response; considerations which led to the inclusion/exclusion of particular aspects; consultations involved in the process of forming a response – internal, political, or other groups; the involvement of local interests and the degree of dialogue with outside agencies; conflicts and compromises; who met the costs of producing the document; factors stressed and why; was any particular strategy involved; and were any problems deliberately omitted from the submission?

Managing the submission: was there a deliberate strategy to manage the representation; were other representations made; how were these organised and which were most effective?

Wider issues: attitude to regional policy over the years; has it changed; other connections between authority/agency and central government agencies as regards local economic development; self-perception of local economic status and future potential?

Reactions to the revised Assisted Areas map: what local reactions occurred; were any further representations made in the wake of the outcome?

None of these dimensions of locally derived policy or of local–central connections could have been analysed without the additional data produced from the survey. A wide range of useful material was generated and this forms an important part of our analysis in later chapters (especially in Chapter 5).

3.3 The Limitations

Against the clear benefits already established we must counterpose the limitations of the review response data source, constraints that apply to both the documentary and the survey material.

Initially, it is worth noting that there has been some work on local policy that used a similar approach. For example, Hudson and Townsend (1992) surveyed local authorities to elicit information on their local tourism strategies. Interestingly, the sample response was less than 20 per cent. Even so, they were able to utilise the data effectively. The research around which the present book is framed was able to build analysis from a much stronger, complete data base.

Despite the 'comfort' of a 100 per cent sample of local authority reactions, it is clearly not possible to 'read' too much from the representations. They are only 'representations' and are designed for a purpose, i.e. to get across a local message about the local economy. Moreover, they reflect a range of unique, complex influences. As Duncan and Goodwin (1988) argue, and as we have already noted, we are not able to 'read-off' policy formation and attitudes directly from the basic 'status' of places.

In another sense, it is clear that the statements made on behalf of localities are sometimes designed as much to 'stir up' local politicians as they are to represent and reflect the area to external assessors (Fenton, 1992). As such, we must take care in what we read into, and draw out of, the submissions.

There is also a 'non-comparability' constraint with the use of the various documents as local representations. They derive from authorities with very different resources and thus potential for active involvement in processes of policy formation. They do not follow consistent formats. For example, they vary in length and content – some are veritable treasure troves of data; others are rather bland statements of intent and/or of local economic problems. As such, it is sometimes difficult to make comparisons – some authorities have really not provided a viewpoint on the policy package, or sought to represent their local economic problems in any particular depth. However, this 'level of vigour' in itself reflects a particular central–local policy stance on the part of the authority involved.

Finally, it is clear that the submissions – and the representations made therein – are framed at one particular point in time. Representations will change over time in accordance with changes in economic circumstances, political pressures, the presence of key individuals and so on. As such, there is a potential problem of outdatedness, although as long as this is accepted then there need be no real limit on the data source. That said, there is much more that we can do with submission documents than simply to explore the anatomy of the review exercise and, in some cases, constraints can be turned to advantage – for example, representations are valuable in their own right – and that will become apparent as we work through Parts 2, 3 and 4.

3.4 Concluding Comments

In this chapter we have focused on the pros and cons and methods involved in analysing local authority submissions to the Assisted Areas review exercise. We have concluded that documentary submissions are a potentially rich, novel source of information. Especially when supplemented with survey material, they enable us to lock on to attitudes and representations. These can be used to elicit much about the actions and activities of local authorities in the field of regional policy and, indeed, a much wider array of insights can be worked up. There are, of course, pros and cons, and the material is not perfect. However, it offers a way in to dimensions of the policy arena that either are costly to study or, more likely, cannot be so easily accessed or confronted using other methods and materials. In later parts of the book we go on to make use of this material in discussing the *engagement* of local authorities in the review process and the development of local economies and, most important, developing analyses from the review response material, in addressing *attitudes* about the needs of the local as expressed in views about regional policy, and *representations* about its specific problems.

PART 2

Documenting and Explaining the Local Authority Responses

4

ENGAGING WITH THE 1992/1993 ASSISTED AREAS REVIEW

Southampton did not make a formal submission . . . there was little chance . . . of success (and) we were also concerned that an application for Assisted Area status may send the wrong signals to potential inward investors when the City Council and its partners are promoting the area as having the foundations of a strong local economy.
(Southampton City Council, Department of Strategy and Development, 18 February 1994)

The role of Assisted Area status is clear. It provides the vital incentive for companies to invest in an economy which is capable of halting decline and steering in the direction of growth.
(Mansfield District Council Submission, p. 11)

The quest for Assisted Area status, and the access to regional policy support that it provides, is not a universally popular pursuit. For a variety of reasons, some local authorities do not seek to acquire it. Others, however, seek it with vigour. It is, in that sense, immediately highlighted as a potentially controversial issue.

This chapter is the first of two on the level and distribution of responses to the consultation phase of the 1992/1993 Assisted Areas review and the processes through which the submissions were formulated. It looks at who responded and who did not respond, and describes and discusses the basic nature of the submissions. There is some analysis of liaisons between authorities, other local agencies and the private sector, together with an evaluation of the quality and approach of the local submissions. The chapter also deals with the 'why' element in as much as it can be discerned from the submissions material. It investigates what motivated local responses to the review exercise and, aside from the actual engagement, what factors governed the submission strategy – including what material was included, and in what style and approach.

4.1 Who, How, and Why Does it Matter?

The engagement of local authorities in the review process is important in a number of ways. From a policy analysis perspective, it opens up the area of local–central relations in spatial economic policy. As regards the 'local', it reveals the insider viewpoint, perhaps signifies local liaisons between local interests, and helps to contextualise the ways in which authorities function as facilitators. Who engages and who does not, and their motives for doing so, can be deployed as a surrogate for understanding other aspects of local attitudes to development, policy position, and operating style. Aggressive involvement spells a determination to develop, perhaps to regenerate the local economy and sends signals to the outside world. A lack of engagement suggests complacency or compliance, and also sends signals, of a different kind. Within the context of these variable approaches, it is important to chart variations in reactions to problems such as unemployment or to the potentials that access to regional policy could unleash. Particularly important is the fact that the review response data used in the book enables us to range across the full width of local attitudes, economic and political complexions and geographical settings in exploring this aspect of the policy arena.

Aside from the fact of engagement, the style in which the submission is produced is also likely to be (even more) revealing of local authority approaches to local economic development. The packages of arguments generated, the emphasis placed on particular factors and so on, is clearly indicative of wider attitudes to development.

From a resource access perspective – something of direct interest to practitioners – engagement style is hypothesised and perceived to be particularly important. The image projected may or may not influence resource acquisition, but in a policy arena where competitive bidding is predominating as a method for the distribution of regional and urban aid, such matters cannot be ignored.

4.2 'Nailing Your Colours to the Mast'

The documentary submissions to the DTI and the various regional offices were dominated in number and depth of material by those stemming from local authorities (Appendix 1, Table A.1.1). Moreover, much of the non-local authority response was engineered by authorities in support of their submissions and the bids that they contained. As such, these take on the guise of collusions of an indirect nature. There was a range of interesting non-local authority responses – and many contain illuminating ideas which will be drawn into the analysis later in the book – but they are relatively few in number.

Submissions were made on behalf of 214 of the 322 Travel-to-Work Areas (TTWA) in Great Britain (67 per cent) (Tables 4.1 and A.1.2). Thus, in over 100 local labour market areas, no local voice – local authority, Chamber of Commerce, local businesses, or even MPs – was forthcoming as regards the review of the Assisted Areas. There was some regional and local variation in this pattern. This is unsurprising given the nature of the geographical economy on the eve of the review (Figure 4.1). If we take this distribution of unemployment as a 'benchmark' figure for assessing engagement, then we would expect wide differences in response.

Relatively few representations were made for TTWAs in East Anglia, with less than 50 per cent of those in the South West represented. Regions such as the South East, the East Midlands and West Midlands had around 50 per cent of their TTWAs represented, but in the more peripheral regions where regional

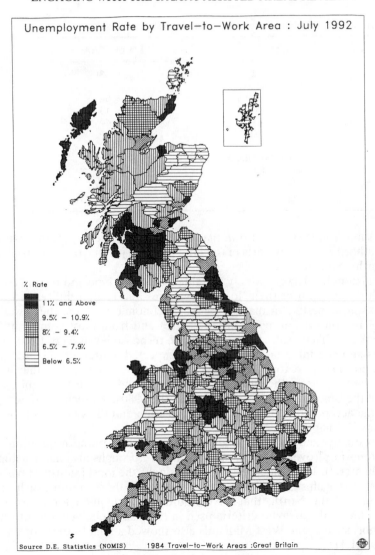

Unemployment Rate by Travel—to—Work Area : July 1992

% Rate

11% and Above
9.5% – 10.9%
8% – 9.4%
6.5% – 7.9%
Below 6.5%

Source D.E. Statistics (NOMIS)   1984 Travel—to—Work Areas :Great Britain

Figure 4.1 The geographical distribution of unemployment on the eve of the Assisted Areas review exercise.

policy is something of a traditional pursuit – the North, Wales and Scotland – the level of representation was very high (Tables 4.1 and A.1.2). Engagement with issues of regional policy, it seems, strongly reflects north–south differences, although, as we will show, matters have changed (Chapter 7).

Over 60 per cent of local authorities – 317 in total – presented some level of response to the Assisted Areas review consultation paper (Tables A.1.1 and A.1.3). There is no benchmark against which to assess and evaluate this level of reaction, but, perhaps in view of the low profile of regional policy at the time of the review, it seemed initially to be a rather high level. However, further analysis

Table 4.1   Level of TTWA representation at the consultation phase

Region	% of TTWAs
South East	53
West Midlands	52
East Midlands	52
East Anglia	19
South West	44
North West	82
North	100
Yorkshire/Humberside	68
Scotland	95
Wales	85
Total	67

of the submissions (Chapter 6 in particular) reveals the importance with which local authorities in many parts of the UK – and not just the old industrial areas of the North – view regional policy.

Submission levels were widely variable by locality type and region. Reflective of both the breadth of their 'local' economies and responsibility, and their resources and expertise in matters of local economic analysis, there was a high level of response from major urban centres and from most county authorities (Table A.1.3). That aside, the most notable response levels were from industrial districts and coastal areas. The former is expected – after all, regional policy is geared up to support for industrial activity (Chapter 1). On the other hand, the strong 'showing' from the latter is less expected, and reflects the demise of many parts of the 'sea-sector' over the course of the 1980s. As such, more will be said about the acceptability of this area identification and the vagaries of the coastal economy in Chapter 6.

Interestingly, and reflecting the sensitivity of the 'southern question', a sizeable proportion (over 50 per cent) of London Boroughs also made submissions (see Chapter 7). That aside, and not surprisingly, the most intensive level of local authority (as against TTWA) response occurred in those regions, such as Wales, Scotland and the North, that have traditionally qualified for regional policy support under the array of criteria used in the past. Relatively recent recipients of support such as the West Midlands also showed a high level of local response (Table A.1.4).

Simply charting the submissions is clearly of great interest and importance in any understanding of spatial economic policy, particularly as it pertains to the interaction of the local and the regional. Beyond that, the submissions also allow us to consider the groupings that produced them. Many were submitted by individual local authorities; but a large number were the product of liaisons, and that connects the review exercise with the subject of coalitions (see Chapter 1).

4.3 Whose Submission? The Incidence of Liaison and the Coalition Factor

Another aspect of the submissions concerns the level of liaison involved in their production. To what extent were coalitions involved in the process, what kinds of internal and external liaison occurred, which local authorities liaised and why, and what was the role for coalitions that included local business representation? Building on the discussion in Chapter 1, there is an opportunity here to delve into the whole area of local coalition – something that is such an important part of life for British local authorities in the 1990s.

4.3.1 The extent of local authority liaison in the submissions

There were a large number of jointly produced submissions (Table 4.2) – in fact, nearly half of the total representation for local authorities involved some type of direct liaisons in the production of the 'bid' document. Around half of those

Table 4.2 Liaisons in the submissions

Type	Number	% of all submissions
LA independent	169	54
LA grouping	77	24
LA+ grouping (TECs)	71	22
All	317	100

were liaisons between groups of authorities representing either the whole of a particular Travel-to-Work Area (TTWA) (for example, the submission for the Goole and Selby TTWA jointly produced by Boothferry Borough Council, Selby District Council and North Yorkshire County Council). The other half were wider groupings. These normally involved the direct involvement of the local Training and Enterprise Council, Chamber of Commerce, local Enterprise Agency and so on. For example, there was a joint submission for the Manchester conurbation core which was produced by the four Metropolitan Boroughs plus the two TECs and the two Development Corporations. Others were joint submissions covering more than one TTWA, for example, the submission for the two TTWAs in south east Hampshire (Portsmouth TTWA and Gosport and Fareham TTWA) which was jointly produced by the four local authorities, the Hampshire TEC and the South East Hampshire Chamber of Commerce. In sum, there were many joint submissions. By virtue of their combined effort, submissions involving a number of authorities who liaised to produce a co-ordinated approach – and often with vital financial support from partners – were amongst the best-produced documents. This is significant for playing the 'bidding game' (Appendix 2).

There tended to be more joint submissions for local authority areas that were potential seekers, in other words for localities aspiring to Assisted Area status. Some 147 local authorities that were non-Assisted at the start of the review process, submitted material. Nearly 60 per cent of these involved some direct liaison, whereas for existing Assisted Areas, less than 40 per cent involved joint approaches. These aspirant authorities were seemingly marshalling their forces in the quest to 'get on the map' or, at least, to flag up problems.

Notably above-average levels of direct liaison in the submissions occurred in the South East, Yorkshire and Humberside and the South West (see Appendix 1, Table A.1.5). In the South East, the calculated figure is biased by the inclusion

of two large group submissions amongst a smaller number of independent responses – an East London group (a less formalised liaison and more typical of
the joint submissions) and the East Kent Initiative (a more permanent coalition
structure) both of which involved several authorities.

Of course, the incidence of overtly joint submissions does not pick up all
liaisons. There is an additional layer of inter-authority and inter-agency liaison
that operates through the officer working groups and similar joint arrangements
between groups of authorities. That cannot be identified by analysing the submissions, but it can be isolated by direct investigation as reported in the cameos
in Chapter 5.

The occurrence of liaison is important because it reflects the development of a
degree of partnership and, as such, tells us a little about the local economic
policy profile of the area involved. However, that is all it tells us and we need to
explore further if we are to capitalise on this material. We can of course deduce
more from personal communication. In at least one case, Gillingham and the
East Kent Initiative (see Chapter 5), a local authority left out of a particular
coalition by choice, regretted it when the policy review began to work towards a
decision (Gillingham Borough Council, personal communication, 12 February
1994).

In most cases, the liaisons were not part of a wider growth coalition of the type
discussed in Chapter 1, but were simply liaisons geared towards the particular
review event. They were, in this sense, quite different from the growth coalition
model. That said, a number of existing growth coalitions – for example, Furness
Enterprise, and the East Kent Initiative – did co-ordinate the submissions for
their areas.

There were also some interesting examples reflecting an apparent lack of full
liaison in a strategic sense, or at least a questionable strategy. For example, the
case for the Mansfield TTWA was delivered by three sizeable submissions.
Independent submissions were made by two District Councils – Mansfield, and
Newark and Sherwood – while another county-wide response covering various
Nottinghamshire TTWAs, and including Mansfield, was put in by the County
Council. This may be seen as a 'grapeshot' strategy – hitting the government with
submissions from three directions – but it can be called into question on grounds
of cost of production, and information overload. Although all submissions were
scanned by civil servants at the various (DTI/Welsh Office/Scottish Office) Regional Offices, there was generally a benefit in synthesising the arguments –
keeping them to manageable proportions. All were of good quality, all claimed
liaison, but inevitably there were differences in the emphases and nuances in the
documentary presentations. This serves to cloud the issue to a degree. Not least
of all, in what appears to be a local political compromise, the county-based
submission sought Assisted Area status for all six TTWAs within its boundaries
and was less discerning in its focus. There are at least three sets of implications
here, all of them linked to the 'bidding game'. First, it is clear that there are
political sensitivities involved and that authorities may be in 'defensive mode'.
The review response submissions were often made with multiple objectives in
mind. For District Councils in declining coal mining areas, there was probably a
genuine attempt, but certainly a political need, to be seen to be defending the
area. Second, there are implications for economy of effort in producing (expensive) documentation. Third, and linked to this, there is the whole question of the

efficacy of authorities involvement in the game – the submission of too much information cannot be a sensible strategy.

Although it is not possible to assess the conditions under which the varous liaisons functioned, we can set up aspects that might be investigated in Chapter 5 when we focus on a handful of areas. Clearly, the processes could be illuminating. For example, a temporary liaison for the purposes of progressing the bid is rather different from a permanent liaison. In some cases, it is quite likely that the review itself was the catalyst for coalition formation. Again, that is something, information permitting, to be picked up in Chapter 5. More generally, it seems that, while we can find out much of use from the submission documents, we need fuller material if we are to be able to judge the impact of coalitions and the review process. We need to know about key individuals, processes of policy formation and so on.

4.3.2 Liaisons involving local authorities and the private sector

There has been a gradual recognition that the solution to local economic problems lies at least partly with local business, revealed in the shift towards a focus on indigenous industrial policy (Taylor, 1992). Such a move has itself fostered a closer association between authorities and the private sector, and alongside this has been a move towards local corporatism that has often involved the local authority as a partner (Martin and Townroe, 1992). Local business involvement in local economic development is not always beneficial or, certainly, smooth in its operation. There certainly are cited cases where business, given its sensitivity to image, did not concur with policies that overtly recognised local economic problems (see Sadler, 1993). As such, and as we will argue later in the chapter, the business lobby has tended to pull authorities away from an overt stress on problems in the local economy, to a strategy that focuses rather more on area potential. This shows itself in some of the submissions, especially where they involved local businesses as more than ephemeral members (e.g. where Chambers of Commerce were directly involved in producing the submission).

The submission documents reveal some aspects of business involvement. Around 13 per cent of them actually included supporting documentation from private sector interests in the locality. Perhaps more significantly, in total, there were 76 examples (24 per cent of all local authority-led submissions) of direct private sector involvement in the submission. For the authorities, the benefits came in the image of partnership that was projected, in the contribution to the costs of the submission, and in the detailed arguments and, occasionally, analysis put forward by businesses.

The kinds of material from the private sector range from detailed arguments to simple supporting letters. The Isle of Wight Development Board explicitly requested local business comments on aspects of the island economy – in particular, the impact of the Solent 'barrier' – and their responses form a useful insight (see Chapter 9 on peripherality). For Portsmouth, letters were requested from local businesses involved as defence contractors in order to demonstrate the reality of the 'threat' from the 'peace dividend' (see Chapter 6, p. 97, on the defence industry). In urban centres, there was a tendency not only for key manufacturing businesses to submit supporting documents, but also for commercial and retail business reactions to be sought and included. This was all part of the authority response strategy.

As with many of the aspects explored so far, we need to investigate further. We need to determine the sensitivity of local businesses in different economic contexts, and to pick up on any tensions and how they were resolved. There is likely to be business antagonism as regards the fruits of regional policy if these are beyond the reach – applicable to other businesses and so on (see Chapter 1 for a review of the 1992 Assisted Area 'benefits'). Any tensions between businesses and the authorities are certainly not discernible from the documentations and await fuller investigation. The whole question of tensions and the submissions production process will be discussed in Chapter 5.

4.4 The Nature and Style of the Submissions

The actual engagement of authorities in the review exercise is only one side of the issue. Having detailed the distribution of responses, and investigated liaisons between local authorities and other agencies with which they worked in partnership, we turn to an evaluation of the submissions themselves. What form did they take; which factors were stressed and which underplayed; were any apparent strategies prominent; and what images were portrayed in the quest to be 'recognised'?

4.4.1 The quality of the submissions

There are potential pitfalls in discussing the 'quality' of the submissions. Clearly, there must be some element of subjectivity in any evaluation. However, it is possible to utilise stringent criteria to establish at least a crude measure of quality that can stand the test of criticism. The quality of the submissions – as reflected in the resources required to produce them – is important because it links to essential questions: to what extent is the size, research underpinning and 'glossiness' of the submission connected to success in the bid and how cost-effective is it? (See Appendix 2.)

The submissions are categorised in terms of scale, level of local economic substance, and production quality into three types – modest (often just a letter); reasonable documentation (a report with some illustrations but with only a little background research); high quality (a fuller, perhaps synthesised report, containing analysis, quality maps and diagrams, etc.). The findings from the review response data set are in Table 4.3. The majority were mid-range submissions. However, a small number reflected the deployment of substantial resources and the production of a high quality submission. These tended to be large urban and industrial authorities with more resources available or traditionally committed to this type of quest (e.g. Bradford; Scottish regions; county councils; Manchester) or those who had made a decision to invest in the submission (bid) in an attempt to defend or seek what was viewed as a potentially vital source of external resources (e.g. coal producing areas such as Mansfield and Selby), perhaps with the financial or administrative support of partners in the submission (e.g. Stoke-on-Trent).

Table 4.3 Submission quality category by type of locality (%)

Local authority locality type	a	b	c
London	18	76	6
Other large cities	11	52	37
Districts with new towns	14	86	–
Resort/retirement areas	25	75	–
Coastal areas	13	78	9
Urban and mixed urban/rural areas	14	76	10
Industrial districts	15	70	15
Remoter rural areas	42	49	9
County/regional authorities	6	79	15
All	16	70	14

Note: a = modest quality; b = reasonable quality; c = high quality. See text for criteria.

4.4.2 The factors used

Clearly, the representations made by local authorities in their submissions was, to a significant extent, governed by the specifications in the DTI consultation paper. This requested that submissions addressed a range of considerations (see Chapter 1), from unemployment levels to peripherality, and, presumably as a sop to areas with impending change – for example, coal producing and defence-related localities – including any known future closures.

In this sense, it is probably more interesting to consider how such information was presented and portrayed, rather than simply recording its inclusion. That is a detailed task for Chapters 8 and 9. In this section, we simply and briefly chart the nature and repetition in the occurrence and use of arguments put forward, in particular linking this through to, and thinking about, the apparent strategies that were used via the presentation of material and constructed (or concealed) images about localities.

Clearly, it is useful to document local perceptions of local economic problems and potentials – via the identification of strategies – as it provides a route in to local attitudes and, ultimately, policy actions. Moreover, there is a benefit in charting the broad spectrum of material and arguments included, especially where they go beyond the minimum effectively required by the DTI.

In general, we can analyse the most cited factors, also considering any regional variations that seem apparent. From an overall count of the ten main lines of argument from each submission we arrive at the distribution in Table 4.4.

Not surprisingly given the adherence to DTI guidelines, unemployment and associated local labour market issues predominate. These were the key elements in the DTI guidelines, and dominate the past designation of Assisted Areas. Of course, the TTWA itself is an approximation of the local labour market area.

4.4.3 Packages of arguments

From Table 4.4 it is clear that the submissions tended to focus on a range of key areas (but distinguished themselves within that structure in the ways that they built arguments around the quantification). For example, more than simply

Table 4.4 The emergent lines of argument (% of responding local authorities)

Key factors stressed in submissions	Selected regions					All submissions
	SE	Wales	NW	Sc	WM	
Problems						
Unemployment	96	95	100	82	91	93
Other labour market problems	62	61	94	73	67	71
Declining key industries	67	49	65	61	55	58
Peripherality	13	67	27	73	3	41
Transportation constraints	51	37	18	31	21	27
Urban deprivation	29	30	41	28	18	25
Premises	29	5	18	10	21	22
Low wage problems	9	61	0	10	12	17
Out-migration	0	28	6	31	0	13
Quality of inward investments	7	23	29	8	6	13
Outcompeted by AAs	6	9	24	12	12	11
Opportunities						
Inward investment	38	51	44	28	67	35
Indigenous industry	49	28	38	29	73	31

Note: Figures refer to the proportion of the submissions that included a section on the key factors listed.

addressing the vagaries of unemployment, submissions tended to delve into local labour market issues, producing material on:

- unemployment or impending unemployment;
- conventional unemployment rates and long-term unemployment;
- poor quality of labour force;
- demographic growth threatening labour market;
- activity rates;
- problems for particular social groups;
- local labour market problems as a threat to future local economic performance/survival.

Outside the key unemployment issues, it is interesting to focus on other apparent prioritisations. Those that had the strongest showing presumably reflected those that had greatest comparability, or that were, at least by inference, viewed collectively as central issues. An expectedly key factor was the problems confronting the local industrial base. These issues tended to be articulated around questions of:

- overspecialisation;
- especially problematical sectors – for example, coal; shipbuilding; defence; tourism decline;
- the need to diversify but the need for resources to encourage it;
- the lack of small firms.

Again following the DTI guidelines, geographical location was widely represented in the submissions. Here, there was a tendency to lock on to:

- unrecognised peripherality in the past;
- the aggravated position with infrastructural developments;
- the impacts and implications of marginalisation.

Other lines of argument drew attention to overtly (in the self-estimation of respondents) unharnessed potential and detailed local constraints – shortage of venture capital/lack of business confidence in the area; overinsularity; poor record of attracting inward investment; and so on.

There are clear regional variations in the factors stressed. In terms of problems cited, there were expected differences in factors such as peripherality (stressed by submissions from Wales and Scotland), but some other variations that presumably reflect differing attitudes to problems. Despite high levels in the region, unemployment tended to be played down by some Scottish authorities who were, by inference, more image sensitive and potential-orientated. Similarly, the demise of key industries was avoided by some Welsh authorities who tended to focus more on other problems (migration; low wages). Sensitivity to competition from areas with Assisted Area status was greater in the North West, and relatively low in the South East.

In terms of opportunities cited, there were some variations. Not all submissions discussed these issues. However, where they did build in the 'potential' angle, authorities in regions such as the South East and the West Midlands focused more on indigenous industry, while, not surprisingly, those from traditional areas of assistance were locked into inward investment potential. Clearly, perhaps explained to a degree by inter-authority liaisons at a regional level, there were regional differences in the sensitivity to problems and the perceptions of opportunity.

4.4.4 Apparent emergent strategies – unpacking the packaging

Clearly, the submissions reflect a range of strategies on the part of their origin authorities and groupings. Against a background of past history and present position in regional policy terms – for example, whether they were defenders or seekers – and the local economic policy attitude, we can determine at least two groups of approaches. There is a 'standard needs package' that sets out the key problems in a locality as seen from the local perspective; and, there is a 'standard needs plus' approach that focuses not only on the local needs for external resources to support development but also on the potential of the area to utilise such support.

Coupled with this, we should add other elements into any typology, such as the inclusion of a private sector viewpoint, and the resources invested in the submission.

The 'standard needs package' involves a standard coverage of unemployment with some comparative analysis, and a building in of associated problems . It is very much focused on the problems of the area with only a minimal discussion of local economic potential. Some of the smaller District authorities (for example, North East Fife; Easington; Merthyr Tydfil) but also some larger, better resourced authorities such as Blackpool, adopted this type of approach.

The 'standard needs plus' approach addresses both needs and potentials. It has a similar coverage as the standard package, but with a much fuller emphasis on local potentials. In the main, it was the larger authorities or joint submissions – where more resources and expertise could be generated – that adopted this rather more sophisticated and better informed strategy. A stress on potential as well as on local economic problems may serve to allay fears of projecting a negative image; it will certainly gell more with decision-makers allocating aid if it can show an effective use for any support. Although we cannot be sure about criteria and decision-making processes, there are distinctive lessons here for 'playing the bidding game'.

An interesting spin-off from this analysis concerns the strategies adopted by authorities that were potentially under threat from the review by virtue of their much improved unemployment performance. In cases such as that of Corby and of Telford, the strategy was to argue that the 'job is not yet complete' and that loss of status could be a serious problem. Such a view was in contrast to the political rhetoric in the wake of the outcome. Thus, 'we recognise that the time had come for other areas to receive some of the benefits given to Corby' (W. Powell, MP for Corby, House of Commons, Assisted Areas debate, 26 July 1993, Hansard, CD36, p. 757).

Clearly, the incidence of these 'packages' depends on the local economic approaches adopted by authorities – are they aggressive, defensive and so on. Some submissions virtually demanded support; others were more subtle in their quest, although we still need to know what considerations – conflicts, consensus agreements within coalitions and so on – underpin the public pronouncements. Our analysis so far, in particular the points about the potential of places and the notions of 'selling' a case, connects with Part 3 where we investigate attitudes to regional policy. Of course, some deductions can be made even at this juncture. However, we really know little about what local factors condition the style and approach in the representations – at least, nothing like as much as we can say about the engagement itself. This can also be rectified, partly by using more specific survey material as in Chapter 5, and partly by delving into individual aspects of the representations as in, for example, Chapter 8 on unemployment.

The feel of the submissions can perhaps be best put across with a few brief examples (with many more to come in later chapters). Some are full and de-tailed; others are more concise in design; some are selective and more closely targeted. An example of each type has been selected – and suitably condensed – to illustrate the kinds of material and the arguments being made.

Fuller review: Borders Regional Council

An example of one of the fullest submissions is that produced by Borders Regional Council. The County and Scottish Region submissions tend, natu-rally given their geographical coverage, to be fuller, wide-ranging docu-ments. Offering a really detailed review of the regional economy, this submission offers a basic package of analyses.

These cover: economic structure, stressing the manufacturing specialisa-tion of the region (textiles), something that is perceived to be unrealised by outsiders; the performance of Borders manufacturing; the low level of services employment; recent employment changes and the accelerating growth of unemployment in the region; the sensitivity of key sectors such as agriculture; the low relative GDP per capita, earnings and disposable income; the imbalanced age-structure with an ageing population; the problems of depopulation from some parts of the region; the acute peripherality of the region *vis-à-vis* major European markets.

Assisted Area status is needed to 'unlock' the opportunities that exist in the region.

(Other examples – many of the County authorities.)

Concise/synthesis type: Newcastle-upon-Tyne

A concise, targeted submission was made by Newcastle-upon-Tyne City Council (as the lead authority representing the Newcastle-upon-Tyne TTWA). This focuses more tightly on unemployment, the future demand for jobs, structural change, and peripherality. It seeks to retain the existing Assisted Area status of the TTWA and thus is defending rather than seeking. The basic argument is that, despite years of assistance and major improvement, ' fundamental structural and deep seated economic problems remain, requiring . . . the retention of full Development Area status' (p. 25).

(Other examples – Manchester – appears to have been a deliberate strategy to offer a condensed, streamlined representation that would make an impact.)

Selective, targeted type: Isle of Wight

Many submissions were more specifically targeted on particular problems confronting some or all of the locality involved. For example, in the case of the Isle of Wight Development Board, the overriding concern seemed to be with the relative isolation of the area because of the barrier of the Solent. Problems with the local economy, difficulties encountered by major employers on the island, coupled with the vulnerability of the island tourist industry, were given prominence.

(Other examples – areas with a particularly prominent problem sector, e.g. defence; tourism, or with a viability threatening issue, e.g. major coal mine closures.)

Clearly, in analysing the submissions we are dealing with strategic decisions about how to influence the course of policy change. We have already been able to make some critical comments about the kinds of approaches that appear to be used. In Appendix 2, and in the light of all of the book material, we will be able offer a more considered judgement on their efficacy.

4.4.5 Images and impressions – the visual projection of the local

Earlier in the book we discussed the rise of place marketing as one strand of the greater local competitiveness that pervades the spatial economic policy arena in the 1990s. We linked that trend to changes in the policy package and the way that it is delivered, and discussed the ideological bases around which the local responds to such challenges. Now, clearly, all representations, written or visual, can be construed as part of building an image. However, some of the higher quality submissions went to some lengths to 'get the message' across by developing logos specially for the Assisted Areas review.

The style of the logos allows us to draw inferences about the image being projected. Three examples can be used to demonstrate the use of imagery and to assess the kinds of message being put across. It is likely that such logos were used to deflect the negative impression that a bid for 'support' would be perceived to generate, especially by local business interest. As such, logo production may well be a central part of any strategy of representation. In these ways, we expect problems to be highlighted but we would also anticipate some images of potential or quality and attractiveness being worked into the image.

In their particular focus, the constructions hint at impending problems, the need for support, and, often, area potential. The Great Yarmouth logo (Figure 4.2) neatly demonstrates our expected use of imagery. Here we have an overt representation of the local economy as needing to be 'unlocked' – 'unlocking the area's potential'. The emphasis is not on the local economy as problematical but on the local economy as a place of potential. More subtly, the logo for Hastings portrays a simple landscape, with an indication of peripherality and coastal confinement (Figure 4.3). This may be just a 'pretty picture' but it nevertheless is 'read' and evokes an image of tranquillity and, perhaps stretching the reading a

A submission for regional aid for the

Great Yarmouth
Travel-to-Work Area

To unlock our area's full potential we need the extra leverage only government can provide

Great
Yarmouth
Borough
Council

Figure 4.2   The Great Yarmouth submission logo.

Figure 4.3   The Hastings submission logo.

little, of quality. A final example, that produced by Mansfield District Council for the Mansfield TTWA, is more explicit in its orientation. It nevertheless still carries the notion of combining problems and potentials in the visual case for assistance. This interprets the acquisition of Assisted Area status and the benefits that go with it as providing the missing piece of the development jigsaw (Figure 4.4). In other words, this is a local economy beset by economic constraints, not least of all the closure of coal-mining capacity, that has the potential to regenerate but needs the grant aid for new businesses to make progress.

An interesting point to note is that all three authorities generating these visual images – as most others cited elsewhere in the book – were what we have labelled 'seekers' (and 'winners', see Chapter 10). They were seeking Assisted Area status from a position of hitherto non-assistance. As such, they were making a special effort to overcome what they might have perceived to be conventions, predispositions – inferred in the DTI consultation document – towards existing areas of assistance. The logo construction could thus be seen as part of the 'attack' on the conventions of Assisted Area designation.

A number of other images attached to the local reactions are included in the book, taking the form of either logos, or, sometimes combined with a logo, specific visual representations of local economic features as problems. These are included in the analysis of the engagement (Chapter 5, East Kent Initiative), of attitudes to regional policy (Chapter 6, Portsmouth; Dorchester and Weymouth), or of representations of the local economy (Chapter 10, Isle of Wight; Lancaster; Lowestoft; and Allerdale). The images constructed for Great Yarmouth and Mansfield both reflect the notion of policy support as assisting potential. Elsewhere, as we will find later, the visual images developed for the exercise were rather more explicitly stated and more overtly targeted on the 'problem' message. Together, all reveal the working in of distinct images designed to enhance the case for status, to project images for future reference or whatever.

This type of analysis offers some rich insights into local–central relations and the 'marketing' of places, but it unfortunately does not tell us whose image was

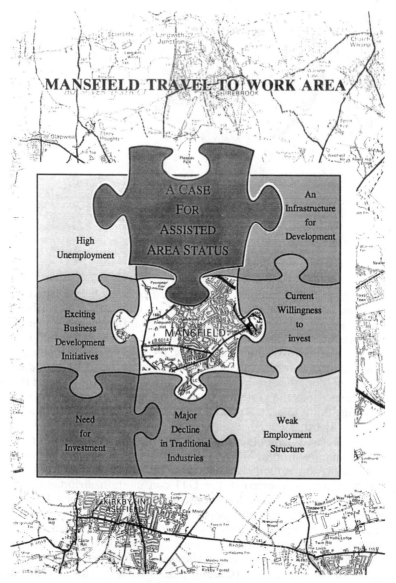

Figure 4.4   The Mansfield District Council submission logo.

being projected, who decided and so on. We also have no knowledge of the impact and effect of such imagery. This reflects a wider issue – the effects of the submissions in general. Were the images (and submissions) simply in the end devices for 'throat clearing' on the part of local authorities (although useful for the analysis in this book) or were they genuinely influential? Of course, these various issues need a research project of their own, although we can, in exploring some of the submissions, say a little more on the motives behind such representations in Chapter 5, and, perhaps, draw out their impact in the concluding part of the book (Chapter 10).

Having explored the anatomy of the local authority submissions, we now turn to the 'why' issue. In the following section, we move towards an explanation, assessing the distribution of engagement by authority against the expected influences discussed in Chapter 2. We also discuss the style of engagement, drawing out ideas about the motives and strategies involved. Later, in Chapter 5, we will go on to investigate the processes of policy formation in a series of cameos, looking in more detail at the motives behind the representations made and how the policy responses were formulated.

4.5 Towards an Understanding

Initially, we can make use of the submissions, first, to look at engagement and second, to assess the nature of the representations. In addition, we can draw on the explanations offered by responding authorities and groups on the reasons for their lack of involvement. To recap on our discussion in Chapter 2, section 2.1.2, we expected to find that engagement is connected to local needs, the status of the local economy, authority attitudes and approaches to local economic policy, the experience of local–central relations perhaps as reflected in involvement with existing government spatial policy, personnel factors, historical policy factors and position as regards existing regional policy designation, and the functioning of local policy processes.

4.5.1 Was the review a concern of the less prosperous localities?

In this section, we briefly draw together evidence from the distribution of the local authority responses to the review exercise.

Local needs and engagement as reflected in local prosperity variations

The review data set allows us to assess submissions that came from areas classified as prosperous in the 'booming towns' approach (section 2.1.2) (Champion and Green, 1990). This can then lead us into a more informed view about involvement.

As revealed in Table 4.5, there is a significant variation between local authorities by the rank of the LLMAs (local labour market areas) in their areas. Engagement in the review was only 11 per cent for the 75 authorities representing areas with a high ranking; it was 33 per cent for intermediate and 87 per cent for low ranking LLMAs. Clearly, the engagement links closely to objective notions of local prosperity.

As expected, there is a clear association between the level of prosperity of areas in the early 1990s and their engagement in the review process. However, there are some interesting exceptions. For example, a handful of submissions were made by those representing high ranking localities, and some low ranking authorities did not submit. In the former case, we cannot specify precise explanations although we can surmise that the explanation may reside in a fear of decline, or in motives that go beyond the simple bid objective (Chapter 2, section

Table 4.5 Local responses to the consultation document by LLMA status

LLMA rank (excl. counties)	No response	Response	Total No.	%
High	67	8	75	11
Intermediate	112	223	335	33
Low	6	39	45	87
All	196	317	513	62

Note: High ranking LLMAs (up to rank 50) are those with the highest levels of prosperity as defined by the 'booming towns' multivariate method. Low ranking LLMAs are those below rank 250. Counties and Scottish Regions are excluded from the categories but not the total. Where variations are said to be significant, unless otherwise stated, this refers to a significant chi-squared test at the 99 per cent level.

2.1). It may also have been viewed as a passport to potential European Commission regional policy or other funding. It is certainly likely that the exercise itself acted as catalyst to 'nudge' authorities into self-analysis of their relative economic positions.

The lack of involvement of expected participants is potentially rather more revealing and is discussed in section 4.5.2 below, using some additional material obtained from non-participating authorities.

Local unemployment and engagement

Unemployment is included within the 'booming towns' approach. However, given its centrality in the whole policy arena, it is worth a brief assessment. As expected, there is a relationship with local engagement, although it is not clear-cut. The basic level of engagement connects significantly to the basic unemployment level (Table 4.6). This is a wholly expected pattern, but it is nevertheless useful to be able to demonstrate it across the full array of British local authorities.

Table 4.6 Unemployment and the engagement of local authorities in the review exercise

Percentage level of unemployment	*Degree of engagement
5.0–7.5	35
7.6–10.0	57
10.1–12.5	76
12.6–15.0	100
15.0–20.0	100
All	62

Note: *Percentage of authorities responding to the review.

We get a rather garbled picture when we look at unemployment change in the 24 months preceding the review (Table 4.7). Most of those local authorities with falling unemployment levels – many of these being in Scotland – responded with bids for assistance. Most of those with relatively modest unemployment growth submitted bids. Yet, none of those with a three-fold increase in unemployment over the period actually bid for Assisted Area assistance. These latter authorities were almost wholly located in the south, including places such as Buckinghamshire, Guildford, Horsham, Tunbridge Wells and Wycombe. The reasons for not bidding perhaps included a perception that the unemployment levels were still modest, complacency or an informed belief that the 'problems' of the suburban south were transient.

Table 4.7 Unemployment change and the engagement of local authorities in the review exercise

Percentage change in unemployment rate June 1989 – June 1992	Degree of engagement
−30.3–0	77
1–50.9	89
51–100.9	76
101–200.9	45
201–300.9	17
301+	–
Total	62

It does seem that the persistence of a basic unemployment rate above or below the national average is a better predictor of attitudes to regional policy. In other words, traditional beliefs about the case or the need for support have not been broken down by unemployment growth – at least, not in the south.

Attitudes and approaches to local economic policy and engagement

Rather less can be discerned from the submissions on this set of influences. We have already noted that the political complexion of a local authority might be expected to condition, in some cases at least, its overall approach to intervention, local economic development, etc. We know that liaisons between political groups are sometimes important (Boddy, Lovering and Bassett, 1986) but still expect to find differences occurring. From Table 4.8 it is clear that Conservative-controlled authorities are less interventionist and involved (54 per cent responded) than, for example, Labour-controlled authorities (84 per cent). However, the differences may well be solely related to differences in prosperity levels – indeed, they are likely to be linked in this way. That said, and while it is difficult to 'tease out' such variations, we can make an 'at a distance' judgement on political influences in terms of the review engagement. In differentiating between levels of unemployment it emerges that authorities with a higher level showed a stronger tendency to engage with the review, regardless of political control.

These are useful findings: they confirm at a macro-level what has often been claimed in individual authority and area studies. However, rather more in-depth analysis is required if we are to get the full picture on political influences of this kind. We will make some progress on that in Chapter 5.

Experience of local–central relations and engagement

This cannot be read from the submissions. However, and as a crude surrogate only, there was some evidence that participation in existing schemes led to

Table 4.8 Engagement, unemployment and political control

Political control of local authority	Percentage engaging in review at different levels of unemployment		
	Lower	Higher	All
Alliance/Liberal	26	54	36
Labour	71	93	84
Conservative	25	75	54
No overall control	51	71	54
Others	71	75	72
All	48	79	61

Note: Lower = up to 10.0 per cent. Higher = 10.1 per cent or more.

involvement. For example, 'coal closure areas' and those receiving other central government support (e.g. urban policy) were active participants (Table 4.9). It may, of course, be simply that these are, by the fact of their designation, 'problem' areas of a sort.

Table 4.9 Engagement in the review by other central government area policy links

Type of link	Degree of engagement (% of relevant authorities)
Coal closure area	89
Other central government support*	89
All	62

Note: *Urban Programme; Enterprise Zone; Urban Development Corporation, etc.

Personnel factors and engagement

It is not possible to tease out evidence of local individuals or groupings from the submission documents. However, it seems that the submissions were virtually all local officer-led and less politically sanitised than some other public documents. They were often approved by local politicians but rarely with any changes. Moreover, in many cases, submissions came direct without political control. The timing of the review announcement and the due date for submissions (late September) meant that responses simply could not go through the usual Committee structure. Some submitted documents actually specify that they had not been to 'committee' (Wolverhampton; Anglesey). Other evidence can be discerned from some local media (newspaper) reports which state that reports were written by key local officers (e.g. Fenland). Again, the supplementary survey should throw some light on this aspect.

Historical policy factors and engagement – the past history of Assisted Area status

We expect that local authorities with a past history of Assisted Area status will be likely to engage in the review process. There is certainly evidence that some authorities tend to cling on to traditional ideas about local economies and their role and that these are difficult to dislodge (see Gordon, 1988).

Table 4.10 Engagement in the review by 1979 and 1984 Assisted Area status

Assisted Area status	Degree of engagement by previous Assisted Area status (%)	
	1979	1984
Non-Assisted Area	40	44
Intermediate Area	87	94
Development Area	88	92
Special Development Area	87	na
All		62

From Table 4.10, it is revealed that the majority of 1979 non-Assisted Areas did not respond, but that many did. The majority of 1979 Assisted Areas did respond, but some did not. This may be due to complacency, or to the cost when such areas expected to be given status. There was no apparent fear of failure and a strategy that there was no need to defend existing status.

It is easier to consider the engagement response against the distribution of 1984 Assisted Area status. More 1984 non-Assisted Areas did respond. Clearly, some were seekers while others were defending their existing status. Virtually all authorities with Assisted Areas at the time of the review responded – a reflection, perhaps, of defensive pressures heightening in the 1990s.

Local policy processes and engagement

How the submissions were put together and what processes of liaison occurred cannot be picked up from the submissions. Earlier in the chapter we have discussed this topic in as much detail as the material allows. More will be said on this in Chapter 5.

4.5.2. Notable by their absence: the distribution of non-engagement

Another dimension in all this are the notable absences from the exercise. Who were they, why did they not submit a 'bid' and what does that lack of submission tell us about central–local relations, attitudes to development and so on?

Around 200 local authorities in Britain did not respond to the consultation paper. In many cases, they were authorities located in prosperous southern and eastern Britain (Table A.1.3). But that was not always the case, and some areas that we might have expected to respond did not. The reasons behind the non-submission are undetectable from the data set. However, some of the non-responding authorities did respond to the original request for material by saying why they did not engage with the process. In addition, a wide selection of others were contacted in order to discover the circumstances of non-response.

A compilation of these information sources (Table 4.11) allows us to investigate the factors behind such a non-response and, once again, this offers insights into the style and attitude with which authorities operate policy.

It is unsurprising that many authorities in the South East, East Anglia and the South West failed to make representations (Table A.1.3). In most cases, these authorities had a low expectation of success or a lack of interest in acquiring

Table 4.11 An analysis of the reasons for non-involvement in the review

Reasons stated	Number of local authorities in sample		
	County	District	Total
First tier authority			
(County) will do it	–	6	6
No hope attitude	2	17	19
Avoid stigma of			
designation	–	3	3
Ignorance of review	1	4	5
Focus on Obj 2 submission	–	1	1
Combination of			
considerations*	2	19	21
Total	5	50	55

Note: *Mainly a combination of no hope/stigma.
Source: personal communication with a sample of local authorities.

Assisted Area status because of the negative connotations that they perceived it to carry. Even in the coastal areas that proved to be such vociferous camapigners for status, there were omissions. While prominent coastal economies such as Portsmouth, Brighton, Eastbourne, Dover, Southend-on-Sea, Lowestoft, Hull, Penzance, Blackpool and virtually all of the coastal areas in Scotland submitted responses to the consultation document, in other areas, neither the local authorities, private business, industrial associations nor MPs or any other agency or group submitted representations. Amongst these 'non-combatants' were Bournemouth, Cromer, Minehead, Poole, Southampton, Stewartry, and Worthing, places that we might have expected to have a view about regional policy.

Personal communication with over fifty non-respondents allows us to draw out some explanations and to gain insights into local attitudes to the whole process.

Set in the context of the costs and benefits of producing a submission document that would need to be sophisticated and extensive if it were (perceived) to be influential, many decided against involvement. Where authorities with relatively high unemployment or other local economic problems did not engage with the review, there was a likelihood that these areas, again given the costs of submitting, simply expected to be given support. However, no examples were found of such high expectation or complacency. Authorities in the 'expected to submit' category did not get involved for a number of other reasons (Table 4.11). In several cases, administrative oversight was the reason (e.g. Argyll and Bute; London Borough of Southwark); more often though, the key factor was a fear of the stigma that might follow from such a designation. Several authorities (e.g. Gillingham, Derby, Dartford) were preparing an application for Objective 2 status under the European Structural Funds which they felt (rightly or wrongly) did not carry the same negative images. This was particularly mentioned by Ipswich, Southampton and Carlisle. The case of Derby is a particularly interesting one: the authority did not respond as the political leadership felt that a stigma would be attached to any designation, giving the impression of a declining, struggling economy. An application for Objective 2 status was, however, made – on the basis of manufacturing losses in defence-related manufacturing (nuclear engines, army uniforms, and engineering sub-contract work). However, local officers felt that an Assisted Areas 'bid' would have been a useful prelude to this, and was an opportunity missed (personal communication).

Clearly, just as they were important in conditioning submissions (see Chapter 2), many local factors underlay the decision not to engage in the review or to seek Assisted Area status. Whether authorities could be seen as defenders or seekers, the extent of their regular involvement in and attitude towards local economic development, and developments in the complexion of the local economy over the preceding period, were all relevant factors in the process.

4.6 Conclusion

Using the unique opportunity afforded by the material assembled from local submissions, this chapter has been able to document and assess in some detail the structure of the response to the 1992 Assisted Areas review. This offers a remarkably wide potential. To be able to identify and analyse response and non-response to the review, and to evaluate the substance of the response (and, occasionally, the reasons behind the lack of response) and the liaisons and groupings that produced them, is novel. Moreover, it enables us to investigate aspects of the spatial economic policy arena that have not been touched before.

The analysis of review responses has identified, by the sheer weight of response that included reference to them, a number of key issues.[1] In particular, it seems that controversy and debate revolved around the perennial unemployment/local labour market question and, in particular, how that debate was articulated, the issue of peripherality, the particular problems of certain areas – for example, not only London and the south and other metropolitan areas, but also, interestingly, coastal economies, and the issue of local industrial change in sectors such as defence. For example, analysis of the distribution of the submissions reveals that certain areas – high in the 'booming towns' index: places such as Ashford, Hastings, South Lakeland, Teignbridge, West Dorset, and Weymouth and Portland – submitted or participated in 'bids' because of their self-perceived vulnerability as coastal areas, places whose local economy is defence-laden, or places feeling threatened by peripherality. In Part 4 we will go on to explore some of these aspects of engagement in more detail.

Prior to that, however, there is a need and an opportunity to delve deeper into the processes of policy formation. We have only been able to take the analysis and explanation so far using the review response data. We can lock on to unemployment trends in the localities, assess past histories of support status, and even touch on political complexions. However, we need some local detail if we are to really understand the reactions and responses to the review and, hence, the attitudes towards regional (and indeed other forms of spatial) policy. Using the information generated by detailed surveys in five case study areas we can explore these issues further.

Note

1. This, incidentally, is part of the real pay-off in collating and using the review response data because it represents a dimension that could not even be identified, let alone investigated, in its absence – at least not without the use of substantial resources.

5

UNDERSTANDING AND INTERPRETING THE RESPONSES

In this chapter we make use of the supplementary survey in order to gain fuller information on reactions to the Assisted Areas review exercise, and to explore aspects of the review process that have been raised in our analysis of the submissions (Chapter 4) or in the background contextual discussions (Chapters 1 and 2), but which cannot be isolated and explored from such sources. The cameos presented in the chapter provide additional insights into the policy process and open up the topic for a more complete analysis. First, we consider what aspects of the review process we still need to know about having completed our assessment of the submission documents, and in this way assess the potential role for local case examples.

5.1 Beyond a Quantitative Analysis

The key angles that would substantially add to our understanding of the policy process have already been flagged up in earlier parts of the book, in particular in Chapters 1 and 4. These can be summarised in the following questions.

- What were the reaction motives – the influences and the strategies? What exactly were the objectives in responding to the DTI consultation paper, and what does this reveal about central–local relations and local economic objectives?
- How was the policy position formed? How were decisions made about what 'line' to take in the submission and what information to include?
- What about the local politics of it all? What is the significance of review reactions, etc. for the survival of local coalitions? How was a consensus attained and were there any conflicts, between or within local authorities and/or local businesses?
- What are the specific relationships between local coalitions and the review exercise?
- What was the role of key individuals in the process?

- Were there other activities around the submissions, other channels in central–local relations that could not be detected from analysing the submissions?

(Reasons for opting out of the process have already been explored in Chapter 4.)

The main quest, then, is to answer some important, hitherto inaccessible and unknown questions, not just in terms of what the policy positions were (attitudes, approaches, intentions, etc.) but also how they were established.

5.2 Opting In – the Formation of Policy Positions

This section discusses the supplementary information that was obtained from direct survey with the lead officials involved (Chapter 3). Five main areas were chosen for this fuller coverage:

- Stoke-on-Trent and the Potteries
- Chester, Alyn and Deeside, and Clwyd
- Bradford
- Hackney and East London
- East Kent coastal area

Some additional areas (Ellesmere Port and Neston; Dumfries and Galloway) were originally surveyed but, given space limitations, have been omitted from the detailed analysis. The results from these areas are nevertheless included in the general discussion in section 5.2.2.

The mix involves areas traditionally reliant on regional policy support; aspirant areas; and those situated in economic environments known to have been 'pressured' over the course of the late 1980s/early 1990s. Three of the examples are based around single local authorities – a Metropolitan District, a large urban District, and a London Borough; one covers a number of authorities and their deliberations as well as the approach of the umbrella growth coalition (EKI) that co-ordinated their main submission; and one covers a group of areas in south west Cheshire and north east Clwyd. The idea behind the last of these is to give a fuller coverage of a cluster of authorities in a sub-regional setting, with a view to picking up any inter-area competition between them, or at least to evaluate any liaisons and to identify attitudes to adjacent authorities. The survey explored the issues from all sides and did not rely on the claims of a single authority. However, the selected grouping makes no claims for representativeness – it is just a set of adjacent authorities that it was felt would not be unrepresentative.

The rationale for such an approach is simply the need to add local colour and local background if we are really to understand local economic issues (Axford and Pinch, 1994; Duncan and Goodwin, 1988). It is not just an excuse for some local empiricism.

The policy issues are analysed in terms of these areas, first by focusing on them individually, setting the 'problem and potential' context, background to the area and so on, as well as discussing the policy process, and second, by drawing together the material into general observations about processes of policy formation, outcomes and so on.

5.2.1 Motives, processes and the management of representations at the local level

The five cameos that follow are each presented in a number of sections. We focus on the area and its economic problems, the response background and motives, the response formulation, the elements used in the response, and the management of the representation, and offer some general concluding points about the approach and outcome. The details of each area example are related to the ideas discussed in Chapters 1 and 4 and an attempt is made to explain and contextualise the findings.

The Stoke-on-Trent TTWA

This area, covering the North Staffordshire conurbation, was represented in the review process by a partnership led by Stoke-on-Trent City Council (the Stoke-on-Trent Partners Group). There was also a Staffordshire County Council submission in the form of a letter on coal mine closures and a response from the Staffordshire Development Association.

A long time aspirant for Assisted Area status, the Partners Group submission in 1992 reflected a new, more positive and integrated approach to lobbying for external funding – a direct result of the review process itself. The quest for external funding through regional or inner area policy has long been a contentious issue in this area given past decisions (Figure 5.1), and the status of surrounding areas (Figure 5.2).

Economic situation. This is a specialised, dependent local economy, reliant on global markets in product areas (in ceramics, tyres, engineering, for example) that are under intense competition (Phillips, 1993). The nature of the industrial base has brought a legacy of a poor environmental image and relatively high development costs in a fractured industrial terrain, capped by mine closures and typified by poor quality development land. The main problem is that industry is vulnerable in a global operating environment.

The area has a negative environmental image but has never been seen from the outside as a high unemployment economy. Unemployment tends to be hid-

Figure 5.1   Local sensitivities to Assisted Areas change.

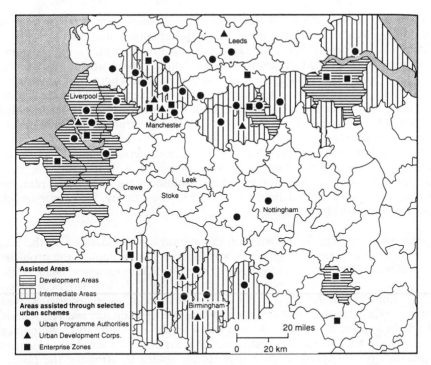

Figure 5.2 The Assisted Areas map in the early 1990s: the Stoke-on-Trent 'doughnut'.

den to a greater extent in this area than in most because of the nature of the traditional workforce. Many workers displaced from the ceramics industry never registered and thus did not appear on the unemployment register. This is essentially the perception of area problems from the local authority perspective.

Stoke-on-Trent City Council has been a persistent applicant for various types of spatial economic policy assistance, and has a long history of denial. Rarely have applications been made on a sub-regional (TTWA) basis; inter-authority antagonisms between Stoke-on-Trent and the neighbouring Borough of Newcastle-under-Lyme (all of which is in the TTWA) are well-known but, to a degree at least, were breached for the occasion with a joint (Partners) approach.

Response motives. The submission was genuinely seeking Assisted Area status, but was also attempting to get on to the government agenda. There were no expectations about success, given past history and a DTI-stated reduction in areas of coverage.

Response formulation. A temporary coalition was formed for the response, with liaison between TTWA local authorities, Staffordshire TEC and North Staffordshire Chamber of Commerce and Industry. The initial move was by the Staffordshire TEC, but the submission was led by Stoke-on-Trent (the authority with the key economic problems) and was orientated towards conurbation centre problems. Initially, Partners included the British Ceramic Manufacturers Federation but they withdrew during the formation of the submission. They were not prepared publicly to state that the ceramics industry was in poor condition *vis-à-vis* global competition, and duly submitted their own views.

There was no formal report of the submission to Committee – the response was very much officer-led. In terms of local dialogue, there was no use of local MPs who, it was felt, would not pursue the precise line. There was an informal debate within the authority and local businesses were represented by the Chamber. There were also some discussions with the pottery industry trade union (CATU). There was informal discussion with the spectrum of political groups resulting in general support.

Although there was a problem with the short notice given, an early consensus was reached via two Partners group meetings on points likely to score. The main contributors in order of importance and contribution were: Stoke-on-Trent, the Chamber of Commerce and Industry, the TEC, the County, Newcastle-under-Lyme and Staffordshire Moorlands.

Response elements. The final content in this submission was decided by the lead officer. The broad consensus approach was to stress both potential and problems and to offer only key points in a concise format. The features stressed included the area's successful track record, competitiveness problems, the low wage/low educational attainment needing support for skills development, overdependency, wish to attract inward investment at key sites, and past partnership success. The submission sought to show how Assisted Area status would accelerate the regeneration process. There was little liaison with adjacent areas as none were Assisted Areas.

The strategy attempted to show a proactive stance by stressing the (anticipated) demise of the local coal industry.

Managing the representation. Given time horizons there was no attempted lobbying to pursue the argument further. The endorsement, and indeed the financial contribution, of the TEC was viewed as a valuable element.

Concluding points. This was a submission dominated by a lead authority/officer, and with a minimal involvement of some (compliant) authorities within the TTWA. The private sector was involved, but there were tensions and some squabbling over image projection.

North Staffordshire – Stoke-on-Trent in particular – has been a long-term aspirant for assistance, building a policy of attrition that has yet really to bear fruit. The proposal was unsuccessful, but part of the area was later awarded Objective 2 status under the European Structural Funds and Single Regeneration Budget support. These 'successes' may stem from the spate of coal closures that confronted the area in 1993. However, there is also a belief on the part of the Partners that the markers set down at the Assisted Areas review stage just might have been significant. This, unfortunately, is impossible to verify.

Despite the dominance of the lead authority, there was an element of coalition inducement through the response. It created a forum for local economic review and self-assessment; and thus functioned as a catalyst for greater local partnership and the production of a more conciliatory path to integrated local economic development. What emerged was a semi-formal TTWA-based policy – something that had not occurred in the past.

South West Cheshire and North East Clwyd

This part of the supplementary survey involves the drawing together of material from a number of local authorities with the aim of assessing the submissions profile for a wider area of interest. It is not designed as representative; the cluster of areas was selected on the grounds that it would be a valuable and not especially unrepresentative contribution. In section 5.2.2 all survey data is grouped for analysis. Here, we focus on two areas, Chester and Alyn and Deeside, drawing in some evidence from other adjacent areas as appropriate.

Chester

To the uninitiated, the idea of Chester as an Assisted Area seems odd, yet all but the rural south of the District was designated as a Development Area in 1984. This was largely as a consequence of a high unemployment profile, not only within Chester itself but more so in the Travel-to-Work Area which includes the Wirral and its economic problems.

Economic situation. Chester's image nationally and internationally is one of affluence, heritage and a tourism/retailing destination, but what is masked is the unbalanced structure of the economy and a high level of both aggregate and long-term unemployment. Visitors provided an estimated £45 million of revenue and supported 16,000 jobs in 1993. In the recession of the early 1990s, the dependence of the local economy on finance, retailing and tourism proved a disadvantage and there were substantial employment losses. Major industries such as Shell, BICC and British Aerospace, in or close to the TTWA, also contracted over the period.

In the late 1980s and early 1990s, Chester was successful in securing significant overseas manufacturing investment and this success was ascribed to the availability of regional industrial grants under the Assisted Area designation. The feared loss of status, the perceived threat to future European Structural funding that had precipitated important infrastructural developments, and the feeling of marginalisation in the face of European competition coupled with the threat of further defence sector job losses (see Chapter 6) were the catalyst for an aggressive submission to the review. The projected positive tourist and inward investment image of Chester as 'a beautiful, historic walled city, surrounded by superb Cheshire countryside' (promotional brochure) seems curiously at odds with the 'persistently high unemployment . . . high levels of economic deprivation . . . (and) structural imbalance' (submission, pp. 1–2). But this is the vernacular language of persuasion.

Response motives. Against the above background, we would expect the Chester response to seek to retain some level of Assisted Area status and this, indeed, was the case. The authority was supported by the Cheshire County Council submission, but the latter also sought the extension of status to the Crewe and Nantwich TTWAs. In a sense, this diverted some of the attention from the Chester case.

In addition to retention, the submission sought to continue the strategy of stressing to central government that the perceived affluence of Chester was a myth rather than a reality and that there was a largely 'hidden' dimension to the area's economy.

Given past successes and antagonism from the UDCs over designations, the authority was hopeful rather than expectant about retention. It was especially hopeful as, in the 18 months preceding the survey, Chester District had received £120 million in regional grants.

Response formulation. The response was formulated by the Economic Development Officer in liaison with elements of the business community. There was a strong partnership element – the Chester Economic Development Forum (CEDF) helped to co-ordinate responses. Within this structure, there were three or four key co-ordinators. Some informal debate occurred within the Economic Development section, but not beyond.

MPs were supportive but had no participation in the construction of the document. There was virtually full cross-party support at local political level. Although there was support from local businesses they were not involved in the production.

There were consultations with adjacent areas in the TTWA, and also with the TEC and Chamber of Commerce. The draft documents were submitted to these various groups (Chamber of Commerce, Chamber of Trade, Chester Business Club). Local trade union groups were involved through the CEDF. Although there was no formal link-up, copies of the submission were sent to Alyn and Deeside and Wrexham.

Response elements. This was solely the domain of the Economic Development Officer. The submission was deliberately succinct, focusing on the DTI 'checklist' of problems and the potential use of support funding.

Managing the representation. The authority encouraged local businesses to make representations and supplied a draft letter. They also asked local MPs to lobby as subtly as possible. Two of the three did, but one, as a Minister at the Foreign Office, distanced himself from the exercise. The local press were encouraged to generate debate. Informal networks were used to check on how the review was proceeding.

Concluding points. The Chester submission was clouded a little by a perception of the area's adjacency to Merseyside. The TTWA runs into Merseyside and there is some in-commuting into the area from the conurbation.

The local economy was viewed by officers as growing, service-based with a high potential – and this indicates a positive impetus for the development effort. There were some tensions between local attitudes and one of the MP's cavalier, political prognostications over the success of the local economy. Officers viewed the post-1984 Assisted Area designation as central to successes. They feared but were not surprised by the shift of attention to the South.

Alyn and Deeside

While the Chester submission was supportive of separate but complementary responses from other areas – such as Ellesmere Port and Neston – that liaison was confined to other Districts within Cheshire County. As the submissions were co-ordinated through the County Council, adjacent areas in Clwyd were not party to the deliberations of the Cheshire authorities.

At the time of the review, this District was included within Development Areas designated for the Shotton, Flint and Rhyl TTWA and the Wrexham TTWA. Its submission to the review was co-ordinated by the County Council (Clwyd) which used consultants Touche Ross to produce a County-wide document. The processes involved in the production of the Clwyd partnership submission are interesting in terms of the methods used to integrate a range of competing demands and positions. In discussing this case we can also draw on some information collected from Clwyd County Council itself.

The economy. In the wake of major steel-making plant closures and a range of linked rationalisations, the Alyn and Deeside local economy has undergone substantial restructuring in the period since the early 1980s. Typified by heavy industry around the Dee estuary, the early 1980s saw what the Clwyd Regional Economic Development Strategy saw as 'a dramatic fightback . . . An aggressive policy of attracting inward investment was adopted.' These 'successes', an influx of new manufacturing businesses into places such as Deeside Industrial Park, were in large part a result of Development Area status granted in 1984. In the mid-1990s, job shedding from some of the growth industries of the 1980s, for example, British Aerospace, was seen as further jeopardising the viability of the local economy.

The title of the Clwyd submission, 'Rebuilding the economy of Clwyd – a task unfinished', reflects the line of argument adopted in the Clwyd approach. This is that despite successes via inward investment and subsequent expansion since the mid-1980s, a further spate of closures (steel-making, and coal-mining in particular) has generated job losses. The image presented is of a fragile economy, dependent on regional policy support.

Response motives. From this point, we discuss the Alyn and Deeside contribution to the Clwyd submission, at the same time drawing in some responses from the Clwyd survey.

The motive was the retention of Assisted Area status for the existing TTWAs with the argument that to remove status would be wasteful of previous resource injections. There was uncertainty over the outcome. Initially, the review anouncement was met with a negative reaction in the District but later, as the debate panned out, there was hope that the area would retain some level of assistance.

Response formulation. For Alyn and Deeside, the Planning Department led the representations. This mainly involved the Economic Development Strategy Group liaising with the County. The content was consultant-led. There was some liaison with Cheshire County Council in order to avoid any conflicts in the approaches.

Local (Clwyd) political groups were not involved in the presentation, but the Labour-controlled council felt that review should have been delayed until after the TTWA review. In the District itself there was a Labour-controlled council intent on intervention and regeneration, and a pro-economic development Tory group. As such, there was a consensus and no conflict over the line and approach taken, although the Conservative group initially favoured a joint submission with Chester.

Response elements. The authority felt that they were 'coming from behind' in the race to secure/retain status and therefore deliberately presented unemployment and other data in a form other than simple percentages. The final document was consultant-led but Districts, etc. fed in their arguments. Alyn and Deeside stressed the need to launch small business development (with a high vacancy rate at a local starter unit development) and to 'home in' on unemployment, but Clwyd had a wider range of criteria, including non-employment. This was a classic case of consultants searching for a 'different' angle.

Generally, the authority was keen to promote a 'good news' strategy and this influenced the style of the presentation. In a separate letter supporting the County-wide submission, and in advance of its endorsement at Committee, Alyn and Deeside argued that, although the unemployment rate was below the national average and the area did not fall within the worst third of the country, there had been a 35 per cent increase over the preceding twelve months and the economy was much less robust than official figures would indicate.

Managing the representation. The local MP was seen as a person who could attract publicity and was therefore used as a lobbyist. The authority organised a delegation to the House of Commons, but generally there was little representation.

As with many local submissions, opportunities for publicity and pressure were sought. The Economic Development Officer grasped the opportunity to appear on BBC2's *The Money Programme.* This compared Alyn and Deeside with Brighton and Margate and, although there was some 'flak' from local partners, it was felt to be a useful additional activity. Businesses were asked to write independently to voice their concern over threatened removal of assistance – a draft letter was suggested by the authority.

Concluding points. In the lead up to the review there had been mounting pressure in Clwyd for attention to be given to the west of the County. This must have influenced the difficult 'balancing act' that the County authority, via its consultants, had to make.

Although regional policy was seen as less important in 1992, Alyn and Deeside argued that without it there would have been little development in the area. There was a general feeling that they had been 'lucky to have had a steel closure in 1981' because that brought regional assistance, although it had not been the panacea that some claimed.

There was little contact with the Chester neighbour, even though a decision on one area would affect the other. A letter from Alyn and Deeside to the DTI stressed the links with west Cheshire and Merseyside, arguing that east Clwyd would be disadvantaged if Chester were to keep Development Area status. Although suppressed for the most part, this reveals the competitive edge that prevailed.

Of course, there was 'dismay' and great disappointment over the outcome: a loss of status for part of the area and a downgrading to Intermediate Area status for the industrial districts.

The Bradford area

Bradford Metropolitan Borough Council was involved in joint submissions for both the Bradford TTWA and the Keighley TTWA. In this cameo, we concentrate on the former. In both cases the 'lead' authority was Bradford itself.

The case of Bradford at the time of the review is a classic example of being on the fringes of potential problem status. To be in the worst one-third of unemployment areas (as specified for the review by the DTI and bound by European Union limits) a TTWA had to be ranked higher than 108th; the Bradford TTWA was 111th. It was expected that Bradford would have developed a strong strategy in an attempt to seek retention of the Assisted Area status that had generated over £4 million each year since designation.

Economic situation. The problems of the Bradford area stem from the rationalisation of the textile industry in the 1970s and 1980s and it was this that brought Intermediate Area status in 1984. Manufacturing is still the dominant element in the local economy, with textiles and clothing (over 25 per cent of all employment), mechanical engineering, and paper and printing at the core. It is a predominantly small firm economy, with over 90 per cent of firms employing less than 50 staff. Some growth in financial services employment in the 1980s was curtailed by the 1990s recession.

While unemployment had risen rapidly during the 1990s, there was a clear convergence towards the national average. The main problems projected in the submission were the vulnerability of the local economy coupled with a rapid growth in the working age population. With a poor new firm growth rate and little inward investment the prognosis for the economy was perceived to be poor.

Response motives. There was a dual motive with the submission. This was primarily to retain status, but also to put down 'markers' for the retention of Objective 2 status under the European Union Structural Funds. These were seen as linked, and, as such, the authority was playing a wider 'bidding game'. There was uncertainty of the likely outcome at the time of the submission. The local business community were blasé.

Response formulation. The response was co-ordinated by the Strategy and Research section of the Bradford Economic Development Unit (EDU). The EDU assembled the main players – the TEC and the Chamber of Commerce. The strategy and content of the submission was discussed by the Economic Strategy Sub-Committee, but generally rushed, and it was difficult to get the submission draft into the authority Committee cycle. There was some informal debate with the Labour group on the Council. The local MP was not involved in the production. The authority did consult with the DTI at various stages.

Outside the EDU, it was found difficult to get local Council members/ officers involved. The same was initially true with local businesses. There was a continuous dialogue with key local firms, and the authority gradually won over textiles and engineering with the Objective 2 argument. In addition to this liaison, there was arms-length contact with Task Force and City Challenge representatives.

There was all-party support at the local level – the Labour group plus a sizeable Tory group generated an all-party delegation to make representations.

With regard to adjacent authorities, Bradford made approaches to Craven District but there was no interest. Leeds (with two wards in the Bradford TTWA) stressed an urban case and played down regional policy.

Response elements. The authority realised that the submission would be weak on key indicators and described unemployment figures as the 'Achilles heel' for the area. It thus tried to ameliorate that weakness by looking at the potential created by past regional support. The unemployment issue was confronted by trying to link with urban problems, stressing 'pockets of deprivation' (see Chapter 8).

The submission deliberately cited peripherality, land and premises, and a low new firm formation performance as problems. It was stressed that Assisted Area status underpinned City Challenge: there was a partnership but a problem if the government were, in effect, to pull away one partner. The response played upon the importance of regional aid – it had been used by 16 per cent of local manufacturing firms in the period since 1984.

The strategy was to show how assistance had supported businesses – and so several case studies were included in the submission (see Figure 5.3).

Managing the representation. A deliberate strategy of representation/lobbying was set up. This used the Vice-Chancellor of Bradford University, local MPs and a carefully planned route.

The Bradford lobbying strategy was set up at a July 1992 meeting. This sought the involvement of all players; co-operation with neighbouring authorities; involvement of local MPs; a visit by the Minister. Following the production of the submission document, the Chamber of Commerce requested all members to write to the DTI. In October 1992 there was an all-party delegation to the DTI; in November 1992, a letter to Baroness Denton (the Minister at the DTI with responsibility for Bradford) stressing the case; in January 1993, a letter to the Minister stressing the importance of status for economic regeneration and inviting a Ministerial visit; in March 1993, a letter from the Chief Executive of Bradford City Challenge to the Minister expressing the importance of assistance, and a letter from the authority setting out additional points to back up the case – high District unemployment, high unemployment in the ethnic minority community and low local income levels.

Concluding points. The decision to remove designation was seen as a 'huge blow for jobs in Bradford . . . with . . . Bradford and Leeds . . . as . . . the only major cities in England and Wales without Assisted Area status (*Bradford Economic Review*, no. 2, Summer 1993, p. 1). There was an immediate backlash from the, hitherto ambivalent, business community, and local political tensions resurfaced with claims that the submission had been mishandled. Consensus it seems was a little superficial in the case of this Assisted Area review submission.

A statistical survey was initiated by the local business community and submitted to the DTI as 'A statistical analysis of the new Assisted Areas list', Economic Strategy and Research Team, Bradford City Council, July 1993 (see Chapter 10). In the aftermath of the decision, officers switched their focus on to the drive to retain Objective 2 status.

KOSSET CARPETS LTD.

Kosset Carpets Ltd. was a management buy-out from the receivers of Coloroll Group PLC in July 1990. The Company manufactured both tufted and axminster woven carpets in two completely separate but adjacent factories in Bradford. The buy-out saved the jobs of 670 people employed at the site. The DTI expressed the ability to help at the time and this was a great confidence booster for a management team in receivership.

At the end of that year a significant opportunity arose to secure the future of the axminster woven operation in Bradford which had previously been unprofitable as a result of poor volumes and margin. This operation was actually the most labour intensive at Kosset, directly employing nearly 300 out of a total of nearly 700 employees at the time. The opportunity was the purchase from the receivers of Coloroll of the Crossley Carpets machinery, brand name and design rights, but the financial requirement, including working capital, could not be met without Regional Selective Assistance.

The total cost of the project was £4.4m excluding working capital and a £1m grant was obtained. The additional working capital was provided by an additional £3m of overdraft facility. It was originally anticipated that the project would create 190 jobs and safeguard a further 30. However the carpet market has been in severe recession since January 1991 and this has meant that the outcome has been even more significant. Without th additional investment we now believe we would have had to close the original axminster business with a potential loss of nearly 300 jobs. As it is we have created 118 jobs on top of safeguarding the former. Axminster output has nearly doubled. Exports of Crossley products have grown from zero to £700,000 per annum already.

BIRKBYS
SHAPING THE FUTURE

BIRKBYS PLASTICS LTD

In 1988, Birkbys Plastics of Liversedge entered into a joint venture with the German Group Kautex Werke, to produce plastic blow-moulded components for the car and packaging industries.

The venture involved investment of £11.6 million at the Liversedge site. This comprised £3.1 million on a 40,000ft2 extension to existing premises, and a new 65,000ft2 factory, and £8.4 million on plant and machinery.

The project attracted RSA from the DTI of £1 million, 12% of the cost of plant and machinery.

Junior Industry Minister, Robert Atkins, commented at the time, "This is a significant new development and is a success for our policy of attracting investment into the Yorkshire and Humberside region".

SPRING RAM

In 1987, the Spring Ram Corporation, which makes bathroom and kitchen furniture, received Regional Selective Assistance towards the first phase of a new factory development at Birstall.

This involved the construction of two factories, with a total floorspace of 275,000ft2 at a cost of £11 million. Some 270 jobs were created.

The project has triggered further development at the Spring Ram Business Park. Spring Ram have invested £20 million in another two factories and warehouse buildings (680,000ft2), bringing total manufacturing employment to over 600, A further 500 jobs will be provided in retailing at Toys R Us (already built), and in planned developments by IKEA, Comet, MacDonalds and other operators.

On laying the foundation stone in 1987, Industry Minister, Giles Shaw, commented "I am pleased that my department has been able to help the projects go ahead in assisted areas by the provision of financial assistance under the Government's regional policy".

Figure 5.3 The Bradford TTWA submission – making a case for assistance with a record of achievement.

Hackney and East London

As we have already noted, there was substantial pressure exerted on the part of various London authorities in the drive to 'get on the map'. Submissions were made by 18 of the 33 London Boroughs, either independently or in liaison with each other and/or other local interests (Chamber of Commerce, TEC, local enterprise agencies, etc.).

The Hackney area was included in three separate submissions – one by the Borough itself; one in conjunction with the adjacent Boroughs of Tower Hamlets and Newham and the private sector-led East London Partnership; and one as part of a wider pressure grouping involving the six Boroughs of Barking and Dagenham, Hackney, Haringey, Newham, Tower Hamlets, and Waltham Forest. In this discussion, we focus on the London Borough of Hackney angle as it threaded its way into the various submissions.

Economic situation. The Hackney economy has undergone major structural changes over the 1970s and 1980s, resulting in a substantial decline in manufacturing industry and a smaller growth in services. It retains its manufacturing specialism – clothing, furniture, and printing, for example – and has a vibrant small firm economy, but it tends to lose firms to decentralisation if they expand. Given its congested central location, a lack of quality premises, and the attractions of Assisted Area benefits elsewhere, mobile manufacturing investment is unlikely to seek a Hackney location. In its deliberations on the review, the Borough perceived a resistance to inner city locations.

At the time of the review, unemployment in the area was recorded as around 22 per cent, more than twice the national average. This was a consistent pattern over the period since the mid-1980s. In fact, Hackney had been recommended for Special Development Area status by the GLC in its 1984 submission at the time of the previous regional policy review (Greater London Council, 1984; DTI, 1983) but had not been granted any level of status. Its support came with the receipt of urban aid through the Urban Programme and other urban schemes.

In the 1992 review, substantial emphasis was put on the localised patterns of high unemployment, in an attempt to encourage the DTI to break with the convention of assessing TTWAs and not areas within. Much of the analysis was in terms of either Hackney or one of the other two groupings and the highest scoring TTWAs elsewhere in the UK. It may well be that the drive behind an East London area submission was motivated by the aim to show that there were unemployment problems in a swathe of areas and not just in a few isolated inner city pockets (see Chapter 7, Figure 7.3). Specific methods for representing the problems were adopted and these are discussed in Chapter 8.

Response motives. The authority perceived a submission to be just one more pressure on the government for area support – this time for Assisted Area status. However, as one of the worst performing local authorities as regards unemployment, it felt that status might be achieved. In addition, the submission was motivated by the quest for Objective 2 status. Success in the former was expected, but only if the case for accepting London as a bona fide area for support was won at a political (European) level.

Response formulation. Interestingly, the review acted as a catalyst in the formation of a (six authority) coalition for the purpose of making a joint submission. The main (six Borough) submission was led by Tower Hamlets.

Hackey's own submission can be used as an example of the general approach and inclusions. The detail of the response was produced by the Economic

Development Officer and went to Committee only after submission. There was no real dialogue with other sections of the authority, or with many outside agencies. The Chamber of Commerce was merely informed of the submission. The main outside agency involvement was with a business support network – the Enterprise Policy Group – and the local TEC.

By its own admission, the Borough 'hedged its bets' – it submitted independently, but also linked itself with submissions that included the problematical and sensitive potential development site of the Lea Valley.

Response elements. The key problem – and the central plank of all submissions involving the Borough – was unemployment. This was combined with the limited development potential in the area as reflected in the high start-up rate but low retention of expanding firms. The Borough's independent submission deliberately confined itself to focusing on these two factors.

The wider six-Borough coalition built on this with a more extensive array of arguments, including employment decline over the 1981–89 period; investment starvation by local small and medium-sized firms; dereliction and the poor quality of much vacant industrial floorspace; social deprivation; poor infrastructure; and a series of 'potential' aspects – the East Thames Corridor, and the Lea Valley, with new transport proposals on the east flank of the conurbation. In this way, a strong line was taken that the six boroughs had a continuity in their problems and their potentials (see Chapter 7).

Managing the representation. There was some lobbying by local MPs for the six-Borough submission. An additional case for assistance for London was made by the Association of London Boroughs, although it was described in Hackney as a 'quiet' case. There were important party political constraint implications in lobbying, and a recognition of the sensitivities between Hackney and other Labour-controlled Districts in the North, Midlands, etc. In general, Hackney avoided confrontation in what was effectively a zero-sum game.

Local officers perceived that Conservative-controlled Boroughs in London (for example, Enfield) lobbied hard for support via a shift in the attention of regional policy southwards; some coastal areas also did this.

Concluding points. The East London response – Hackney included – amounted to a strong representation. It was three-pronged, and important in its link to the East Thames Corridor and Lea Valley areas. Although long typified by some of the highest unemployment levels in the UK, any positive decision required a major change in political attitudes to support for the south (see Chapter 7) – and, particularly important, an acceptance of an argument long voiced in London (see GLC, 1984, Appendix 1) that using the TTWA system as the base for delimiting Assisted Areas effectively led to the by-passing of many local economic problems.

East Kent coastal area

The East Kent coastal area represents one of the more fascinating locations to be involved with the 1992/1993 review. However, assembling an overall idea of how the submission was produced, what issues emerged and what debates occurred is difficult given the number of players, even more so than for a typical County approach such as Clwyd because there is rather more of a sense of informal liaison – as against executive power.

The task in East Kent was to balance a range of interests. There was some history of prognostication over policies. Thanet, for example, is no stranger to debate and controversy over local economic development (Buck *et al.*, 1989); it had regional policy support for a time in the 1950s and had made a number of submissions over the years.

The economic development 'fears' of coastal East Kent are founded in early deliberations on the Channel Tunnel. Much attention has been directed towards the establishment and effect of the East Kent Initiative (EKI) – a local development agency. There has been a growing realisation of relative position/ disadvantage across East Kent. The Kent Impact Study was commissioned in 1987 to investigate the economic impact of the Channel Tunnel on the Kent economy. The 1991 Review of the impact study – also taking into account the impact of the Single European Market – concluded that only 2,000 jobs would be created and that there would be a net loss of jobs in East Kent of 8,900. It recommended the setting up of a task force to bring together resources of central government, local authorities and the private sector and EKI was the outcome. EKI is jointly funded by the public and private sectors and predominantly staffed by secondees from local government and the private sector – it is a growth coalition (Chapter 1).

The southern coastal lobby has been gaining momentum over the 1980s, the catalyst being the growing unemployment problem and a fear of the Channel Tunnel impact on some key industries. In the face of continental competition, the ambivalence of some non-interventionist (often Conservative) authorities towards spatial economic policy has been eroded.

For the book, surveys were conducted with EKI and three Districts – Dover, Thanet and Swale. The results are presented as an EKI view/approach, although as we note in a few places, Swale made a separate, small-scale submission.

Economic situation. The East Kent coastal strip includes the four TTWAs of Sittingbourne and Sheerness, Thanet, Dover and Deal, and Folkestone, plus the coastal area around Herne Bay and Whitstable in the north of Canterbury TTWA. The economic problems of the strip are, given its geographical expanse, complex. However, they can be crudely summarised as the decline of employment in the key industrial base (tourism, agriculture, manufacturing and transport industries) combined with the feared threat of competition from the French Nord Pas de Calais region – one of France's most 'highly assisted' areas – in the wake of the Channel Tunnel development.

In general, the strip is seen as insufficiently diverse in its industrial base, poorly supplied with development sites, poorly perceived by business leaders as a potential location for inward investment, with low new business birth rates and high business death rates, overdependent on low quality seasonal jobs, and relatively 'peripheral' to main centres (see Chapter 9). These problems were reflected in the early 1990s in high unemployment – Thanet, Sittingbourne and Sheerness, and Folkestone TTWAs had average unemployment rates placing them in the worst one-third of the UK and Thanet was in the top 10 per cent. The position in Dover and Deal TTWA was less problematical but here there was the threat of job losses following the completion of the Channel Tunnel, the rationalisation of ferry and port-related industry and continental competition, as predicted by the Kent Impact Study.

Response motives. The central task set for the EKI in making a joint submission was to secure Assisted Area status, and success was expected. For some of the District participants there were additional motives, although these were not always known to the coalition. Thanet sought to boost the case from previous attempts and simply to get on the central government agenda; Swale had similar motives. Initially at the formation, Swale had deliberately linked with EKI rather than with its most 'natural' neighbours (in economic terms) to the north. Expectations of success were mixed across the partners.

Response formulation. The response was formulated by EKI, with a Committee responsible for each area. Consultants were used to produce the case. There was a very active, organised procedure. For example, in Thanet, apart from formal Committee support, there were fortnightly meetings between key officers. Each District fed its content, perceived problems and so on to the consultants. The submission was produced and then edited by EKI and representatives.

There was generally wide political support, although some felt there might be a stigma attached to any success (especially pro-tourism councillors in Thanet and some local MPs). There were strong allies for Assisted Area status in the Chambers of Commerce in Thanet and in Swale. With EKI, there was substantial private sector involvement. The proposed submission went through various committees in each constituent authority.

Response elements. In the spirit of imagery, EKI devised a logo for the submission (Figure 5.4). This reflects the potential-orientated emphasis in the submission by depicting the area as a bridge to continental Europe.

More generally, the emergent strategy was for there to be a joint case plus individual cases. Given the range of localities involved, this was a political

REVIEW OF
ASSISTED AREAS IN GREAT BRITAIN

——— THE CASE FOR ———

EAST KENT

Figure 5.4 The East Kent Initiative logo for the Assisted Areas review submission.

necessity. Aside from potential, there was a stress on unemployment, with threats from expected job losses in ferry and port-related industries. Perhaps the major element of the strategy was an attempt to raise the awareness of East Kent in relation to the rest of the County, and to stress its poor image and relative peripherality. The independent submission from Swale stressed factors not specified by the DTI, for example, out-movement of branch plants. In general, infrastructure problems and needs were played down in the submissions as they were believed to be both sensitive and unattainable goals.

Managing the representation. There was a substantial effort put into lobbying and management of the submission. This was aided by the wide array of political representations on EKI, and the involvement of central government. EKI managed most lobbying, proving to be a powerful agent with cross-party support and substantial private sector involvement. A number of activities were attempted. There was a stall at the Tory Party Conference, a stream of letters to the DTI, and a coachload of Chamber of Commerce members from Thanet to lobby MPs in the House of Commons. Thanet District Council itself set up an exhibition in the House of Commons using a Hornby Hobbies car and railway model set-up (Hornby is a local Thanet firm). In Thanet – the local Chamber also set up a sub-group to press for status.

Concluding points. In general, the survey uncovered a sense of vigorous construction of this submission. Major resources were deployed, and officer time especially was injected into the bid.

With the successful inclusion of much of the coastal strip on the revised Assisted Areas map, there were recriminations on Canterbury City Council. This reflected the feeling that status for the strip would, potentially, divert development from other parts of Kent.

There is, finally, a sense that key local officers were particularly important in conditioning the structure and content of the submission and, through the EKI, orchestrating the lobbying strategy. In this respect, the local political consensus across the strip certainly assisted the formation of a clear line of approach.

5.2.2 General comments – the approach to policy response formation

The five cameos – and additional material – allow us to delve into the submissions and generate some useful insights into the policy process. Local circumstances are clearly important in conditioning local approaches and strategies, but it is still possible to make some useful generalisations. There are potential difficulties for larger authorities having to balance what may be competing local interests (this was mentioned by Dumfries and Galloway). Moreover, we have detected different levels of willingness and ability to commit resources and to 'enter the fray'. The assistance status at the time of the review emerges as a very important factor conditioning the approach. Defending existing status comes out as a particularly forceful factor (Bradford). There have been some interesting impacts – the review turns out to be a catalyst for local economic co-operation (a binding or integrating force) in some areas (Hackney and East London; Stoke-on-Trent). Alternatively, it has been a divisive force in others (with some sensitivity between Districts within the EKI area, and the split between local business and the local authority in Stoke-on-Trent and Dumfries and Galloway). The competitive nature of the whole process reveals itself in places. Where there are joint submissions, we have naturally found substantial liaison occurring. Where independent submissions have occurred there has been little liaison with adjacent authorities (Chester; Alyn and Deeside). In an indirect way, competition has surfaced, although in a relatively suppressed form.

Beyond these general results, we can draw out a range of insights into the key factors set out in section 5.1, all features that will advance our understanding of this part of central–local connections and spatial economic policy.

Motives – the local confronts central government

All submissions were primarily designed to 'win' Assisted Area status, although some had relatively low expectations and were, in effect, making representations with a wider, longer-term benefit in mind (Chapter 2). Most had important secondary objectives – to raise an awareness of local problems, for example – and many were effectively pandering to local pressures. The southern localities may well have been in that category. There was certainly a strong movement towards the acquisition of status during the 1992 review. In addition to the short-term goal of Assisted Area status, the EKI submission – at least as given direction by the local authorities – was certainly trying to construct a new image for the coastal strip with longer-term issues in mind. The review exercise was thus a channel through which the arguments and pressures of the local on the central were exerted and mediated.

Formation of the policy position – the local forms its policy and develops a strategy

Policy formation as reflected in reactions to the review exercise was the domain of the lead authority in joint submissions. There were intricate systems devised to enable a flow of information and return comment to be made. The coalitions between authorities and external agencies functioned as consensus mechanisms. There was relatively little political involvement; a wide consensus formed, with many cross-party agreements and, it seems, relatively little dissent.

There was little liaison outside the authority, or in some cases, within it. Local strategies tended to be very much local officer-led. Naturally, these stressed what were perceived to be key elements. There were stated attempts to develop standard indicators to reveal local economic problems (see Chapters 8 and 9). Some strategies were potential-orientated; others were more problem-orientated; most mixed the two lines. Where more resources were committed there was some use of consultants, but these were not particularly impressive documents, tending to follow a very conventional line of argument. There were some attacks on the lack of assistance in the south, in particular using the arguments about acute unemployment and competition from French coastal areas.

The existing status of authorities not only conditioned their approach. There was also an apparent advantage in the experience factor. These authorities may well be geared up for connecting with DTI, it being difficult for 'seekers' to break into the 'game'.

Arriving at consensus – the local draws together?

The analysis so far projects an image of a rather sanitised process. However, there were tensions lurking just beneath the surface of the submission approaches. Even where there were apparently no problems, it emerged that any groups or authorities opposing the line taken either dropped out or submitted their own separate document. It must be the case that some dissenting voices were simply not heard.

There were, across the surveyed authorities, widely different local policies as regards incorporating local interests – for example, the contrast between Bradford which worked hard to incorporate any local interest, and Hackney which generated an authority view. In essence, there was either careful liaison with groups, or no liaison at all. This was aided by the fact that there was little apparent local political controversy in a time of economic stringency.

It seems that there was a clearly emergent consensus, or alternatively a submission from a group within an authority which, effectively, avoided the need to draw together a consensus view of assistance.

Key individuals – the local 'leaders' and influence reveals itself

As with previous studies, key local individuals – more often local officers – emerged as vitally important in this area of policy. This was picked up in the submissions analysis (Chapter 4), where it was stated by some authorities that the responses were officer-led (e.g. Wolverhampton and the Isle of Anglesey), and not politically sanctioned. From the supplementary survey there was clear evidence that much of the local response was orchestrated by key local officers, sometimes in liaison with the controlling political group on the local authority. Whatever the detail of the local situation, policy responses were very much officer-led.

Coalitions and the review process: the local marshalls its forces

There were various links between coalitions and the review. The review was a catalyst for coalition formation or consolidation; it generated a new impetus for not only coalitions within authorities, but also those between authorities and local business interests. Coalitions involving external agencies were brought into action in response to the review, and, in some cases, the character and complexion of spatial coalitions was adjusted as a result of the review process. In these ways, the review process precipitated a marshalling of local forces and necessitated closer coalitions of interests, within or outside authorities. Such coalitions would be in place for future activity.

Other activities: the local lobbies and manages

The arena of central–local relations, at least in respect of the marshalling of local interest and involvements, was directly implicated by the review process. There were implications also for the myriad of other channels through which the local challenges and cajoles central government.

The management of submissions often involved an elaborate strategy for lobbying the DTI (e.g. Bradford). However, some did virtually none. There was thus substantial variation between authorities. This appeared to follow from previous experience, and was related to the activities and contacts of key individuals, and whether there were effective contacts available – perhaps a government Minister as local MP, or a particularly news-attracting individual. In some authorities, key officers developed gimmicks – exhibitions and displays, etc. – to 'get the message across'. This showed a level of commitment that ran in parallel with the submissions which, in some similar cases, devised tailor-made logos for the review response (Chapter 4).

5.3 Getting on the Map

In this chapter we have filled in some detail on the processes of response formation, investigating the motives, formation, deliberation and management of the local authority submissions. In building analysis around survey material obtained from lead officers, we have been able to go behind the submission documents. This has offered much information on the processes of local position or policy formation and, in particular, on the local connections with central government. These insights and ideas on processes of policy and strategy formation, on attitudes to policy and on aspects of local–central connections, particularly the local, have not been addressed before in the domain of regional policy.

In addition, we have been able to set up the opportunity to do at least two more exercises with the review response data. As reactions to potential changes in the map of the Assisted Areas, the review precipitated many substantial local assessments and comments on regional policy. Our reading of the documents and our review of their opportunities and limitations, leads to the belief that this can offer an excellent and novel opportunity for studying local attitudes. This is done in Part 3. We have also generated material on the form and style of the submissions, and that will allow us to focus on local authority representations of local economic problems, again an area of the policy process about which little has been written. That is the task for Part 4.

PART 3

Local Authority Sensitivities

6

LOCAL AUTHORITY ATTITUDES TO REGIONAL INDUSTRIAL POLICY

> to combat (colliery) closures without the advantages of Development Area status would be akin to fighting the Battle of Jutland from the decks of HMS Pinafore.
>
> (Sunderland Metropolitan Borough Council, 1992, p. 5)

Emotive words indeed – perhaps a little 'tongue in cheek', but nevertheless reflective of the importance with which some local authorities in Britain view the institution of regional policy. Indeed, one of the most interesting and illuminating aspects of the local response to the review exercise concerns these local authority attitudes to regional policy. Just what were the perceptions of local authorities and their agency and business partners? Were the prognostications linked to a real belief in the principles of regional intervention, or was the catalyst simply a matter of the 'carrot' of potential external resources? In this chapter we address these and other related issues. We focus on the significance of local views about policy, assess the detailed arguments put forward in the various local submissions, and try to move towards an understanding of the standpoints that emerge. In essence, we offer an interesting insight into the local dimension of regional policy – something that has not been addressed in previous work because the data was not readily available. The Assisted Areas review data base has changed all that.

Initially, it is important and instructive to think carefully about exactly what the links are between local authorities and regional policy designation.

6.1 Local Authorities and Regional Policy

The consultation phase of the review revealed the fact that the notion of regional policy as an element of spatial policy is alive and well in the perceptions of local economic specialists. It may have fallen by the wayside in recent years as an element of government spending on spatial economic development, but it is still seen by many agencies to be a potentially important mechanism for regional economic regeneration.

In offering their views on regional policy – often, of course, in making a 'local' case for status and thus not providing an objective, global view of the function of the regional policy package – many local authorities and their partner agencies have, amongst the rhetoric and representation that understandably pervades such cases, spelled out why such status is seen as useful. This provides a bonus in the unique opportunity that it affords to review, compare and contrast the views presented. Clearly, local authorities are inevitably prone to take a relatively insular view and their reactions cannot be read as fully objective evaluations in the wider supralocal arena. However, what they do reveal are ideas about the essentially local value of regional policy outside the context of wider issues of equity, justification or entitlement. In that sense, they are of substantial value.

6.2 The Importance of Local Authority Attitudes

Although it is not an area of research that has been particularly popular or well represented, we are able to cite plenty of evaluative research in the field of regional policy that has documented the positive local benefits that may accrue (for example, see Begg, 1993; Sheehan, 1993). We are also able to document the attitudes of central government (Damesick and Wood, 1987; and refer to Chapter 1) or, more often, to infer an attitude from policy developments (Taylor, 1992). What are not at all well-documented, however, are local attitudes to and perceptions of the value of regional policy. Exactly what do local authorities think about such policy? Equally important, why does it matter?

We make no presumption that local authorities should necessarily lock on to and discuss the benefits of regional policy – indeed, many did not in their submissions – although from the perspective of the local group, a case for designation could conceivably be enhanced if it considered just how policy could support the development of the local economy. Nevertheless, the numerous submissions that did include a viewpoint on policy provide a fascinating insight into local attitudes.

More than this, a local viewpoint on the value and limits of regional policy is of great importance in furthering our understanding of the wider role that such a policy may play, about how local groups perceive and hence support or otherwise deny the value of such policy. Addressing the local dimension generates a 'user' viewpoint; there seems little doubt that local agencies are in a closer and better position than most to judge the local value, certainly to evaluate the local impacts of policy initiatives. Indeed, a similar argument has been put forward for the role of local authorities in local economic development. Attitudes about regional (and other nationally based) policy – certainly those set out in the various submissions – reflect a local consensus and that is worth knowing because it can tell us more about the 'local'. Not least of all, attitudes reflect approaches to local economic planning, the external image that local agencies seek to transmit and so on.

Clearly, the views about regional policy held by local authorities and their partner agencies will condition how enthusiastically they operate it, given designation, and how they support it through associated (planning or other) policies, or resourcing strategies (for Training and Enterprise Councils, etc.) at the local scale. So, in these ways too, the local view of regional policy is of some significance.

Establishing local views about nationally based policies is thus an important contribution to our knowledge of central–local relationships in a whole variety of ways. The next question is exactly what is the 'local' perception of regional policy – what did local groups say about policy, interestingly at a time when such policy was at a low point in its powers, influence and extent (Chapter 1)?

6.3 Some Expectations

It is something of a myth that regional policy is universally on the decline in the British spatial economic system. It has had a 'bad press', it is riddled with 'white elephants', prestigious projects that have failed, and the resources devoted to it have increasingly dwindled to a modest level (Chapter 1). However, it is strongly supported by some (Martin, 1993a) and, as we shall show in the later parts of this chapter, it is, for a great variety of reasons, strongly supported by many local interests. Add to that the fact that it survives 'fit and well' in many parts of Europe (as charted in regular columns in *Regions*, the Regional Studies Association newsletter), and we have grounds at least for questioning – if not seeking to dispel – what may amount to the myth of its total demise. It may simply be a 'sleeping giant', but more than that, it has had, even in its leaner days, an important economic and political impact.

So, we might conjur up an idea of local perceptions and local attitudes to regional policy. For a start we should note that the influence of regional policy extends beyond the confines of the actual designation area – it 'touches on' many local authorities, those that secure some designated areas and those that do not. The latter are implicated in a competitive sense as they are, in financial terms, potentially disadvantaged (the submission for the Midlothian District Council stressed this element). On the other hand, designation may be 'shunned' by some authorities because it is seen as a potentially negative image. Ironically, such authorities may presumably view the designation of neighbouring areas as potentially advantageous.

In these terms, it seems reasonable to conclude that Assisted Area designation is bound-up with the image of places – how they are seen from the outside and, perhaps, how they represent themselves. Interestingly, as we will find later in the chapter (and as was apparent in the degree of non-submission, see Chapter 4), authorities differ in their attitudes towards regional policy and in the interpretation that they place on designation.

6.4 Local Authority Attitudes

Not all local authorities support the notion of regional policy. However, for those engaging in the review, responses were tantamount to 'bids'. It is unsurprising that the majority had a positive view of the impact of such policy. From this local standpoint there were clear perceptions of the benefits of Assisted Area designation, and as might be expected, a strong feeling for the disadvantages of non-designation. There was a strong tendency for areas with Assisted Area status at the time of the review exercise to quote the past successes of the policy and for those 'seekers' to articulate the expected effects. Central among the benefits mentioned were a number of recurring key aspects or associations and these are discussed in the following sections. These amount to the collective views of the 'local'.

6.4.1 Instilling confidence

Some submissions argued that the granting of Assisted Area status would demonstrate the confidence of central government in a particular area (Manchester), it would help to put areas 'on the map' – particularly the hitherto non-Assisted Areas in the South – and raise the external awareness of potential investors. This was an argument particularly prominent in some of the 'Southern' submissions (for example, the East Kent Initiative (EKI) representing the swathe of local authorities along the east Kent coast) where it was argued that local problems were ignored in the (erroneous) assumption that Southern prosperity is geographically all-embracing. This issue – linked to the transience or otherwise of higher unemployment levels in the South East – has generated some debate. This is something that we shall return to in Chapter 7.

In more specific terms, as others argued, designation can have an important effect on the economic image of an area, enhancing its credibility as an investment site (Lincolnshire). In a similar, related sense, some submissions, especially those covering areas on the fringes of the oil-rich localities (for example, North Grampian), suggested that designation would dispel myths about a prosperity that had not reached them but with which they were regularly labelled.

6.4.2 Inward investment

Many submissions stressed the importance of regional aid in attracting inward investment (for example, Newcastle-upon-Tyne; Coventry), especially in the face of the fierce inter-area competition that seems so prevalent in the 1990s (Cleveland). As the Manchester report suggests, inward investment tends to concentrate where Assisted Area incentives are available. Without it, some areas would simply not have recorded any successes in attracting external development (Durham). In areas where the policy effort has concentrated, the effects of regional policy via inward investment are dramatic. In Cleveland, for example, Regional Selective Assistance offers totalling £45 million were made between 1984 and 1992, while the total support (adding in other components such as the, since withdrawn, Regional Development Grant) for the period amounted to almost £130 million. Much of this has been directed at new inward investment, or at the expansion plans of past inward investors.

Looking at the more detailed arguments, local knowledge led several authorities to suggest that branch plants have used Regional Selective Assistance to maintain an edge over sister plants (Knowsley; Llanelli). Moreover, the Chester City Council submission suggests that without the support of regional policy, some of the prestigious new developments in and around Chester would have not located in the UK at all. This global view was supported by other agencies. As the Llanelli submission states, while the support offered through Assisted Area designation is only part of the 'package', such a designation does get areas on to a 'long list' of sites suitable for inward investment. For inclusion on a short list other factors are important (labour, skills, communications, and so on) but Assisted Area status can often be relevant at the point of decision where the costs and benefits associated with a location are finally considered. Of course, it is important to note that regional policy creates its own brand of dependency. This is recognised in some submissions, particularly where they are seeking to retain status. Coupling this realisation with an evident recognition of the competitive situation, the Newport (Gwent) submission reveals that its area is very much branch plant and satellite dominated, with only four company headquarters in the area. From the Newport perspective, a loss of status would mean that the competitive advantage that it has enjoyed *vis-à-vis* the east would be lost, leading to the possibility of a 'hollowing out' process.

6.4.3 Business development and diversification

Although Regional Selective Assistance is often associated with inward investment, some submssions stressed the fact that much of the help given through this and other strands of the regional policy package relates to the expansion of existing (indigenous) companies rather than solely to greenfield developments and this was seen as a vitally important factor in the merits of regional policy (EKI; Cleveland).

6.4.4 Catalyst for private sector involvement

An argument in many submissions, especially those from local authorities with some existing Assisted Areas, was that the resources available through regional policy function in a catalytic way to nurture and attract private sector investment (for example, Rotherham; Birmingham). The support available through Assisted Area designation could operate as a 'pump-priming' device to tempt developers into action.

6.4.5 Building on existing infrastructure

Another line of argument used in the submissions was that regional policy aid works in tandem with concentrated infrastructure projects (Merthyr Tydfil). This was a particularly central line of argument used in some of the former coalmining areas, or for areas where the winding down of a New Town was leading to a lower level of external funding (for example, Renfrew District Council). Many of those authorities feeling, and projecting themselves as, 'peripheral' in 1990s Europe (Chapter 9) used the argument that the denial of regional aid would possibly further erode any potential for infrastructural improvement and consequently an opportunity for active improvement would be lost. Clearly, such localities were assuming that failure to achieve Assisted Area status under the British criteria would also deny access to European Union policy support. This did not turn out to be a wholly accurate assumption (see Coombes, 1994) but it did condition local responses and submissions.

In a related line of argument, some submissions viewed an appropriate scale of designation as offering the chance to target areas of potential, whether within TTWAs or as regards entire towns (for example, Telford).

Very few submissions dwelt on the Regional Enterprise Grant (REG) side of the Assisted Areas policy package as it operated in the early 1990s. An exception was Hull City Council which saw this as assisting with new technology, perhaps helping to build links between industry and higher education.

6.4.6 Reducing some dependencies

At first sight it is a little ironic to note that, far from recording vulnerabilities in their dependency on regional policy or other government support, some authorities, and their partners in a joint submission, argued that it could actually reduce some dependencies. Knowsley, for example, argued that the dependency on local banks could be slackened by the availability of regional aid.

6.4.7 Vulnerability without support

The fear of withdrawal prompted some submissions to offer a strong plea (Central Region (Scotland); Monmouth). There was a clear feel for the vulnerability that could prevail. As one report stated, the loss of status in 1984 had 'placed a shackle on the area' (Llanelli). The high degree of potential mobility of existing investment was at the forefront in several submissions (for example, Huddersfield; Lliw Valley; Fife).

Focusing on the Assisted Areas map as it existed prior to the review, the Calderdale submission stresses the 'damaging and distorting' and ultimately 'unfair' effect on the area if designation were to be denied in the face of local economic problems and the designation of a swathe of areas around the District (the so-called 'doughnut' effect). The negative impacts following any withdrawal of support were particularly pursued in areas where an adjacent authority/TTWA had been receiving the benefits of designation. A classic example of this is the case of the Workington and the Whitehaven TTWAs. Not only was the denial of support seen as detrimental, but it was also argued that much previous investment in, for example, factory building could be wasted if further regional aid was not to be made available (Workington, section 7).

Some authorities deliberately cultivated the 'threat' element. For example, as discussed in Chapter 4, past successes and vulnerabilities were consolidated by a number of submissions that deliberately drew on and cultivated the views of the local business community (for example, Manchester; Portsmouth; Great Yarmouth; Isle of Wight). In many of these submissions, there was a distinctive 'threat' element implicit in the style of presentation.

In tandem with the negative consequences of withdrawal, there was an argument that any loss of status could jeopardise existing initiatives – for example, local economic development agencies would be rendered ineffective if Assisted Area status were to be withdrawn from an area (Workington; Bradford).

6.4.8 Past successes

Past local successes deriving from access to regional policy support were stressed in many submissions. The emphasis was on the number and cost-effectiveness of projects and jobs created or saved by regional aid in the past. For example, the Easington submission (p. 14) claims that Regional Selective Assistance (RSA) had been instrumental in the vast majority of job-creating investments in the district, with grants of £12.5 million supporting 69 companies and 4,000 jobs between 1984 and 1992, aside from any indirect effects. Between 1984 and 1992, the Hull TTWA benefited from Intermediate

Area status to the tune of 247 RSA grant claims totalling £14.5 million and creating or safeguarding around 5,000 jobs. Significantly, a summer 1992 survey claimed to find that over half would consider diverting out of the area if Assisted Area status were to be withdrawn in the review. The Rossendale submission claimed a cost of less than £2,200 per job created/saved through RSA.

Linked to past successes, there was the argument that regional policy directly complements other (local) initiatives (Bolton/Bury). According to the Coventry submission, the high take-up of Regional Selective Assistance in the period since designation in 1984 was, 'partly achieved through the promotional and advisory services of the local authorities' (p. 8).

6.4.9 Hinting at the 'dangers' of designation

Although generating a case for their own inclusion, some submissions focused rather more than others on the negative side of Assisted Area designation. Several (Crewe; North East Fife) cited the problem of jobs being drawn away from non-Assisted to Assisted Areas, even within the same local authority area. Others, such as the City of Edinburgh, stressed the impact of 'unassisted' status.

In this sense, and as argued in Chapter 4, local authorities are sometimes in a real quandary when it comes to the chance to bid for development funding. There is a need to reveal the 'problems' of the local economy and this may well run counter to the image being fashioned by the authority to outside interests. This may generate a sufficiently strong self-image that the chance to secure outside funding is forfeited. As raised in a report to the Carlisle Economic Development Committee, 'all of the Council's marketing and promotional initiatives have been linked to Carlisle as an economic success story. To contemplate a case for assistance which emphasised the city's weak points would run counter to this strategy' (Carlisle City Council, Economic Development Committee, 2 July 1992).

Particularly interesting are the submissions for those authorities on the fringe of existing Assisted Areas. The East Staffordshire submission covering the Burton-on-Trent TTWA cites the 'distortions' caused by regional policy, with motor components firms diverted away from the town after having shown an initial interest. Other examples of regional policy in action – for example, the 'luring' of two firms into the Gwent TTWA from their apparently 'preferred' location in South Herefordshire in order to take advantage of Assisted Area benefits – were seen as negative from the perspective of those areas feeling that they had forfeited development as a consequence (in this case, South Herefordshire District Council).

The style of argument is also of interest. Some representations suggested that local and central state policy could and should be complementary and that regional policy was one way in which this could be achieved. This is interesting in the sense that one of the major criticisms of regional policy in the past has been a lack of strategic direction when it comes to local–regional–national objectives (Armstrong and Taylor, 1987; Damesick and Wood, 1987; Townroe and Martin, 1992).

6.5 Understanding the Attitudes

So far in this chapter we have established the perceived value of regional policy access from the standpoint of the 'local'. In this section, we focus on some of the factors that are likely to have influenced attitudes to policy access.

While it is not possible, in the absence of direct interrogation, to identify definitive causes for the line taken on regional policy (although see the five cameos in Chapter 5), it is possible to draw some inferences from the content and style of the submissions and from the background characteristics of the areas represented. In addition, we can assemble the submission content and attitude analysis for different groups of areas. As found in the engagement analysis (Chapter 4), some types of locality, although crudely defined, were vigorous respondents in the review exercise. In the latter part of this section, we briefly focus on two of them – local authorities in first, coastal economies, and second, defence-laden local economies.

6.5.1 Some explanations

We have already considered the circumstances leading to non-response by local authorities. In some cases this was found to be a reflection of a self-perception of modest problem status. As a corollary, we find that the opposite tends to govern the motives behind responses. In fact, at least five sets of factors seem relevant and these can be identified in the arguments assessed in the previous section.

Past history of Assisted Area status

It is evident from the variable content and line of argument adopted in the submissions that this is an important conditioning factor. There was a clear distinction between the arguments put forward by those localities with existing Assisted Area status – those we have referred to as defenders in Chapter 4 – and those without it (seekers). For example, in some non-Assisted Areas there was the argument that regional policy should experiment with short-term designations to alleviate problems in 'deteriorating' areas (Nottingham). There was also the suggestion that special assistance and tailored designation should be afforded to defence-related local economies (Bristol) (see section 6.5.2).

For those local authorities with recent experience of Assisted Areas designation, there was a distinct stress on the benefits and successes of that designation, on the need for continuity, on the tendency to utilise the support of local business via what might be reasonably interpreted as a 'hint of withdrawal strategy'.

Local competition

Attitudes towards policy designation changes seem to have been to a degree conditioned by the status of adjacent authorities or TTWAs. In some cases in fact, projects supported by regional policy in a neighbouring area are actually documented in what amounts to a 'rival' submission. For example, the submission for Whitehaven cites the opportunities foregone (and accruing to near neighbours) in previous rounds of policy assistance (Figure 6.1).

RSA OFFERS MADE IN WORKINGTON TTWA SINCE 1984					
	Offers Made	Total Assistance	Project Costs	New Jobs	Jobs Saved
1984	10	404,420	3,564,225	201	-
1985	4	232,000	2,796,000	138	-
1986	7	2,803,000	68,632,000	192	234
1987	5	2,426,700	9,790,470	79	350
1988	3	245,000	3,034,000	71	-
1989	7	306,000	3,003,430	172	41
1990	15	2,945,000	15,623,306	323	122
1991	15	989,000	6,467,296	282	146
1992 to date	12	2,217,000	10,437,400	113	183
	78	12,568,120	123,348,120	1571	1076

Source: Dept. of Trade and Industry   Table 9

Figure 6.1 The perceived 'benefits' of Assisted Area status as reflected in the policy 'successes' of neighbouring authorities.
Source: Copeland Borough Council (Whitehaven).

Local competition between areas also shows itself in classic divisions; for example, between the South Wales valley economies and the more prosperous coastal plain economies – the western end of the so-called 'M4 corridor'. The Rhymney Valley District Council submission, covering the Merthyr and Rhymney TTWA, reveals a clear sensitivity to the differing problems of places such as Cardiff on the coast and the valley economies. In this submission, the inclusion of Caerphilly in the analysis with Cardiff (the Cardiff TTWA) is claimed to underrepresent the problems of the former, which is much more akin to a problematical valley economy than to the coastal strip. This is one of the most regularly occurring criticisms of the designation approach and something which we will return to in section 6.6.

The role of local officers and the degree of local partnership

It is not possible to pinpoint the role of local officers precisely using the review data. However, from the analysis in Chapter 5 we have been able to conclude firmly that they are the crucial element in the style and often the fact of engagement with central government over issues such as regional policy.

The regional setting

Perhaps one of the most interesting aspects of the present analysis concerns the approaches adopted by authorities and agencies in London and the South. The ultimate granting of Assisted Area status to a swathe of coastal areas in the South and to parts of London has, of course, itself generated some controversy (Martin, 1993b; and see Chapter 10). The other side of the issue is the attitude of London and Southern authorities and linked agencies towards regional policy (Chapter 7). Perhaps the major group of 'winners' in the process were what we have labelled the coastal economies (see below; and Chapter 10).

As we have already intimated in Chapter 5, there is nothing new in southern representations with regard to 'getting on the Assisted Areas map'. For example, the Greater London Council submitted a strongly argued case in 1984. The difference in the 1992/1993 review was that there were more and stronger southern representations, and some successes!

The local economic base

Subject to a 'fear' of overstressing the problematical condition of a local economy, the nature of the local economic base emerges as the key factor conditioning attitudes to policy acquisition. Given the nature of the regional policy package in the mid-1990s, this is not surprising. What is interesting, however, is the extent to which the economic specialisations and, to a degree, locally perceived role for places, influenced attitudes to regional policy. That is the subject of section 6.5.2.

6.5.2 The character of the local economy

Given the importance of the local economic base in conditioning attitudes to regional policy, there is some value in exploring this a little further. In this section, we focus on two groups of authorities – those on the coast and specialising in the 'sea sector', and those that we might describe as defence-laden, specialising to a substantial (self-perceived) degree in defence industries. Both were strong voices during the review exercise.

The coastal economy

> Left high and dry by a turn of the economic tide.
>
> (Guardian, 26 July 1993)

Coastal authorities were prominent in their level of engagement with the government during the review (Appendix 1; Chapter 4). Moreover, many of the strongest submissions came from coastal authorities in the South, South West and East making their voices heard, sometimes for the first time as regards regional policy. It is useful to investigate attitudes to regional policy from the perspective of this group.

Britain's coastal localities have eked a living out of the coast and the sea, as physical resources or as access locations, for hundreds of years. However, the post-war period, particularly since the 1960s, has brought problems for virtually all the traditional specialisms, with ailing tourism industries in the face of overseas competition, rationalisations in the fishing industry as a result of competition, quotas, etc.; the demise of sea transport; the 'peace dividend' and the closure or cutback of naval installations and defence industries (see further below), many of which are located in coastal areas (Cooke, 1986; English Tourist Board, 1992; Brindle, 1993; Pattinson, 1993). In addition, reinforcing the 'fear of decline', many coastal authorities view themselves as peripheral to major markets (for example, Great Yarmouth Borough Council; see Chapter 9), and, in a connected sense, at a disadvantage in the new, more open competitive conditions in the European economy of the 1990s (East Kent Initiative). In effect, Britain's coastal resorts have been facing decline precipitated by shifting markets, and this has reflected itself in a range of problems – declining employment, rising unemployment, ailing infrastructures, and limited prospects for developing alternative economic activities.

If unemployment records and reveals the demise of places, and that is questionable (Murphy and Sutherland, 1992), then it is undoubtedly the case that local unemployment variations in Britain reveal a fairly high incidence of coastal areas amongst the worst 'performers'. Many of these problem localities are located in the South (East and West). From Figure 4.1 we found the appearance of places such as Clacton, Skegness, Penzance, Hastings, Sheerness, Brighton and Portsmouth amongst the worst performing Travel-to-Work Areas in mid-1992. The unemployment 'blackspots' had shifted to the seaside!

In addition, it is regularly claimed, the seasonal demand profile for labour in many coastal labour market areas serves artificially to reduce the impression of long-term unemployment as unemployed people tend to get drawn into seasonal work at certain times of the year. This has been forcefully argued as a problem (of understatement) for many Kent coastal strip economies such as Sittingbourne/Sheerness, Folkestone, and Thanet (e.g. East Kent Initiative) and for east coast localities such as Whitby (North Yorkshire County Council) and Skegness (Lincolnshire Training and Enterprise Council). However, as shown in an English Tourist Board report, while basic unemployment rates are relatively high in many coastal resorts and ports, the long-term unemployment rates are often much less pronounced, even relatively low in some cases (Coopers and Lybrand, 1992, para 105); for example, the Newquay TTWA ranks 8th worst in the former but 316th (out of 322) in the latter, reflecting the short-term nature of unemployment so typical of seaside tourist resorts (see Amstrong and Taylor, 1983). Conversely, some 'resorts' (e.g. Hastings; Thanet) scored relatively badly on both criteria.

Of course, the demise of Britain's coastal economies has been well recognised in the past. In general terms, the mix of proposed locations put forward for the ESRC – funded localities research in the 1980s included six coastal areas, one of which, Thanet, was ultimately selected for research (Cooke, 1986). However, Thanet was the only locality put forward that could claim any resemblance to a coastal resort economy. In more specific terms, research has locked on to the inherent problems of coastal economies, whether it be the job instability of the local workforce (Gordon, 1988), the seasonality that often implicates coastal resorts (Ball, 1989), or the environmental and developmental problems that confront such areas in the wake of economic decline (Pattinson, 1993).

The review simultaneously generated two reactions on the coast; first, it unleashed sensitivities about local differences in prosperity, about the lack of government support for the local problems noted, and about the ongoing plight of areas; second, it provided such places, and the agencies that represent them and their industries, with a golden opportunity to engage with the government in the quest to secure some level of regional support (Chapter 2, section 2.1). Many local authorities and other groups did just that, and the consultation process even generated some local action groups.

Past recognition or not, the demise of the coastal economies has been brought to the fore in the last few years and that has led to a more vigorous campaign on the part of interested agencies – local authorities and others – for government regeneration support. Nearly three-quarters of Britain's coastal authorities submitted reactions to the review exercise (Chapter 4, Appendix A.1.3).

In discussing the nature of the response to the consultation document, it is interesting to note some liaisons of support. In a small number of cases, these took the form of local campaigns orchestrated by local newspapers and other agencies. For example, 729 responses representing the defence-dependent Weymouth and Portland TTWA were received, 719 of them from members of the local population. A campaign led by the Ilfracombe and District Development Status Action Group submitted a petition to the DTI with 4,200 names. More commonly, liaisons of support were formed between local authorities and one or sometimes all of the following: Training Enterprise Councils, Chambers of Commerce, local industry and other groups.

Against the background of economic decline, it is not surprising that we find many coastal authorities representing their areas as problematical on a number of classic bases – from unemployment to the narrowness of the local economic base.

An important part of the local case for Assisted Area designation concerned the actual need for such status in terms of its potential use. Some responses from coastal authorities offered detailed plans for an effective use of regional policy support. Others simply set out the standard claim that status would reduce the reliance on a limited range of industries through the encouragement of inward investment, including access to internationally mobile companies and the enhancement of local business development; facilitate infrastructural development; enhance sites to overcome peripherality problems; and provide a trigger for other sources of (European Commission) funding.

Local arguments were more revealing. These tended to promote the point that designation would increase or enhance the chances of turning area potential into reality – a kind of catalytic role. A number of specific points were made in the various submissions, that Assisted Area designation and the access to financial support that it implies would:

- Promote excellence in an area of potential diversification (this was argued by authorities for places such as Grimsby) with potential in the fishing heritage industry and in the development of the fish processing industry into higher value-added products, or even in terms of access to the spin-offs of Channel Tunnel development by authorities such as Hastings.

- Enable new investment in, and bolster the role of, existing key industries such as tourism (Great Yarmouth).
- Allow past partnership successes to be built upon.
- Offset the danger of losing existing economic activity – a strategy and line of argument apparently engineered and prompted by consultants working on behalf of several coastal authorities. It was argued, by, for example Tendring (representing the Clacton and Harwich TTWA) and Torbay, but also by East Yorkshire Borough Council (representing the Bridlington and Driffield TTWA), that designation would offset the plans that some local firms had for shifting some existing activity into the existing Assisted Areas, or developing new activities in them.
- Remove an important barrier to development, either where adjacent areas had Assisted Area status or where a locality was wedged between two growth areas without gaining spin-off benefits; the former was argued by authorities north of the Humber (Bridlington and Driffield) as regards those south of the estuary; the latter was raised by Moray in terms of the Aberdeen and Inverness 'growth points'.
- Offset the negative consequences of the loss of designation at the previous review in 1984 (Teignbridge; Bridlington and Driffield; the Shetland Isles).
- Lend credibility to the area as a locus for investment (East Kent Initiative).

The line of argument was almost universally that there was little alternative source of funding available, that in many cases, coastal authorities were not eligible for urban policy support and, often, not part of rural development programmes – they therefore fell 'between two stools'.

In essence, these various arguments represent the collective views of coastal local authorities submitting material to the review process on the problems and the potential of their localities. They provide us with a useful insight into both the plight and potential of such areas, and their attitudes to regional policy. Central state acceptance of coastal economy problems was reflected in the fact that many were successful in securing designation under the revised map (Goldring, 1993), either recapturing the status lost in earlier revisions or getting on to the map for the first time (see Chapter 10).

Defence-laden areas

Whether through business accruing to local or nearby firms, jobs for locals, or via the impact of military installations, defence economic activity pervades many localities in Britain. It has generated great prosperity in some, and notable 'benefits' in many. However, the 'defence dividend' is gradually being superceded by a 'peace dividend' that is chipping away at the defence-related elements of these local economies. Jubilation over the relaxing of the 'cold war' has been tempered in those localities that are, in some way, dependent on the defence industries by the economic implications of such changes in world politics. The review provided an opportunity for defence-related local authorities, amongst many others, to 'flag up' their problems and, of relevance to this chapter, to reveal the ways in which they perceived regional policy to be of potential assistance (Ball, 1994a).

Defence-laden local authorities, as well as many other respondents, viewed Assisted Area status as a potentially important catalyst. For example, the

Barrow-in-Furness submission (Furness Enterprise) made reference to the previous period of assistance (1960 to 1980) and to the inward investment that was secured. In areas such as the Bristol region, designation was seen as a 'major step forward towards redressing the structural economic problems of the area . . . (enabling the area) . . . to attract new manufacturing jobs . . . (and) . . . foster indigenous growth' (submission by Avon County Council *et al.*, p. 4). In this way, many authorities were keen to demonstrate the potential impacts of Assisted Area designation.

Even more seriously, some authorities viewed the prospect of descheduling from the Assisted Areas map with trepidation. As one submission urged, there was a need for:

> the retention of Intermediate development area status for the Cinderford and Ross-on-Wye Travel-to-Work Area to enable them, as key facilitators in the area, to complete the task orginally set in 1984. The job of diversifying the TTWA's economy remains, the need for local jobs is still apparent despite falls in unemployment, and future threats, particularly from reductions in defence expenditure and from European trends, will make those tasks more difficult. Incentives for private investment are still required and any reversal to the pre-1984 situations (*vis-à-vis* South Wales) could undo much of the progress that has already been achieved.
>
> (Forest of Dean, p. 2)

Serious words indeed – but the TTWA lost its Assisted Area status altogther.

Defence-laden local authority responses fall into two categories in terms of scale. Most focused on the defence sector as just one threatened element of the local economy. These tended to be modest reports with limited analysis (Bristol; Wirral/Chester; Fife). Where defence was a more prominent element of the local economy the situation was very different. Authorities or groups representing areas such as Lancashire, Weymouth and Portland, Portsmouth, and Barrow-in-Furness clearly invested substantial resources in producing extensive, and potentially powerful, responses to the government paper.

Some County responses mention defence and pursue a case for the entire local authority area of jurisdiction (Lancashire; Blackburn; Kirkaldy). Others drew on County support (e.g. Cheshire County Council presented the case for the Wirral/Chester TTWA). Most impressive were a handful of responses produced by liaisons between the local authorities and other local interests. These include the following: Dorchester and Weymouth, with Weymouth and Portland Borough Council producing a response in liaison with Dorset County Council (the 'lead' authority), West Dorset District Council and the Dorset Training and Enterprise Council (TEC); Portsmouth City Council leading the response for the Portsmouth TTWA in liaison with Borough Councils in Gosport, Fareham and Havant, the Hampshire TEC, and the South Hampshire Chamber of Commerce and Industry; the Barrow-in-Furness TTWA represented by Furness Enterprise – a partnership between the local authorities (Cumbria; Barrow-in-Furness; South Lakeland), the Enterprise Agency itself, Vickers Shipbuilding and Engineering Limited, Scott Limited, the Cumbria TEC, and English Estates.

The failure of government policy to respond to the needs of areas such as the Portsmouth defence economy is nothing new (see the comments of Bateman, 1986). However, the review provided a real opportunity for such areas to force themselves on to the agenda and a variety of strategies were employed to achieve this. Particularly dramatic was the use of imagery – at its most prominent in the Portsmouth and Dorchester, Weymouth and Portland submissions. Substantive and well-produced, these carry a defence-related message on their covers. In the Portsmouth case, this is in the form of a prominent, carefully engineered defence/unemployment logo (Figure 6.2). In the case of Dorchester, Weymouth and Portland this is a representation of the need for diversification in the wake of defence cutbacks (Figure 6.3).

Local authority perceptions of the problems that rationalisation in the defence sector might generate connect with the perceived needs of the areas. The crux of the issue is seen as the threat of substantial job losses coupled with unemployment growth; the overdependence of the area on defence-related industries; and the fear of a negative multiplier effect hitting related industries and the locality in general – for many, a new and very unwelcome 'spatial fix'. The submission from the Isle of Wight claimed that two firms, both with strong defence links, employed 3,000 staff or 34 per cent of the island's workforce. In addition, perhaps partly as a consequence of the 'Solent factor', both had strong island links through subcontracting and hence large multiplier effects. Assisted Area designation was seen as providing the stimulus to new investment and jobs in the area – a source of assistance for reducing the dependency, modest or otherwise.

The Portsmouth response focused on the recent substantial rise in local unemployment to well over the national average. In contrast, the Dorchester and

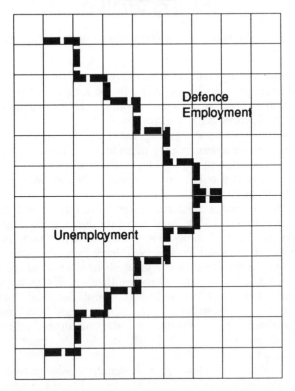

Figure 6.2 Portsmouth's defence-related graphic.

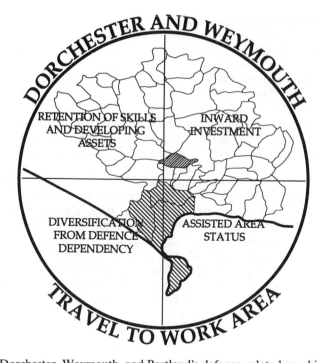

Figure 6.3   Dorchester, Weymouth, and Portland's defence-related graphic.

Weymouth submission argued that unemployment – at the time of the review below national average – was likely to rise in the future. In that sense, it sought to engender a more proactive approach from the DTI in its deliberations over the refined Assisted Areas map.

The review of the Assisted Areas map came as a 'window of opportunity' for many defence-connected areas. It gave them an extra chance to make representations to central government over their medium-term economic predicaments. Moreover, regional policy could provide much needed finance to support restructuring in the local economy.

That is the conventional wisdom; some would not concur, arguing that problems of economic fragility might not be served by the according or retention of Assisted Area status. There was clearly some scepticism about the real benefits of regional policy. We have already noted the effective abstention of some authorities on the grounds of stigma, or the self-perceived remote chance of success. In the Portsmouth case, for example, one of the local MPs admitted to much initial unease about the local 'bid' for designation, related to the perceived risk that status might send out the 'wrong signal', that 'our area is pessimistic and dependent on others rather than independent and enterprising' (Willetts, in the Portsmouth and Gosport TTWA's submission, update, 1992).

In general, however, Assisted Area designation was viewed as potentially beneficial on a number of, largely familiar, bases. These are summed up by the Furness submission as:

- attracting inward investment and improving the inquiry-conversion rate by providing a key promotional asset;
- fostering the indigenous growth of existing companies or the formation and development of new firms;
- assisting modernisation and the introduction of new technology;
- assisting in the targeting of manufacturing companies in key areas for each locality;
- extending the chances of securing access to European Commission regional support (Furness Enterprise, 1992).

It is of interest to relate the perceived problems of defence-related localities to the potential that Assisted Area designation might bring. In this we might take a rather more critical line. For example, according to the Plymouth submission, the hypothetical closure of the Devonport Dockyard would remove £521 million of income from Devon and Cornwall (5 per cent of the region's total), and 29,900 jobs; it would implicate some 600 local firms and £38 million of orders, take away 30 per cent of Plymouth's local income and 20 per cent of its work opportunities, and raise local unemployment by 15–20 per cent (Devon County Council submission, p. 8). Against this kind of impact, any benefits that a modestly funded regional policy might bring would be limited, even negligible in a relative sense. At best, the benefits – if they emerged – would accrue over the medium and long-term. Yet, significantly, there was an almost wholly positive view taken of regional policy in the local authority and other local agency submissions. At a time when regional policy had clearly faded as a policy element, at least as regards central government agendas, there was a plethora of local authorities, not surprisingly but nevertheless vociferously, stating the merits of such a tool of spatial economic regeneration. Moreover, most of those who did not respond were discouraged by circumstance or the fear of stigma, rather than by being unsupportive of the benefits to the individual locality (Chapter 4).

The consultation process generated some innovative ideas – new ways of thinking about area assistance. Wary that the new Assisted Areas map might well apply to a smaller number of areas than those designated from 1984, and probably in the expectation of failure to secure Assisted Area status following the review, the Bristol TTWA submission (p. 5) suggested the introduction of 'a more flexible and discretionary approach . . . (offering) . . . assistance . . . on a short-term basis'. This would involve the designation of a 'defence priority area' for the TTWA which would allow regional policy benefits for a specified period as part of a broader package of measures addressing the problem of structural decline in the defence sector. Unfortunately – for Bristol at least – this suggestion was not taken up by the DTI.

6.6 Recasting Regional Policy

Unsurprisingly, many submissions to the Assisted Areas review exercise took the opportunity to offer a critical appraisal of the regional policy structure and approach in place in Britain in the early 1990s. This adds an extra dimension to the analysis already completed in the chapter.

There were a number of general disadvantages cited in the submissions. Regional policy was described as a system in need of overhaul (York City), needing to be recast (Amber Valley). Others cited the lack of continuity in the policy, its ad hoc nature (Glasgow), and the need for a more focused form. Some submissions decried the loss of Special Development Areas, the upper tier of the policy package pre-1979, and noted the benefits in reintroducing the automatic Regional Development Grant that had been successful, but phased out as too uncontrollable in the late 1980s (Strathclyde).

Both access to the 'benefits' of regional policy and its denial were variously viewed as problematical. Without it, some areas claimed they could not easily attract development. However, even with it, there was the problem already cited in this chapter, of the dependency that regional policy has generated in some places – in particular, a dependency on inward investment in the local economy and a vulnerability as a result (Newport (Gwent)).

The 'boundary effect' looms large as a critical comment – either in terms of a general drawing of resources away from non-Assisted Areas, or in the 'doughnut' effect of a TTWA surrounded by Assisted Areas (Calderdale). There is a clearly stated need not to focus on pockets of problems, but to take a more carefully selective line. In a veiled criticism of 'fear' that the policy focus would 'drift south', Ceredigion argues that regional policy is essentially a long-term policy that needs to target areas of long-standing and continuous problems. It should not be allowed to bow to 'short-termism' and political sensitivities.

Some criticisms were also levelled at the concepts of regional policy. In particular, as in previous reviews of regional policy, there was widespread criticism of the TTWA basis of policy area delimitation – perhaps the 'opening arguments' in an ensuing debate as TTWAs were known to be due for revision and the review provided the opportunity to make some early points. There has long been antagonism in Luton, where the TTWA combines a prosperous southern section that reduces the area unemployment rate but conceals the problems of Luton itself (Barnes, 1992). In Scotland, East Lothian's partial inclusion within the Edinburgh TTWA was felt to deflate the picture of local economic problems. Similar arguments were forthcoming from North East Fife, Perth and Kinross, and Cumnock and Doon Valley.

As with the GLC in 1983, several of the London Boroughs were sensitive to the TTWA issue. The three-Borough submission by Hackney, Newham and Tower Hamlets, in association with the East London Partnership, argued that the East London resident looks to a more localised labour market when searching for work, and that the TTWA designation works to the disadvantage of inner London Boroughs. The London Boroughs Association submission (joint with the London TECs and the ALA) argued that London was a special case where the TTWA was inappropriate and where there was a need to delimit smaller pockets of high unemployment (see Chapter 7, Figure 7.3).

The other main concept criticism concerned the criteria for granting status. For example, there was a need to expand the criteria to include cyclical patterns of employment change and the impact of migration on unemployment levels (Strathclyde), and to use industrial land and floorspace availability as an indicator of potential (Merton). The latter reflects a comment made more widely that the strategy for policy areas could be designed to select areas for assistance that can accommodate growth, and not those with unemployment and the need for development. Again, this is a problem that has pervaded regional policy – to support potential or problem areas? Rarely has it been possible to cover both objectives simultaneously.

There were also some criticisms of the operational side of regional policy. In particular, and again revealing the sensitivity of some areas to the forfeiting of investment to the Assisted Areas, South Bedfordshire argued that there was a need to scrutinise applications and awards more carefully.

In a different vein, although a long-term policy, several authorities suggested that regional policy should contain or develop a short-term element; for example, short-term aid to deteriorating areas (Nottingham City; South Somerset). In general, there was felt to be a need for a more integrated, variable and finely tuned policy structure.

6.7 Concluding Comments

In this chapter we have focused on local authority and local partnership attitudes towards regional policy, and how its role and effect is perceived at the local level. Such a perspective – made possible by using the Assisted Areas review data base – has not been addressed in the past. Obviously, in using the submissions made to the review process, we are focusing on a form of 'bidding' and the cases made are clearly representations designed to secure funding. In that sense, there is a need for care in interpreting the material. However, there is an equally clear objectivity in much of the documentation. Most were not public documents in many senses of the term, and virtually all appeared to offer a critically aware line of argument. There is no doubt that the ideas about regional policy put forward in the various documents did reflect a genuine view of this element of spatial economic policy.

In the analysis we found a general acceptance that regional policy has been a significant force in the development (and constraining) of a wide range of local economies. The attitudes of local representatives are clearly influenced by their local history of access to regional policy funding, the nature of the local economic base and so on. However, in general, there was substantial evidence that regional aid has had a whole range of positive impacts where it has been applied. For some submissions – in particular covering the more peripheral, industrial areas – the role of regional policy was seen as very much inward investment orientated and the value was seen in this globally competitive sense. For others – some of the presentations from areas in the South – indigenous support was seen as the key strength of the policy package. In this sense, there appear to be many viewpoints about the uses of policy. What is clear is that the demise of regional policy is certainly viewed with alarm in many of the more peripheral or industrially rundown localities in Britain. That renders it a hot political potato – and not just in 'traditional' Assisted Areas.

7

SOUTHERN ATTITUDES TO REGIONAL POLICY

Pockets of disadvantage within the south east warrant serious national attention because they compromise the region's capacity to lead the country out of recovery and rein back the region's – and thus the UK's – competitive position in Europe . . . In Brighton and Hove, the leverage offered by regional policy will turn the place around.

(Brighton Borough Council *et al.*, p. 6)

Indicators overwhelmingly show that London authorities should be considered for Assisted Area status . . . (in fact) . . . the case is incontrovertible.

(London Boroughs Association, London Training Enterprise Councils, and the Association of London Authorities, pp. 2–3)

Hackney Council has a successful record in working . . . in the fields of urban regeneration and economic development. But success requires more than close working relationships, imagination and experience; it also needs the major injection of additional resources that Assisted Area status would bring.

(London Borough of Hackney, p. 5)

These are powerful statements; they evoke a real sense of the strength of feeling as regards the need for development resources that pervaded parts of the South in the early 1990s. In discussing the arguments put forward by various local authorities and their partner agencies in response to the Assisted Areas review it is of importance and interest to focus on some of the key underlying debates (see Chapter 1). Prominent amongst such debates in the early 1990s has been the 'Southern' question – the problems confronting the economic development of London and the South East. The review material allows us to delve into the (level of) representations made by such southern interests and to deal with questions that lie at the heart of contemporary debates about spatial economic development and policy needs. As we have already documented (Chapter 4, section 4.2; Appendix 1, Tables A.1.2 and A.1.3), some 32 per cent of Southern localities (using the South East region as the measure) and over 50 per cent of London Boroughs took the opportunity to state their view of the Assisted Areas, most often to set their particular local or sub-regional problems before central government. So, what are the problems as perceived by Southern interests? What representations were made, by whom and with what perspective on spatial economic, and especially, regional policy?

7.1 Perceived Self-Image and Economic Problems

As we have already demonstrated in the cases of Hackney and East London, and the East Kent coastal strip (Chapter 5), there is a certain sensitivity amongst some local authorities and other interests in the South to the problems of local economies. This connects with views about the nature of central state intervention and support through spatially sensitive policy actions, and the perceived self-need of the areas involved. The South East and, to some extent at least, London are held to be universally prosperous and growth-orientated, with little constraint on their long-term potential. At least, that is the essence of the 'myth' feared by representatives in the South. It certainly conditions attitudes and reactions to events such as the Assisted Areas review.

What arguments were put forward by those Southern authorities and partnerships who responded and what were the reasons for the non-submission of others? Of course, in a way, the very fact of submission reflects a desire to bring an area's problems to the attention of central government. However, non-response is also of interest, especially if the reasons for such a lack of submission can be teased out.

The most effective way of assessing the situation is to select a small number of authorities for attention and, we will therefore draw on the responses of some of the coastal and other areas in the South – the group of East Sussex localities including Hastings and Brighton, the East Kent submission, Luton, and some of the London Boroughs. Assessment is based on the array of factors identified in the fuller range of submissions discussed above. What is the local (Southern) view of labour market problems, peripherality, the potential for southern economic growth and so on? How does the view of Southern localities differ, if at all, from the representations of localities outside the South? What was the 'Southern' line of argument?

7.2 London and the South East – Who Submitted?

In the South East and London there were a number of 'pace-setting' submissions. The scene-setting submission for the London economy came from the London Boroughs Association (LBA). This argued that there was a clear case for extending Assisted Area status into many parts of the London economy, in particular comparing unemployment levels in the locality to the existing Assisted Areas (Table 7.1).

It is against the background of this submission that we should assess the London case. Elsewhere in London, there were other powerful submissions. For example, there was the joint East London submission that we have already discussed in Chapter 5. This argued that, with unemployment in East London higher than in 41 of the 42 Development Areas and all 56 of the Intermediate Areas, there was a virtually irrefutable case for designating the area for assistance. Other London submissions came from the West London group (Brent; Ealing; Hammersmith and Fulham; and Hounslow) and from authorities such as Merton, and Kensington and Chelsea.

Outside London itself, the submission by the East Kent Initiative (covering areas such as Dover, Thanet, Shepway and Swale (Chapter 5)) stands out as one

Table 7.1 Unemployment in London relative to Intermediate Areas

	June 1990	June 1991	June 1992
Intermediate Areas in:			
South West	7.2	11.4	13.4
West Midlands	7.6	10.8	13.1
East Midlands	5.4	8.4	9.9
Yorkshire and Humberside	8.9	11.3	12.4
North West	7.3	9.9	10.9
North	8.0	10.3	11.1
Wales	7.5	10.2	11.0
Scotland	10.1	11.1	11.7
Average of above figures	7.8	10.4	11.7
22-borough area	7.6	11.9	14.6

Source: Department of Employment Gazettes for August 1990, 1991 and 1992 for Intermediate Areas; Unemployment Unit for London figures.

of the fuller, more considered representations. In addition, there was a group of submissions from coastal localities in East Sussex (Brighton and Hove; Hastings; Worthing and Eastbourne). The Isle of Wight Board generated a detailed, formidable submission, particularly focusing on what they refer to as the 'Solent factor' – the physical and economic barrier of the Solent estuary that, in effect, peripheralises the island, or so it is argued. There were, amongst others, also submissions from Luton District Council, in liaison with Bedfordshire County Council and South Bedfordshire District Council. All argued for the consideration of parts of London and the South East as Assisted Areas.

A number of Southern submissions reflect on, and probably were stimulated by, defence sector changes. Rationalisation in the defence sector – actual or feared – has touched many parts of the UK spatial economy, not least several Southern localities, and not only the obvious areas such as Portsmouth and Plymouth (see Chapter 6). Parts of the London economy are clearly implicated. For example, in Kingston-upon-Thames it is estimated that around 7,600 manufacturing jobs were lost between 1981 and 1992, largely as a result of the major restructuring of the defence industry. The closure of the British Aerospace factory would, it was argued, itself create a 40-acre development site in need of investment (Royal Borough of Kingston-upon-Thames). In Hounslow and West London, the local authority claimed that much of what remained of the manufacturing sector had been involved in the production of defence end-products. Planned workforce reductions by firms such as Fairey Hydraulics, the Thorn-EMI Defence Group, and Dowty Maritime, together with reductions outside the locality but within its commuting hinterland (British Aerospace; Lucas Aerospace), would inevitably generate local problems (London Borough of Hounslow).

So much for the submissions. Elsewhere in the book we have argued that non-submission is itself interesting. Of course, in the case of London and the south it is perhaps less revealing. Many authorities in the South simply did not bother to respond as their economic circumstances did not seem to warrant it (as stated in correspondence with, for example, Dartford and Reading). It was the defence-laden areas, or parts of inner London, that felt a need to highlight their problems via a representation. Non-submission becomes significant where authorities might have been expected to respond, when, for example, they carried particular local economic problems. In fact, there were few such cases – Southampton, with a TTWA unemployment level of 11 per cent refrained from reacting on grounds of limited chance of success and a fear of sending the 'wrong signals' to potential inward investors (letter, 18 February 1994). For others, the failure to respond reflected administrative oversight (Southwark) or a decision, later regretted, not to respond but to go for European Structural Fund support (Gillingham). Clearly, in some cases, we might suggest that it was a matter of what we have labelled the 'representational detail' – resources, expertise and the ability to construct cases and tease out opportunities, as much as any more ideological factors, that were at the core of an explanation.

7.3 The 'Southern' View of Regional Policy

The 'Southern' view can be explored in two ways – first, through a general comment on Southern attitudes, and second, through a brief comment on a number of specific aspects that should provide us with an idea about the self-perception of the South. Building on the discussion in Chapter 6, we can consider what was said about southern labour markets, peripherality, the economic base, and the future potential of the South. We can also note some of the 'Southern' gripes about the 'institution' of regional policy itself.

7.3.1 General comments on Southern attitudes

Perhaps the central line to emerge from the 45 London and South East submissions was that there are localised pockets of severe economic 'distress' within what is perceived to be seen by those outside (and even inside) the South as a widely prosperous regional economic environment (East Sussex; Brighton and Hove; Luton; parts of central London). Some places in the South, it is claimed, have never 'overheated', and have never really been a central part of Southern prosperity. Moreover, places have been, and are being, 'passed by' in development terms, or at least that is the evident 'fear' of some localities. More generally, there is the explicit argument that resources are needed to 'unlock' the region's potential. The claim for some is that places have changed – from an image of 'underperforming', claims Brighton and Hove, the local economy has shifted towards being more typified by 'structural disadvantage'. This is exemplified elsewhere in the South. In London, for example, the growth of the finance sector in the 1980s is held to have been a temporary phenomenon, while the demise of light manufacturing and engineering/metal-based sectors – losing 150,000 jobs between 1990 and 1992 – is cited as evidence of structural problems (London Boroughs Association et al., 1992).

Against such a perceived position, the value of Assisted Area status (or indeed, any other recognition via spatial economic policy) would serve to raise the awareness of localised economic problems in London and the South; perhaps even to explode this 'myth' of global southern prosperity. This is the key 'benefit' cited. In addition, any support decision would generate resources for the development effort. More specifically, the availability of regional incentives would potentially pull in inward investment (Swale), providing an added impetus for development.

In general, Southern authorities viewed the potential access to regional policy support as a major regeneration opportunity. There was, in some cases, an acceptance that support would not, perhaps should not, be provided indefinitely. For example, the joint Bedfordshire, Luton and South Bedfordshire submission seeking status for Luton, Dunstable and Houghton Regis, argued that assistance would reap tangible benefits within a five-year timescale. Perhaps circumventing the transience argument, certainly suggesting a new departure of assistance for a fixed period, they sought status only for a limited period. The argument was that with assistance, the area's inherent strengths (export-based manufacturing) could be realised, while without assistance, there was the prospect, emotively framed, of being 'trapped in a spiral of continuing decline'.

7.3.2 The detail of the arguments

Attitudes about Southern local labour markets

Unemployment has undoubtedly reached new levels in the South since the late 1980s, but to what extent is there any evidence that the problem is other than transient? That is undoubtedly a key issue. The response comes in at least two forms – sustainability, and some consideration of the basis of the changed position.

Table 7.2 Unemployment in the 22-borough area relative to the national rate for July of each year

	22 boroughs %	United Kingdom %	Rate in 22-borough area as % of national rate
1983	12.8	10.6	121
1984	13.4	10.7	125
1985	14.1	10.9	129
1986	14.7	11.2	131
1987	12.9	10.0	129
1988	10.4	7.9	132
1989	7.9	6.2	127
1990	7.5	5.7	132
1991	12.0	8.3	145
1992	15.0	9.7	155

Source: Department of Employment.

On the basis of unemployment and other indicators, some 22 London Boroughs would be eligible for Assisted Area status under the DTI criterion of falling within the 'worst third of the country' (Table 7.2). Over the ten years previous to the review, the relative position of this group of areas had deteriorated. Other figures were produced to show that long-term unemployment in London (12 months or more of persistent registration) had increased from 9.4 per cent of the UK total in 1983, to 17.0 per cent in 1992 (London Boroughs Association *et al.*, 1992, Table 5).

The submissions include some mention of 'unemployment blackspots' with surprisingly little apparent concern (e.g. Eastbourne) for the images that such a label carries. We have already noted the 'stigma' issue in considering the reasons behind a non-response in some areas that we would have expected to find bidding for Assisted Area status. In other cases, there is a clear acceptance of the need to promote such problems.

In Hastings, it was shown that the 'unemployment gap' had opened up since 1990 (Figure 7.1). However, it is clear that the 'gap' is recent and may not be a permanent feature. Although in the submission there was no direct consideration of the 'transience' question, the unemployment point was accompanied by a linked argument that implied a greater permanence in the problem, with much of it seen to stem from local economic weakness combined with branch closures (Figure 7.2).

The data in Figure 7.2 obviously represents a modest array of job losses, certainly relative to some of the problems of urban industrial economies (see for example the submissions by Cleveland or West Lothian). However, its significance is that it presents a different view, by the local authority involved, of the Hastings locality, as a place where there is decline, and for reasons other than simple recession.

Attitudes about peripherality

There may be a general presumption that the South is in many ways central and accessible. Later in the book (Chapter 9) we will show, in more detail, that many local authorities in the South dispute that presumption, and that others also 'feel' peripheral. For now, it is worth noting that several submissions argued that developments had by-passed them. There appears, for example, to be an innate

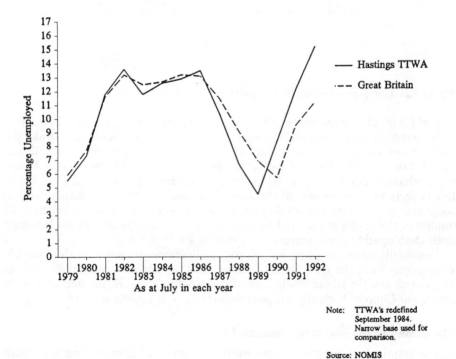

Note: TTWA's redefined
September 1984.
Narrow base used for
comparison.

Source: NOMIS

Figure 7.1 Hastings and Great Britain unemployment rate, 1979–1992.

COMPANY	NATURE OF BUSINESS	NO. OF JOBS LOST	DATE	REMARKS
Ibex Engineering	Manufacture of pumps	150	1989	Company amalgamation. Relocation to Eastbourne.
MK Electrical	Electrical component manufacturers	200	1990	Part of larger company Picked for closure as one of MK's smallest factories.
Newtime Foods	Food Production	200	1990	Transfer of production to Histon, Cambridge.
Derritron	Electrical Engineering	48	1990	Company taken over, relocated to Worcester
South East Computers	Computer Systems Equipment	30	1991	
W. M. Still	Catering Equipment manufacture	160	1991	Company now part of P.M.I. Food Equipment Group. Production moved to Barnstaple.
Knowles Electronics	Electronics Engineers	50	1992	Taken over by larger company. Closed due to rationalisation.
Michelsons	Shirt manufacture	45	1992	Closure due to rationalisation. Consolidated at Sittingbourne

Source: Hastings Borough Council
Planning Department
September 1992

Figure 7.2   Companies closing branch plants in Hastings, 1989–1992.

fear of Channel Tunnel inaccessibility from those areas that perceive themselves to be marginalised by either the tunnel itself or by the emergent routes linking it to the motorway or rail system (real fear or representation is not easy to determine). For example, Swale (east Kent) quotes the 1992 Medway Ports Handbook which refers to the port of Sheerness as Kent's 'hidden asset'. To Swale, this reflects the remoteness of the Isle of Sheppey (within the district) and to some extent, given the low level of road construction expenditure in the area (£3 million in 1991 against a district average in Kent of £10 million), of the Borough itself (Swale, additional submission to that by EKI).

Arguments about peripherality and communications problems are also found in submissions from the East Sussex coastal areas. In addition, authorities such as Weymouth and the Isle of Wight argued strongly that they are, in effect and as we explore in Chapter 9, clearly peripheral to the central growth areas of the region.

The demise of the Southern economic base

Representations about the various local economies of London and the South dwell heavily on the demise of key sectors. Prominent amongst these are defence, coastal tourism, inner city manufacturing, and vulnerable producer service activities. The 'branch plant economy' – so often cited as a problem for the Assisted Areas in the North and West – is revealed as an issue in some unlikely places (in Hastings for example, see Figure 7.2).

Elsewhere, economic problems are highlighted in a tone that implies they are unseen outside their areas of location. In Brighton for example, there is the argument that a 36 per cent decline in manufacturing jobs between 1981 and 1989 compares very unfavourably with that for the South East as a whole (–22 per cent) and the national picture (–15 per cent). In Brighton, the submission argues, the area's role as an office centre has suffered because of oversupply in the London office market.

Another area of perceived problems is not so much the demise as the actual failure of some localities to lock into the growth of business and financial services (Hastings). The overdependence of localities on key sectors (tourism in the Eastbourne submission; the defence sector in several of the Southern submissions) is also put forward.

The vagaries of the London economy, of course, feature heavily in the London submissions. Here the emphasis is on the demise of hitherto growth sectors. Restructuring in key sectors such as defence, pharmaceuticals, engineering, and a lack of financial and business services growth generating a legacy of unused and unappealing industrial floorspace (Ealing; Merton; East London submission) is accorded some prominence.

Attitudes about the future potential of Southern localities

Perhaps most interesting – and, indeed, difficult to predict in the absence of the submissions evidence – are attitudes towards the future potential of Southern localities. Certainly, there was a feeling that the 'big' infrastructure developments of the day were 'passing by' some places, leaving them with constrained potential (Swale; Brighton and Hove). Related to this, there were numerous instances of the 'infrastructure need' argument being put forward by London authorities (Ealing; Hackney). As the East London submission put it, there is a 'plethora of land-locked sites' in the inner London area, and large areas of vacant industrial floorspace. As such, the area was seen as having substantial potential with a need for resources to build it further. There was a need, claimed the report, to support key areas within the eastern flanks of the conurbation – the East Thames corridor, the Lea Valley and so on. Looking to the future, there was an apparent fear amongst London and other Southern authorities that the European domain is not being exploited, or even realised, by regional businesses, particularly in the manufacturing sector. Combined with the claimed 'strength of partnership' in the region, especially within the London economy, Assisted Area status for parts of the South would help to unlock potential and signal a prioritisation to both inside and outside interests.

7.3.3 Summing up the Southern view

In essence, the 'Southern' view was largely articulated through three sets of arguments: those associated with the declining economic base – in effect, the 'from transience or underperforming to structural demise' line of argument; the suggestion of a largely unrecognised and unacknowledged peripherality of parts of the South; and 'internal destabilisation' with the knock-on effects of change in the London economic arena (such as office rentals) sweeping across and implicating the rest of the south. As regards resources for development, regeneration, etc., the implicit arguments in many Southern submissions were that resource needs transcend local prosperity variations and that vulnerabilities (to European competition and so on) are just as much a part of the South as elsewhere in the economy, and that the South needs support as much as anywhere else (see East London area submission).

7.4 Concluding Comments

What we have called the 'Southern' view of regional policy is clearly articulated in the various submissions that emanated from Southern authorities during the 1992 review exercise. We have charted a relatively vigorous campaign on the part of the 'South' to dislodge the notion that its economic problems could be solved without government intervention. As part of that representation, a whole range of arguments were put forward by authorities and their partner agencies in London and the South East on the need for and value of regional policy. This offers us a useful insight into Southern thinking on this part of the policy arena.

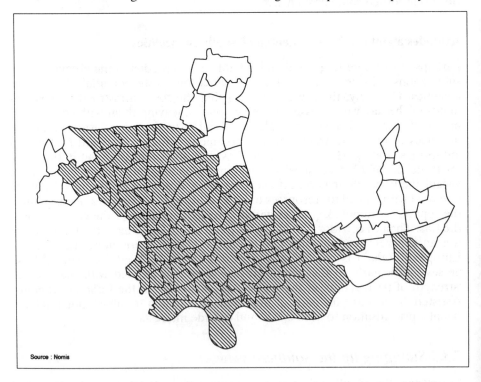

Source : Nomis

Figure 7.3 Wards in East London with an unemployment rate above the Development Areas average (workforce based) in July 1992.

As a final fix on the material, it is useful to evaluate critically the representations made. To what extent did they offer a balanced view, and were there more contentious issues that were 'glossed over' or ignored in the submissions? The submissions did attempt to compare the Southern position with that elsewhere in the country – particularly in terms of unemployment. For example, the East London (6-Borough) submission presented persuasive data on ward unemployment in its area relative to the Development Areas (Figure 7.3). However, only indirectly did they really explore the idea that the problems of the south may be essentially transitory. The arguments from the Luton area, that policy support was required for a fixed five-year period, is an exception. In general, the arguments do not take the analysis of 'problems' such as unemployment beyond relatively superficial levels.

Of all the varied issues to emerge from the 1992/1993 review of the Assisted Areas map, Southern economic change and the attitudes of some Southern authorities to the regional policy arena are particularly prominent. Although some Southern authorities sought regional policy status back in the mid-1980s at the time of the previous (full) review, there was an apparently wider array of submissions in 1992. The state of the Southern economy in its global setting was the catalyst. The effect was to feed the growing competitive environment within which places operate. In making 'bids' for Assisted Area status and a share of a regional policy budget that the government had said would not be allowed to grow by very much, if at all, Southern authorities were effectively seeking to switch aid from other areas – in other words, there was real competition for assistance.

PART 4

Representations of the Local Economy

8

REPRESENTATIONS OF UNEMPLOYMENT

A range of core dimensions and concerns were identified from the basic analysis in Chapter 4. Prominent amongst the various representations were issues – of substantial local sensitivity – connected to unemployment and local labour markets, local industrial change, peripherality, and the decline of particular geographical economies as in a number of coastal localities. Indeed, the decline of many coastal economies and their 'rise' up the league table of unemployment levels (Chapter 6) even prompted one local authority submission (Darlington) to suggest that the heightened awareness of coastal area problems was functioning partly to subsume those of more traditional 'problem' areas. In 1992/1993, these were the issues at the forefront of local–central representations as regards spatial economic policy. In this chapter, we focus on the first of them.

The 'revelation' in Chapter 4 that unemployment and other local labour market problems featured so prominently in the review submissions tells us much about, and confirms, the sensitivities to this key component of the local profile. However, it reveals nothing about the character of the representations made, the lines of argument offered, or the 'feel' with which labour market issues in general are projected externally by such groupings. Consequently, it denies any opportunity to evaluate the effects of such representations. In order to progress, we need and are able to delve much deeper. First, we can usefully establish the importance of representations of unemployment and the local labour market – why does it matter?

8.1 The Importance of Local Labour Market Representation

Representations of unemployment and other aspects of the local labour market are of substantial interest and importance in analysing the various responses in the Assisted Areas review. Unemployment is probably the crucial factor in the local economic profile – certainly as perceived by local authorities and by central government (DTI, Scottish Office and Welsh Office, 1993; House of Commons, 1993) and especially given the 'gathering clouds' of a wider geographical distribution of unemployment that has pervaded the UK in the 1980s and 1990s. The level and nature of unemployment has a real bearing on how places are 'read' and understood; it influences both the perception of places and, crucially, the distribution of resources through spatial economic policies (see Parsons, 1988 for an indication of how central the issue has been over the years in the survival and conditioning of regional policy). It must be the most sensitive of all socio-economic indicators, at political, economic and social levels, at all scales of analysis and, indeed, across the range of policy developments. Unsurprisingly, much local authority economic policy is framed against a background of unemployment concerns (Campbell, 1992, p. 185).

Unfortunately, there has been very little hard research on 'local' attitudes to or views about the local labour market (Campbell and Duffy, 1992), and in particular about local ideas on unemployment. Moreover, much (but not all) published work on local labour markets can reasonably be described as dry and standard, offering a very basic, conventional level of analysis and not really delving into the myriad of issues that confront the jobs and unemployment arena. Texts that are, in many other respects, excellent reviews of the field of spatial economic development (for example, Townroe and Martin, 1992; Champion and Townsend, 1990; Damesick and Wood, 1987), devote little space to the question of unemployment. There is not only inadequate information around which to build analysis, but also a tacit acceptance of unemployment as a basic problem to be resolved, and not so much to be assessed in its various dimensions.

Even in subjects and areas of enquiry that are situated at the frontiers of research investigation – such as place competition and place marketing – researchers have not really broached the kinds of issues confronted here. For example, as we suggested in Chapter 2, place marketing work itself tends to focus on the positive side – evaluating the origins and implications of promotional activity and so on; for example, assessing the ways in which agents have sought to 'gild the smokestacks' as one writer has put it (Watson, 1991) – and has not addressed negative marketing as a leverage device (Chapter 2, section 2.2.2). However, representations of unemployment that are designed to capture available resources must be interpreted as negative place marketing. Therein lies the seeds of local conflict, even though local strategies may well be designed to recover and recapture a more positive image, perhaps by stressing area potential rather than problems. This book is able to rectify the gaps with an investigation of these dimensions of the local economy using the Assisted Areas review data set, but it cannot link findings to a body of existing research. Local authority attitudes to local unemployment and related problems are tacitly assumed to be based on a belief that they are immensely problematical and in need of some response. This is undoubtedly true, but the issues – of how such problems are projected to the outside world, indeed whether they are at all, and so on – extend way beyond such a basic position.

8.1.1 Unemployment: centre stage or sideline?

Whether or not it is an acceptable barometer of a place's problems and/or needs, the basic issue of unemployment takes centre stage in many area assessments (DTI, 1983). For a local authority it may be a key influence in governing the inflow of resources from the central state. It thus has to be a likely candidate for inclusion in any area representation, and it undoubtedly has a real bearing on the impact that is made – ultimately we can surmise, but not prove, success or otherwise in the 'bidding game' (see Appendix 2).

Whether those representing places will necessarily always choose to deploy the 'unemployment' factor in their representations is unlikely. Precisely because it carries 'messages' about a place, we might expect some to avoid playing it up on the grounds of 'image'. A negative image will translate itself into a poor potential for inward investment. A similar attitude is known to have been at the core of the decision of some local authorities not to actively seek Assisted Area status during the review exercise (Chapters 4 and 5). Unfortunately for evaluative purposes, the guidance of the DTI consultation paper (DTI, Scottish Office and Welsh Office, 1992) for potential respondents was that unemployment and local labour market problems would probably be central in any analysis included in the submission. There was therefore, apart from any other considerations, a tendency for most submissions to focus on unemployment and related problems.

8.1.2 Approaches to the use of unemployment as a leverage factor

We can nevertheless perhaps take the point a little further by constructing likely strategies reflecting the extent and style of inclusion of unemployment information that would be expected. We might start with the assumption that areas with a high unemployment problem or profile are likely to use that position in order to seek assistance and then look at those who did not deploy the factor. Against a background of different motives and starting positions as regards the attitudes to involvement, the local economic climate and present status – the representational base – a range of possible baseline attitudes, strategies and approaches seem likely. These might be labelled as follows:

- *Active unemployment-based strategy* – involving a cavalier defence of current status or plea for designation with little overt regard for the negative image that might be promoted. From this, we would expect that a full and detailed exposure of local unemployment problems be included in the submission. This strategy is likely to involve both seekers and defenders.

- *Defensive concealment strategy* – as a legacy of tensions between growth impetus and problem status labelling. Here, unemployment is represented, but the emphasis is on other aspects of the locality – other problems such as threats from existing local firms or lack of diversification, or aspects of potential such as the nature of the local industrial or infrastructural base, geographical location and so on. This is likely to typify mainly those seeking status.

- *Defence of status strategy* – where unemployment issues are avoided or barely mentioned by authorities who are mainly seeking to retain (defend) status gained in an earlier round of designations but where unemployment is presently at a relatively low level (perhaps because of the successes of policy support), in effect, sidetracking to save status by showcasing other local economic problems or potentials.

- *Compromise strategy* – involving a mix where unemployment is represented and discussed but not overplayed – a centre line in the hope of gaining status. This would not be evident amongst those likely to be defending existing status.

In this last strategy, there are likely to be tensions between a quest to promote problems and acquire resources and the place image that it is desired to project. There may even be tensions between different sections of an authority (as a coalition) – a contrast between the images that a marketing department would like to promote and that projected by, say, an economic development team, or alternatively, the images that local officers might present as against those that local councillors or business interests (sometimes the same individuals) would prefer to proffer. Contrast the promotional brochures that many places produce with the kinds of representations being set down in 'bid' documents.

From this, we are led to the question of what alternative strategies emerge and evolve as a result of local pressures? Which win the day – problem or positive image, or some strategy that combines the two? Who decides? And with what effects?

Within these rather broad types, we would expect to find a range of approaches or sub-types – for example, those stressing past or future unemployment growth; or problems compared to neighbouring or comparable areas. As we are able to show, the representations range from those offering a conventional array of material, to those seeking to pursue a less conventional angle, to build in a competitive edge, or to delve into the finer detail of local labour issues, all underpinned by image construction considerations and constraints.

The interesting research questions are thus linked not only to charting which representations included material on the local labour market and which did not, and the strength and mode with which the information was deployed and projected, but also to explaining why there were such differences. The representations data allows us to consider these questions to some degree, and a number of themes may be developed from the information base. This should enable us to consider the representational base, representational detail and method and construction of images (Chapter 2, section 2.2).

8.2 Local Unemployment Issues

In general, it is of interest to explore what use has been made of local labour market (and especially unemployment) material in the representations; what is the degree of inclusion of material on the local labour market area (LLMA). Linked to that, to what degree were representations seeking to advance the case for an area beyond that of potentially competing areas which, in some respects, had a worse unemployment profile? What kinds of arguments were being put forward and why? To what extent are we able to confirm or deny the existence of strategic positions as detailed above?

More specifically, we can pose a range of linked questions that may tell us much about the scenario of, and underlying attitudes to, local economic involvement and that can be extracted from the submissions:

- *Scale of focus* – what is the precise extent (scale) of reference to unemployment in the representation?

- *Attitude* – what is the prognosis on unemployment in the representation? Is it viewed as increasing, static or decreasing? And what is the degree of retrospective analysis? What is the perception of unemployment in the representation? Is it heavily featured, emphasised or played down?

- *Technical detail* – what causes/types are emphasised; for example, structural; fricticnal; seasonal; mixed; industrially linked?

- *Competitive angle* – what is the nature and extent of unemployment comparisons made – interregional; local; sub-local – and to what extent are comparisons made with localities that had the status of Assisted Areas (pre-1993)?

- *Emphasis on specific groups* – what is the degree of detail included and thus the emphasis on aspects of unemployment such as gender, age and duration (e.g. long-term unemployment)?

- *Style of presentation* – what is the style of the representation – tabular; graphics; maps – (reflections of the representational detail) with technical alternatives being used to meet implicit objectives?

- *Outcome* – is there any evidence that the nature of the representation influenced the Assisted Areas review outcome?

Space limitations preclude a detailed analysis of every aspect and here we consider only some of the central dimensions.

Simply by focusing on representations of unemployment, and the comparative basis, we can generate some useful insights into attitudes to local labour market problems in the localities involved. More specifically, such research reveals aspects of place identity, in particular about how an authority may deliberately contrive to construct (or to avoid the construction of) an image of its local economy. This, of course, relates to the representational base, and representational detail and method discussed in Chapter 2. For example, an area with a substantial unemployment problem but a minimal or lack of use of the unemployment 'card' in its representation to the Assisted Areas review might be viewed as defensively 'playing down' the problem in order to avoid the negative images associated with it (the 'defensive concealment' strategy).

In essence of course, the submissions offer a wealth of information on representational detail – on how local labour market problems, unemployment in particular, are presented, even packaged, for outside consumption, what strategies seem to prevail in the style of the presentation, and so on. Such analysis has not been conducted in previous research, and this is somewhat surprising as it is an important aspect of the space economy and its manipulation by government.

8.3 Deploying the Unemployment Factor

Unemployment and, to a degree, other local labour market problems feature prominently in the submissions with over 90 per cent discussing its local extent and significance (Table 4.4). For over 80 per cent of documents, unemployment featured as the key element in the representation. Although that is not at all surprising given the remit presented by the DTI, it does allow us to delve into the representations in terms of the issues listed above.

While most submissions contained unemployment appraisals, the scale of inclusion, the emphasis involved, and other factors varied. Less than 5 per cent of submissions ignored it, about 50 per cent contained a sizeable element of analysis, and about 25 per cent gave it prominence by working in a more substantial analysis (Table 8.1). Clearly, local sensitivities to local labour market and unemployment problems varied by the type of area. For example, remoter rural areas tended to play up other features of the local economy, while coastal/resort areas, with prominent base unemployment problems (Figure 4.1) focused more on fuller unemployment material.

Table 8.1   Local sensitivities to unemployment and local labour market problems

| Locality type | Degree of inclusion of local labour market material* | | |
	Little or none	Sizeable	Substantial
London	29	53	18
Other large cities	20	56	24
Districts with new towns	14	72	14
Coastal/resort areas	24	40	36
Urban and mixed urban/rural areas	20	52	28
Industrial districts	30	61	9
Remoter rural areas	55	36	9
County/regional authorities	15	54	31
All areas	25	50	25

Note: *Percentage of responding local authorities: Little or none = approximately 10 per cent or less of the document. Sizeable = approximately 11–49 per cent of the document. Substantial = approximately 50 per cent or more of the document.

There were local variations in the apparent sensitivity to unemployment. In the representations analysis, around 80 of the submissions either ignored or tended to play down the issue of unemployment, yet at the same time apparently sought to generate a case for retention or acquisition of Assisted Area status. These were in the main remoter rural areas (largely places such as Orkney, Roxburgh and Berwickshire in Scotland) that had not been suffering from substantial unemployment growth, and industrial localities and some of the responding London boroughs where the 'problem' of unemployment was, in effect, being played down. This may well constitute tacit evidence for a defensive concealment strategy as regards this aspect of the local economic character of the areas involved. Elsewhere, the 'problem' of unemployment was played down as it had subsided. For example, the submissions covering Telford in the West Midlands – in the past an area where Assisted Area status applications had generated local conflict with a Development Corporation in favour and local authorities against application on image criteria – tended to play down unemployment as an issue. This apparent 'defence of status' strategy is reflected in submissions from areas such as Corby and Telford/Bridgnorth. Similarly, the submission for Cumbernauld and Kilsyth in Scotland sought to circumvent the 'problem' by focusing on other aspects of the locality. In some cases, the strength of the drive for unlocking potential led to an underplaying of the unemployment card – a likely 'defensive concealment' strategy. The Borders Region submission, while mentioning the problem of comparatively high unemployment in the area, focuses strongly on its potential for development rather than its intrinsic problems.

As regards other aspects of unemployment, only 8 per cent of submissions included a sizeable analysis of long-term unemployment (26 per cent ignored it completely). Long-term unemployment is rather more concentrated than its aggregate counterpart, but this level of omission is quite startling. Most notably, coastal authorities (15 per cent) and metropolitan authorities outside London (11 per cent) latched on to this dimension. Few submissions analysed age (9 per cent) and gender (18 per cent) issues (or both – 4 per cent) in the local unemployment profile.

8.4 Aspects of the Representations

Clearly, we are able to connect representations of unemployment with particular strategies and approaches. We have already identified approaches that indicate 'defensive concealment' and 'defence of status' type strategies (section 8.1.2). These aside, the unemployment representations were dominated by what we referred to as an 'active unemployment strategy'. Further analysis helps to confirm the array of different approaches.

As shown in Figure 8.1, the proportion of each document assigned to unemployment discussion is indicative of a desire to either play up or play down the problem. Of course, there is more to it than a simple identification of an approach and strategy. We can start to draw out evidence for the competitive position. For example, it is possible to highlight a direct competitive element in the representations. Many submissions were relatively inward-looking in orientation – 13 per cent made no external comparisons and over 10 per cent compared only localities within the immediate vicinity. Only 17 per cent of

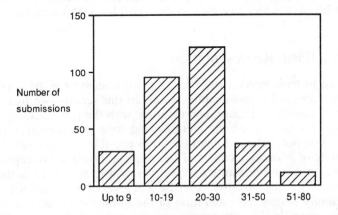

Percentage of document ascribed to unemployment analysis

Figure 8.1 The focus on unemployment issues in the submissions.

submissions used the three most obvious comparative levels – the immediate local, the national picture and that in the then existing Assisted Areas. This is somewhat revealing in terms of the quality and effectiveness of the representations, and suggests a certain degree of missed opportunities.

However, 97 submissions (about 31 per cent of the total) made a direct comparison of their area with existing Assisted Areas, revealing a more direct competitive slant (Table 8.2). Particularly prominent amongst these were first, coastal/resort areas, and second, some London Boroughs, both groups apparently containing a number of aspirant Assisted Areas. Clearly this is simply a strategic decision made by those producing the submission. Perhaps it is a little incongruous to delve into it. Does it merely reflect officer choice? However, it is still important if local policy – local futures – is at least partly conditioned by the whim of local officers.

Table 8.2 Submissions that compared the local situation with existing Assisted Areas

Locality type	Percentage of responding authorities
London	41
Other large cities	33
Districts with new towns	14
Coastal/resort areas	48
Urban and mixed urban/rural areas	35
Industrial districts	12
Remoter rural areas	6
County/regional authorities	29
All areas	31

So far, we have charted the broad use of unemployment information in the projection of local needs (and potentials). Of course, many submissions go some way beyond this baseline, developing a fuller, more precise and targeted exploration. Basically, the unemployment remit was to consider the position of the locality *vis-à-vis* other areas. Beyond that, there was scope for submissions to use unemployment flexibly, as a device to construct particular local labour market images.

8.5 Beyond a Basic Representation

It is instructive to look beyond the basic statistical analysis of unemployment representations covered in the chapter so far. In this section, we focus on the broad nature of the presentations, commenting, with the use of examples from the submissions themselves, on the methods and style of representation, inclusions and general approaches adopted (as far as possible, and in order to give a feel for the style of approach, copies of the original inclusion are reproduced). This all generates some interesting perspectives. Not least, it reveals the extent to which local authorities have the expertise and level of resources necessary to offer a sufficiently strong representation in the quest for funding access. This offers pointers towards the effectiveness of agents not only in the 1992/1993 Assisted Areas review, but also in other developments (such as the SRB) that form part of the 'bidding game' (Chapter 1).

How were unemployment issues represented and what can we say about them? What were the 'messages' and how did authorities 'get the message' across?

8.5.1 Getting the message across

Once the approach is established (representational base), it is important to note that there are two core aspects to 'getting the message' across: the nature, scope and scale of material deployed – the representational detail; and the actual method of representation – a technical issue. Both are important in moulding the image that is projected. A specific method may be developed to get across a particular message and this gives a clear link to expertise (see Chapter 2, section 2.2.3).

The notion of representational detail is closely linked to resources and expertise, innovativeness and creativeness, and probably mainly the former. It is worth noting – especially for practitioners – that there are as many different styles of representation as there are representations. Almost the only exceptions are those submissions prepared by the same professional consultancy where identical approaches have been used (such is the efficiency with which consultants sometimes operate, not of course necessarily to the benefit of their local authority clients). In other words, there is more to it than a simple identification of an approach and strategy. Method of representation, and type of material, etc. is also important.

Moreover, it is worth noting that the objectives in representation may well be wider than the mere acquisition or retention of policy status. Against what is often a core aim to maximise the chances of securing Assisted Area status there will be others – to render local problems overt or to dispel myths (of low unemployment and/or prosperity) about some local economies, at least as perceived by their local authorities (e.g. Grampian; Blackpool).

Authorities have to find novel and notable ways of getting the unemployment message across – or of suppressing a potential image. The imagery can take any of three basic forms – logos; written representations; or graphs/diagrams presenting data. As shown in Chapter 6, both Portsmouth and Dorchester/Weymouth constructed and integrated an image of unemployment growth into their Assisted Area review submission logos.

8.5.2 The strategy, approach and technical style of presentation

Having set up the idea of flexibility in representation and emergent local strategies, we can move to an assessment of the actual submissions. Here we are combining the idea of the representational base with that of detail and method. The representational base conditions the actual base attitude; the representational detail reflects locally specific parameters such as resources and expertise, and both feed into and mould the actual methods used. In simple terms, we can think of each approach as conditioned by the motives discussed in Chapter 4 – defending; seeking; and so on – and by the actual unemployment problem. Given political and ideological attitudes to local economic development, is it necessary to conceal or play down an improvement, or to play up a deteriorating unemployment profile? Are there particular (self-perceived) problems linked to unemployment that need to be flagged up under a particular local economic approach?

Conventional representations

To begin with, there seems to be a 'conventional' approach to representing local unemployment problems. This is to compare the local TTWA with the national picture retrospectively over a few years and to present these in tabular and/or graphical form. It is a line taken by virtually all local authority submissions. Against this background, the notion of representational detail suggests the likelihood of flexibility and that a variety of presentation methods would be deployed. For example, the submission for the Coventry sub-region and for Rotherham/Mexborough TTWA presents an index of trends (Figure 8.2), while that for

Year (July)	Coventry/Hinckley TTWA No.	%	Great Britain No.	%	Cov/Hinckley Index GB=100
1984	37525	15.8	2978893	12.6	125
1985	37402	15.5	3116181	13.0	119
1986	36802	15.2	3150162	13.1	116
1987	32386	13.4	2778526	11.6	116
1988	24945	10.4	2208464	9.2	113
1989	17328	7.4	1663617	7.0	106
1990	16484	7.1	1524105	6.4	111
1991	24261	10.2	2263922	9.5	107
1992	30415	13.0	2663848	11.2	116

Unemployment Rate based on employees in employment + registered unemployed
Index = TTWA % /GB %) * 100

	1985	1986	1987	1988	1989	1990	1991	1992
Rotherham & Mexborough TTWA	156	174	174	193	196	200	162	148
Sheffield TTWA	119	127	132	141	141	148	128	117
Yorkshire & Humberside	113	118	116	121	123	123	108	101
Great Britain	100	100	100	100	100	100	100	100

* Figures at July each year
Narrow base percentages
Source: Employment Service Press Notice, Employment Gazette

Figure 8.2 Unemployment trends in the Coventry sub-region and Rotherham/Mexborough Travel-to-Work Area.

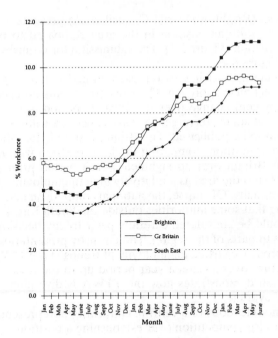

Figure 8.3 Unemployment trends in Brighton and Hove.

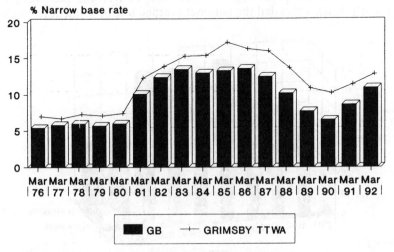

Figure 8.4 Unemployment trends in the Grimsby Travel-to-Work Area.
Source: Department of Employment.

Brighton and Hove (Brighton District Council *et al.*) presents a standard comparison of the deteriorating position in the area compared to the South East region and Great Britain (Figure 8.3). The submission for Grimsby uses the same basic approach (Figure 8.4).

Reflecting varying approaches to representational detail and method, each offers a different technical approach. The Coventry submission generates a local index of unemployment change over the 1984–92 period, revealing an above-average position, but some convergence. This suggests a willingness to allow an improving position to be publicised. The Brighton submission offers an alternative graphical representation, comparing the local position with the South East region and Great Britain over an eighteen-month period prior to the review. This clearly establishes the area as a relatively high unemployment locality, both regionally and nationally. Of course, the national comparison may reflect cyclical factors, something that some authorities outside the South East (Strathclyde for example) felt should be considered carefully prior to any decision to grant Assisted Area status to parts of the region. The Grimsby presentation takes a more retrospective approach, charting unemployment trends in the TTWA against the Great Britain picture over a sixteen-year period up to the review. This visually effective illustration demonstrates how the TTWA is diverging – pulling away from the national average.

These are all modifications of a central, conventional representation, and are effectively vehicles for competition over establishing a position, an image of the 'problem' of unemployment. Yet the flexibility involved generates differences in image that make it difficult to draw comparisons. The question – which is the most effective representation – is not answerable without a clear idea of objectives and outcomes.

The persistence of unemployment levels above a particular regional and national average is perhaps most neatly and effectively represented in an alternative technique in the case of the St Helens/Wigan Travel-to-Work Area (Figure 8.5). This shows the percentage by which the TTWA and the North West region as a whole has exceeded the national average unemployment rate. This is

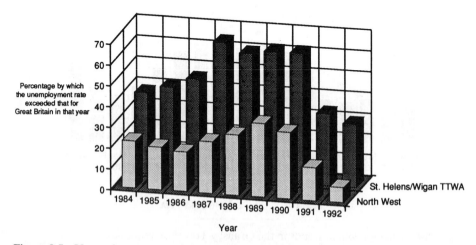

Figure 8.5   Unemployment trends in the St Helens/Wigan Travel-to-Work Area.

just one more technique for presenting a conventional view; it shows some improvement, but still reinforces the relatively poor position of the area.

Clearly, conventional approaches themselves can be very distinctly differentiated by the style, depth and approach adopted. Each is able to offer a slightly different slant on the problem and to project a subtly different image. Such conventional approaches range from the minimalist to the more extensive. The latter included similar representations of other aspects such as long-term unemployment. All would include a selection of indicators from the range required by the DTI in this case but would not go beyond that baseline. The main point of note is that, as we have seen, even within the broadly conventional presentation there is leeway for differentiation via the actual method of presentation of the information.

Looking for the different angle

A number of submissions attempted to set out an alternative, sometimes subtle, angle in order to grab the attention in any assessment. Absolute levels of unemployment, and their distribution within the city, are set out in the Edinburgh submission which offers only limited analysis of unemployment rates. Even where their self-perceived chances of acquiring assistance are low, authorities are still, it seems, tempted to make some sort of bid or case for their areas of interest.

The Blackburn submission, amongst others, focuses on likelihood analysis. This estimates the likelihood of becoming unemployed between October 1991 and April 1992 in various districts in the North West such as Blackburn (120.5 where the national average = 100), compared to Lancashire (112.8), and the North West region (109). Not surprisingly, the town, together with Blackpool and its seasonal variation (175.6), emerges as having a high likelihood.

Other submissions attempt to distinguish their situation by offering information on the unemployment rate for similar areas. This more directly competitive approach is used by some of the coastal/resort localities. Tendring, for example, in its representation on the Clacton and Harwich TTWA, compares the unemployment rate with other English resorts. Clacton and Harwich emerges as the worst area (15.6 per cent in August 1991 as against 10.4 per cent for Newquay, 9.8 per cent for Great Yarmouth, and 8.1 per cent for Blackpool) and with a minor seasonal swing.

In an attempt to demonstrate other, unrecognised problems linked to unemployment and local labour markets, issues such as seasonality are taken up in a number of submissions. This is particularly apparent in areas dominated by agriculture and services such as tourism. For example, the submission by (Scottish) Highlands and Islands Enterprise argues that the 'annual range in unemployment' should be considered as a 'proxy for the seasonality impact upon the local economy'.

Other authorities stress the occurrence of hidden unemployment or non-employment. For example, the submission for the Newcastle-upon-Tyne TTWA argues that the relatively high participation in government training schemes in the North serves to underrepresent the effective level of unemployment.

Some submissions, particularly those for more peripheral Scottish TTWAs, raised the issue of out-migration as an exporter of the unemployed and thus as a vehicle for deflating the image of unemployment and the local economies

TTWA	Unemployment %	Status
Rochdale	12.9	AA, UP, Ob2
Bradford	10.8	AA, UP, Ob2
Keighley	10.7	-
Calderdale	10.5	-
Accrington & Rossendale	9.8	AA, Ob2
Huddersfield	9.7	UP
Pendle	9.3	Ob2
Burnley	9.3	UP, Ob2

Note: AA - Assisted Area
      UP - Urban Programme Area
      Ob2 - Objective 2 Area
Source: Employment Gazette

Figure 8.6 Changes in unemployment in TTWAs bordering Calderdale.

concerned. In offering a different angle, these representations suggest that designations that disregarded migration could potentially switch or avoid designation on questionable bases.

Finally, a number of authorities deployed unemployment representations in an attempt to demonstrate the unfairness of a 'doughnut effect'. Calderdale, for example (Figure 8.6), presents unemployment data for TTWAs bordering it, most of whom had Assisted Area status prior to the review. This is the so-called 'doughnut', with Calderdale as the non-assisted hole in the middle. As part of the Calderdale submission argues, 'investment is sucked out of Calderdale towards Districts which are eligible for regional asistance' (Calderdale submission, p. 3).

The implicit line here is that places that are non-Assisted are distinctly disadvantaged by the opportunities available in surrounding areas. It is a point that we have taken up already (see Chapter 5, Figure 5.2) and one that leads us into another aspect of going beyond the conventional – the competitive edge.

Building in a competitive edge

Building a competitive-comparative edge into the representation offers by far the richest seam of material and insight. A simple scan of the submissions reveals a multitude of methods, all trying to demonstrate a strong relative case for support. These are the more sophisticated strategies of presentation, often reflecting a greater level of local expertise and a more substantial input of resources into the submission.

We are able to identify a number of mini strategies for getting across the message, often comparing all other TTWAs and/or Assisted Areas. In a unique figure, Sedgefield revealed its position *vis-à-vis* all other TTWAs (Figure 8.7). This representation portrayed the 1984–92 unemployment rates for both the Durham and the Bishop Auckland TTWAs, as well as the change in the rankings over the same period. This provides a clear indication of the 'problem' status of the Durham TTWA for much of the period.

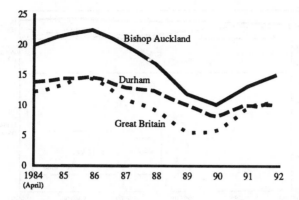

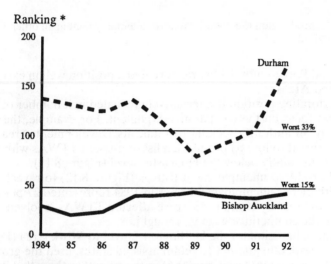

* Ranking is out of 322 TTWAs with rank number 1 having
the highest rate.
To be in the 33% highest band the ranking would be 107 or less.
To be in the 15% highest band the ranking would be 48 or less.

Figure 8.7   Unemployment rates in Sedgefield TTWAs.

A strongly defensive, retrospective representation, again covering all TTWAs
in summary form, was presented for the Central Region (in Scotland). This
demonstrates the 'worst 15 per cent' status of both the Alloa and Falkirk
TTWAs for the entire period and represents an infallible comparative device
(Figure 8.8).

Other methods for demonstrating the relative position of an area in terms of
the then existing Assisted Areas were used by Lancaster (Figure 8.9) and Portsmouth (Figure 8.10). Lancaster produced a listing showing its relative unemployment position in terms of the 1992 Intermediate Areas. Similarly, Portsmouth
located its own unemployment position (for Portsmouth, Gosport and Fareham)
in a ranking of July 1992 unemployment rates for all Assisted Areas. In both

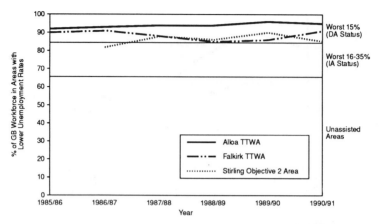

Figure 8.8   Central region (Scotland) – relative unemployment in all other TTWAs from 1985/86 to 1991/92.

Lancaster and Portsmouth the figures revealed a position well in excess of many 1992 Assisted Areas.

The deteriorating position is alternatively revealed in a number of other submissions that focus on the comparative argument. For example, the Doncaster approach (by an authority seeking to retain its Development Area status but under some threat to lose it) produced a list of assisted TTWAs with unemployment rates consistently below the Doncaster level (Figure 8.11).

Sheffield produced unemployment listings (Figure 8.12) to reveal that the 81 TTWAs with higher unemployment rates in 1984 represented 27 per cent of the population, whereas by 1992 the 58 worse affected TTWAs involved only 16 per cent. Again, the competitive edge was sought.

Finally, the submission for the Darlington Travel-to-Work Area (Figure 8.13), perhaps in a desperate attempt to retain assisted status, used the growing problem of coastal economies (see Chapter 6) in an attempt to show that its problems were still there – it was just that other types of area had deteriorated. This begs yet another policy question – is regional policy to be disbursed for need or for relative need?

Delving into the detail

A number of submissions sought to differentiate themselves by delving into the detail. Typically, this involved revealing unemployment blackspots (Burnley; Newcastle; Blackburn), or connecting unemployment to key industries (such as coal in Northumberland and Nottinghamshire).

Specific ward analysis produced by the Nottinghamshire submission combined the two perspectives (Figure 8.14) to reveal unemployment blackspots in the vicinity of the city of Nottingham and in some of the former mining communities.

Finally, delving into the detail in another way, the Great Yarmouth submission deployed the notion of the labour supply gap to present an image of a deteriorating local labour market (Figure 8.15). This was designed to get across a

JULY 1992	Unemployment rate		
	TTWA	Narrow base %	Workforce base %
1	Newton Stewart	18.2	12.1
2	Girvan	16.4	12.6
3	Forres	16.4	12.6
4	Fishguard	16.0	9.3
5	Western Isles	15.8	11.7
6	Bude	15.7	10.7
7	Dunoon & Bute	15.7	11.1
8	Wick	15.3	11.6
9	Doncaster	15.0	13.1
10	Barnsley	14.8	12.9
11	Wolverhampton	14.5	13.0
12	Plymouth	14.1	12.3
13	Bangor & Caernarfon	13.9	11.5
14	Morpeth & Ashington	13.8	12.0
15	Birmingham	13.8	12.4
16	Kirkcaldy	13.7	12.0
17	Llanelli	13.6	11.4
18	Dudley & Sandwell	13.5	12.1
19	Alloa	13.5	11.8
20	Rochdale	13.5	11.5
21	Bodmin & Liskeard	13.4	9.9
22	Walsall	13.3	11.7
23	Haverfordwest	13.2	10.4
24	Stranraer	13.2	10.4
25	Campbeltown	13.2	9.1
26	Sheffield	13.1	11.7
27	Coventry & Hinckley	13.0	11.6
28	Hull	12.5	11.2
29	Gainsborough	12.5	10.4
30	Dunfermline	12.4	10.9
31	Lancaster & Morecambe	12.4	10.2
32	Pontypool & Cwmbran	12.1	10.6
33	Oldham	12.1	10.5
34	Pwllheli	12.1	8.4
35	Grimsby	12.0	10.6
36	Bolton & Bury	11.9	10.2
37	Bridgend	11.8	10.2
38	Blackburn	11.7	10.1
39	Invergordon & Dingwall	11.6	10.0
40	Swansea	11.5	9.9
41	Sutherland	11.5	8.5
42	Falkirk	11.4	10.1
43	Manchester	11.1	9.9
44	Bradford	11.1	9.9
45	Newport	11.0	9.8
46	Cinderford & Ross on Wye	10.9	8.8
47	Darlington	10.8	9.3
48	Cardiff	10.7	9.5
49	Porthmadoc & Ffestiniog	10.5	8.1
50	Telford & Bridgnorth	10.4	9.2
51	Stewartry	10.4	7.2
52	Kidderminster	10.3	8.8
53	Ayr	10.2	8.8
54	Durham	9.9	8.7
55	Accrington & Rossendale	9.5	8.1
56	Skye & Wester Ross	9.3	7.1
57	Lochaber	8.6	7.0
58	Badenoch	8.5	6.6

Source: Department of Employment.

Figure 8.9 The position of Lancaster and Morecombe TTWA relative to Great Britain Intermediate Areas.

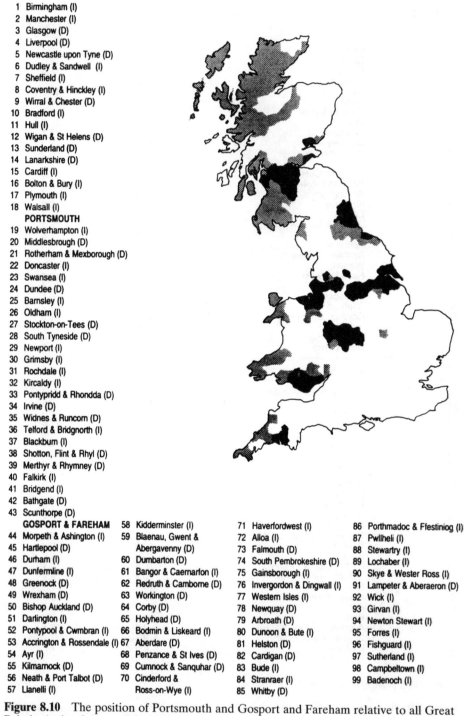

 1 Birmingham (I)
 2 Manchester (I)
 3 Glasgow (D)
 4 Liverpool (D)
 5 Newcastle upon Tyne (D)
 6 Dudley & Sandwell (I)
 7 Sheffield (I)
 8 Coventry & Hinckley (I)
 9 Wirral & Chester (D)
10 Bradford (I)
11 Hull (I)
12 Wigan & St Helens (D)
13 Sunderland (D)
14 Lanarkshire (D)
15 Cardiff (I)
16 Bolton & Bury (I)
17 Plymouth (I)
18 Walsall (I)
    PORTSMOUTH
19 Wolverhampton (I)
20 Middlesbrough (D)
21 Rotherham & Mexborough (D)
22 Doncaster (I)
23 Swansea (I)
24 Dundee (D)
25 Barnsley (I)
26 Oldham (I)
27 Stockton-on-Tees (D)
28 South Tyneside (D)
29 Newport (I)
30 Grimsby (I)
31 Rochdale (I)
32 Kircaldy (I)
33 Pontypridd & Rhondda (D)
34 Irvine (D)
35 Widnes & Runcorn (D)
36 Telford & Bridgnorth (I)
37 Blackburn (I)
38 Shotton, Flint & Rhyl (D)
39 Merthyr & Rhymney (D)
40 Falkirk (I)
41 Bridgend (I)
42 Bathgate (D)
43 Scunthorpe (D)
    GOSPORT & FAREHAM
44 Morpeth & Ashington (I)
45 Hartlepool (D)
46 Durham (I)
47 Dunfermline (I)
48 Greenock (D)
49 Wrexham (D)
50 Bishop Auckland (D)
51 Darlington (I)
52 Pontypool & Cwmbran (I)
53 Accrington & Rossendale (I)
54 Ayr (I)
55 Kilmarnock (D)
56 Neath & Port Talbot (D)
57 Llanelli (I)

58 Kidderminster (I)
59 Blaenau, Gwent &
    Abergavenny (D)
60 Dumbarton (D)
61 Bangor & Caernarfon (I)
62 Redruth & Camborne (D)
63 Workington (D)
64 Corby (D)
65 Holyhead (D)
66 Bodmin & Liskeard (I)
67 Aberdare (D)
68 Penzance & St Ives (D)
69 Cumnock & Sanquhar (D)
70 Cinderford &
    Ross-on-Wye (I)

71 Haverfordwest (I)
72 Alloa (I)
73 Falmouth (D)
74 South Pembrokeshire (D)
75 Gainsborough (I)
76 Invergordon & Dingwall (I)
77 Western Isles (I)
78 Newquay (D)
79 Arbroath (D)
80 Dunoon & Bute (I)
81 Helston (D)
82 Cardigan (D)
83 Bude (I)
84 Stranraer (I)
85 Whitby (D)

86 Porthmadoc & Ffestiniog (I)
87 Pwllheli (I)
88 Stewartry (I)
89 Lochaber (I)
90 Skye & Wester Ross (I)
91 Lampeter & Aberaeron (D)
92 Wick (I)
93 Girvan (I)
94 Newton Stewart (I)
95 Forres (I)
96 Fishguard (I)
97 Sutherland (I)
98 Campbeltown (I)
99 Badenoch (I)

Figure 8.10 The position of Portsmouth and Gosport and Fareham relative to all Great Britain Assisted Areas, July 1992.

Relevant Date Below Doncaster Since	T.T.W.A.	Status	
		Development Area	Intermediate Area
April 1985	Wolverhampton		*
	Portmadoc-Ffestiniog		*
November 1985	Scunthorpe	*	
	Widnes - Runcorn	*	
	Wigan - St. Helens	*	
	Workington	*	
April 1986	Shotton, Flint, Rhyl	*	
November 1986	Bishop Auckland	*	
	Corby	*	
	Telford-Bridgenorth		*
April 1987	Lochaber		*
November 1987	Bathgate	*	

Source: Table 2.4 Employment Gazette.

Figure 8.11 TTWAs with unemployment rates consistently below those in Doncaster TTWA, 1985–1992.

message of persistency in unemployment and inadequate job availability. The implicit argument was that unemployment problems in coastal areas – in this case Great Yarmouth – are not necessarily cyclical but rather more endemic.

Looking to the future

A final aspect of submissions that, in making representations on unemployment, pushed past the conventional, involves the 'more in the pipeline' argument. Especially where faced with a 'no help scenario', some authorities cited a threat of the demise of a dominant employer or sector (for example, Furness and the perceived vulnerability of the defence-reliant VSEL enterprise). In fact, this approach was a central plank in the representations of many defence-related authorities (see Chapter 6) and authorities in coal-mining areas.

8.5.3 Strategies and representations – a review

In section 8.5 we have identified a variety of different representations of unemployment. These range from the overt to the less overt, and from the conventional to the less conventional, the latter in the search for a 'different' angle. There certainly are a wide variety of approaches. However, explaining the

1984					1992			
Pos.	TTWA	Status	Rate	% above	Pos.	TTWA	Status	Rate	% above
1.	South Tyneside	DA	23.8	.0	1.	Cumnock & Sanquhar	DA	19.7	.0
6.	Middlesborough	DA	21.8	.7	7.	Liverpool	DA	15.1	.6
9.	Liverpool	DA	20.4	1.3	8.	Rotherham & Mexborough	DA	14.9	2.4
11.	Lanarkshire	DA	19.6	3.4	16.	Doncaster	IAA	13.7	3.5
13.	Sunderland	DA	19.2	4.1	17.	Middlesborough	DA	13.7	3.9
20.	Rotherham & Mexborough	DA	18.2	5.7	18.	Sunderland	DA	13.6	4.4
30.	Wigan & St Helens	DA	17.2	7.3	21.	Barnsley	IAA	13.2	5.1
32.	Glasgow	DA	17.1	10.7	29.	Wigan & St Helens	DA	12.5	6.3
35.	Wirral & Chester	DA	16.8	11.0	31.	Lanarkshire	DA	12.5	7.0
37.	Wolverhampton	IAA	16.7	12.1	32.	Wolverhampton	IAA	12.4	7.6
44.	Dundee	DA	16.4	13.0	38.	Plymouth	IAA	12.1	8.9
47.	Doncaster	IAA	16.2	13.6	48.	Wirral & Chester	DA	11.9	10.2
48.	Newcastle-upon-Tyne	DA	16.1	14.0	51.	Birmingham	IAA	11.8	11.4
55.	Dudley & Sandwell	IAA	15.8	16.3	56.	Walsall	IAA	11.6	14.9
58.	Swansea	IAA	15.7	17.6	59.	Sheffield	IAA	11.5	15.8
65.	Walsall	IAA	15.2	18.6					
66.	Hull	IAA	15.2	19.2					
68.	Birmingham	IAA	15.1	20.1					
70.	Bolton & Bury	IAA	15.0	23.1					
71.	Coventry & Hinckley	IAA	14.9	23.9					
80.	Barnsley	IAA	14.2	26.1					
82.	Sheffield	IAA	13.9	26.6					

Note: % above = proportion of economically active population covered by TTWA's with higher rates
TTWA's shown in this and subsequent tables are those with over 80,000 population.

Figure 8.12 Sheffield's listing of unemployment rates in January 1984 and 1992. *Source:* NOMIS.

	Ranking	
	June 1990	June 1992
Darlington	82	124
Clacton	70	8
Hastings	174	29
Southend	167	44
Brighton	164	52
Medway & Maidstone	197	72
Torbay	131	76
Isle of Wight	128	85
Weston-Super-Mare	172	102

Figure 8.13 Traditional tourist and service sector TTWA unemployment as produced in the Darlington review submission.

precise thinking behind them is difficult without access to the personnel involved. Of course, we have confirmed in the supplementary survey (Chapter 5) that authorities did quite deliberately construct representations of their local economic problems in order to promote a particular image.

Explanations for the different approaches and representations, the strategy, and the technical style, are difficult to pinpoint without detailed local knowledge.

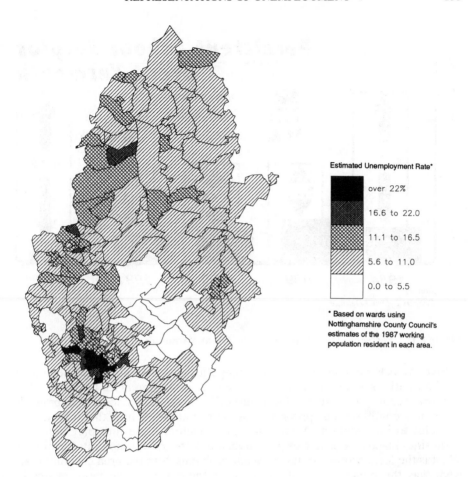

Estimated Unemployment Rate*

over 22%

16.6 to 22.0

11.1 to 16.5

5.6 to 11.0

0.0 to 5.5

* Based on wards using
Nottinghamshire County Council's
estimates of the 1987 working
population resident in each area.

Figure 8.14 An example of ward analysis: unemployment in Nottinghamshire, April 1992.

However, it is clear that some combination of self-perceived needs, expertise and strategy/policy decision are involved. In the preceding discussions, we have attempted to apply the notions of the representational base and representational detail and method. In this way, much of the explanation follows from first, the willingness to reveal, and second, the ability to construct and chart out a representation.

As we have argued, unemployment was not always at the forefront in submissions. For some, there was a clear decision to underplay the 'unemployment' card. This resulted from local fears of lost status and a self-perceived vulnerability (perhaps in Corby for example). In general, the impression gained is that representations also, in combination with corporate authority views about development needs, reflect very much on the local officers who produced them – their ideas, experiences and so on. This is the representational detail.

In these ways, the explanations for unemployment representations are similar to those set out in the analysis of engagement in the review (Chapter 4). First, in

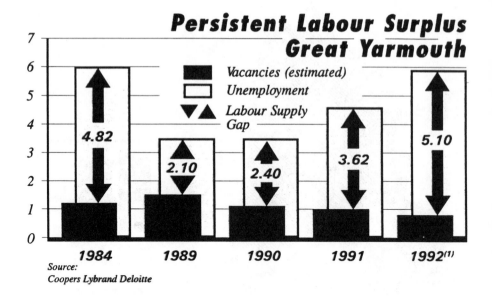

Figure 8.15   Persistent labour surplus in the Great Yarmouth TTWA.

a drive towards a defensive and more competitive inter-area role for themselves, local authorities and their partner agencies are becoming more likely to bid for support. Second, established local authority positions on local economic development condition the approach – the representational base that follows from attitudes to intervention. A host of related factors come into play here. Are authorities inactive, reactive or proactive; interventionist or non-interventionist? What is the local economic status? What problems does the area encounter, and what was the policy status at the time of the review? The more aggressive submissions would tend to reveal much about unemployment. Those defending status would be demonstrating an unchanging situation or playing down change. Seekers would be stressing their high position in the unemployment league table. Third, on top of all this, the local authorities would be influenced by recent economic performance, newly forged partnerships with other agencies (such as the TECs), and local horizons, and, perhaps, nudged into activity by the catalyst of the Assisted Areas review itself. Fourth, we must take into account the likely influence of key local officers and their expertise. In Chapter 8, this has been achieved through applying the notion of representational detail and method.

8.6 Prognosis on the Representations

In the chapter so far, we have been able to identify a range of strategies, methods and technical approaches for representing local unemployment in the 'bidding game'. What is the significance of our investigation and findings?

In a general sense, we have derived a useful checklist of approaches – and this feeds in to our 'playing the bidding game' expertise assessment. Of course, we have also derived a source of well-informed local information on a comparable basis. However, more than that, it is clear that local authority attitudes and representations are influential in both the public and the private domain. How do local authorities perceive their unemployment position and to what extent does that govern local policy and condition the relationships that the locality has with outside agencies? These are very important questions.

More specifically, the strategies adopted and the ways that local authorities and their partner agencies view their problems or perceive their position in terms of unemployment, lead to a great many insights. While it may have been seen as a political necessity to respond on unemployment, the responses offer much of value in understanding local authority self-image, competitive guile, officer expertise and attitude, and so on. We can establish the following sets of linked factors that reveal the significance of all this.

The image projected shows a willingness to expose the local profile to outside scrutiny; marks down the locality and authority to outsiders as 'aggressive', 'defensive' or whatever; gives indirect 'signals' to outsiders such as developers; and reveals the importance placed on unemployment and hence the likely receptiveness to local economic initiatives from many different sources.

The willingness to expose and the importance placed on unemployment, links in a more general way to attitudes to local economic development; it connects with attitudes to policy support and the desire and acceptability of outside resource inputs; it may well be deployed as a predictor of future developments in this policy area. Partly linked to the willingness to put resources into making (more elaborate) representations is . . .

The quality of submission and the perceived nature of unemployment problems reflects the availability of local expertise and resources, projecting an image of an authority that is well informed and well aware of its local economic problems and commitments. Attitudes to local labour market problems at the local level reflect, in a general way, a jurisdictionally derived local sense of place.

A view of best practice, effectiveness and the best representations for each purpose should emerge from all this. We should be able to make some sort of judgement on how best to present a case. Whether or not we can assume that the quality of the presentation governs success in the 'bidding game' is something that we will leave to Appendix 2. However, there are clearly implications for the cost-effectiveness of submissions, indeed for the wisdom, from a local viewpoint, of the whole shift to competitive bidding and an increase of the competitive element in local authority economic activity. Linked to all this is our idea of representational detail and method. Many representations were fairly inward-looking and unadventurous, while others generated a sophisticated, innovative presentation. This suggests that the level of resource and expertise available at the the local level varied quite dramatically across authorities (see Hasluck and Duffy, 1992, p. 3); a matter of some importance for local authorities as they enter a new era of competitive involvement.

The final issue – how persuasive were the arguments – is difficult to judge. Some cleverly conceived representations were successful in that Assisted Area status was granted; others were not. As part of the overall submission quality, there is no doubt that an ability to get across a persuasive message through a particular fix on the unemployment problem would at least make an impact, if not for the Assisted Areas review, for a 'battle' yet to come.

8.7 Conclusions

This chapter has investigated some hitherto unexplored aspects of the local perception of economic problems. It reveals that presenting unemployment information, in this case to a review, is not necessarily a simple process with straightforward outcomes. It is open to all kinds of strategic manipulation as regards the type of information presented, the style and approach adopted and, ultimately, the images that are constructed. There are, in effect, numerous ways of representing unemployment.

Unemployment is the most sensitive of all socio-economic problems and the demands for solutions strike hard at government. In tackling the question of unemployment representations we have connected with issues that go beyond a simple investigation of the review event. There are wider implications to be drawn out from the ways in which authorities represent their unemployment profile. Whether or not the question of unemployment is played up or played down is revealing. For some authorities, it is in tension with the approved image, and thus an issue not to be mentioned. For those seeking government assistance, such as Manchester and others in the Assisted Areas review, it is under-emphasised in order, we can surmise, to lay a stress on potential rather than problem. Of course, given the variety of local attitudes to intervention – and hence what we have labelled the representational base, and the representational detail and method – there are almost as many different ways of representing unemployment as there are representations. Weld together different political attitudes and ideologies at the local level, different local economic circumstances, needs and resources, and we get a good idea of the complexity.

Representations of unemployment relate closely to the image that a place projects. In the 'bidding game' there is a need for negative place marketing and that is bound to be controversial as it is in tension with the other side of place marketing, that of fostering an image of attractiveness and prosperity. How this is viewed rather depends on attitudes to exposing local problems to outside scrutiny.

This is a vitally important aspect of local economic development simply because unemployment is such a key issue and determinant. The questions discussed in this chapter have never really been tackled before. The findings reveal variations between local authorities in the ways that they represent their problems and this says much about the 'local' itself; its sensitivity to local unemployment problems; and the availability of resources and expertise to make an effective case. They reveal the complexion of a local authority, and point to a particular attitude to local labour market development, strategies of representation, and the perceived value of an Assisted Areas review response, for whatever motive it might be made.

What is certain is that representations of unemployment are very important. They condition the image of a place, influencing local populations and potential developers and businesses, and they affect the resources that it may obtain from central government. As such, we find a dual role for unemployment representations. Unemployment invokes defensive reactions but may also be deployed as a weapon.

9
REPRESENTATIONS OF PERIPHERALITY

There is a widespread, indeed international, perception of . . . Barrow-in-Furness . . . as being situated at the end of the 'longest cul-de-sac' in England, a road which at one point goes through a farm yard.

(Furness Enterprise)

Many of the region's problems have their roots in its peripherality . . . Not only does distance from markets and supplies raise production costs, but remoteness has also been shown to reduce innovation within firms, and to curtail the level of new business formation.

(Strathclyde Regional Council)

It is perhaps tempting to think of the Isle of Wight as part of the relatively prosperous South East, despite being separated by a narrow strip of water. In practice . . . this is the most expensive to cross in the UK and possibly the world . . . and dominates the Island's economy.

(Isle of Wight Development Board)

Aside from unemployment, responses to the review consultation phase were testimony to the sensitivity of geographical location in the realms of inter-area competition. In this chapter we assess the 'peripherality' representations made by local authorities, looking at which authorities claimed this to be an issue and a problem and how they generated and presented their conceptions of it. First, we consider the importance of the issue in the attitudes of local authorities.

9.1 A Clear-Cut Issue?

Representations of peripherality are clearly important. They are another dimension in local authority representations of their problems, reveal local attitudes, and serve to project an image that extends beyond the confines of any review exercise. In reflecting matters of geographical position in local and global economic terms, and of competitive disadvantage in access to markets and suppliers, they confront vitally important issues of local economic problems.

Nevertheless, despite the inclusion of peripherality as one of the central factors to be considered (DTI, Scottish Office and Welsh Office, 1992), these are rather less sensitive and less emotive matters than that of unemployment discussed in Chapter 8. The 'problem' of unemployment hits harder at the 'local' in a variety of ways. It reflects a more direct disadvantage for an area in prosperity terms, links directly to people, unleashes political and social sensitivities more readily, and, in general, lies more at the forefront of perceptions of 'problem' status. Peripherality represents a rather more 'matter of fact' issue. It is recognised as an element of disadvantage – hence, it is one of the indicators specified by the DTI. Yet it somehow fails to generate the same emotive feelings. Maybe, as Pickvance (1990a) suggests, the answer is that, in reality, its inclusion owes as much to past lobbying by Scottish and Welsh interests as to pure economic considerations.

Despite this lower problem status, peripherality is important as is demonstrated by local reactions to the review exercise. Peripherality is viewed as a major disadvantage in a wide range of places – many of which we might not, at first sight, think of as particularly remote or greatly inaccessible. There is considerable variability in the notion of peripherality itself – it does not appear to be a clear-cut concept. As with the issue of unemployment, there is again room for manoeuvre in its representation. That renders it another interesting fix on the 1992 Assisted Areas review exercise.

9.2 Assessing Representations of Peripherality

Much has been written on the ways in which rapid developments in transport and communication have affected places, generating a shrinkage of relative space, labelled by Harvey as 'time-space compression' (Harvey, 1989). However, while there is undoubtedly a 'shrinking world' out there, some places either feel 'peripheral' or, at the least, feel able to promote themselves as needing support on the grounds of 'peripherality' (Pickvance, 1990a).

That, in itself, provides a strong rationale for assessment. More specifically though, there are clear returns on an investigation of local representations. First, it provides a range of collective views about the concept of peripherality as a problem. A survey and analysis, especially if it can draw on data from a large number of areas within the UK, offers an opportunity to examine in depth 'popular' representations of the notion of 'peripherality'. Moreover, it is of interest to consider the ways in which local authorities adapt the concept to represent their particular 'spatial fix' – their self-image of local economic disadvantage. Second, as there are, not surprisingly, many and varied representations of 'peripherality', it is instructive, if we are to understand local attitudes to economic development and to changes like the amendment of the Assisted Areas map, to engage with these issues. The analysis offers an important insight into local authorities' perception of the 'quality' of their geographical location and informs us on many aspects of their functioning as governmental units – in attitudes to resources, infrastructure and so on.

In discussing the issue of peripherality as it pertains to locational disadvantage and the representations of local authorities in the Assisted Areas review, there are two angles. First, which authorities cited it, and second, what exactly was it that they cited?

9.3 Who Used the Peripherality Factor?

The problem of peripherality was cited by 137 or over 43 per cent of the 317 local authorities who responded to the consultation paper (Table 9.1). Not surprisingly, the survey data base reveals that these tended to be drawn from a number of specific locality types and regions. At the regional scale, there was a clear picture of representation, with authorities in Scotland, the North, the North West, Wales, and the South West particularly prominent. Conversely, it is also clear that relatively few authorities in the South East and the East Midlands, and only one in the West Midlands, sought to progress their case for designation by claiming any kind of peripherality. Unsurprisingly, something of a 'North–South' divide in perceptions about the importance of geographical location as a factor in economic performance is clearly indicated.

Counties and Regional Authorities (in Scotland) were prominent in emphasising peripherality (Table 9.2) but they clearly draw issues from a wider range, covering a larger area than the District, and it is not surprising that many of these authorities have a perception that parts or all of their area of jurisdiction is in some way peripheral.

Districts tend to 'lock on' to local factors and an analysis of their representations is revealing (Table 9.2). There were particular concentrations of coastal authorities who used and stressed the peripherality factor in their review response. On the other hand, there were authorities representing virtually all locality types who deployed this element. This is significant as it reflects a widespread feeling of peripherality confronting many different types of local economy, not solely those in remote rural areas or those on the coast.

Further evidence for the imprecision in local authority views of peripherality can be derived from a simple comparison between, on the one hand, some objective measure of peripherality (using an accessibility index) and, on the

Table 9.1 Representations of peripherality by local authorities: regional analysis

Region	a	b	c	d	e
East Anglia	7	16	23	6	86
Scotland	51	14	65	37	73
North	28	4	32	19	68
Wales	43	2	45	29	67
South West	27	25	52	17	63
Yorkshire and Humberside	24	4	28	9	38
North West	34	4	38	10	29
South East	45	98	143	6	13
East Midlands	25	20	45	3	12
West Midlands	33	9	42	1	3
All	317	196	513	137	43

Key:
a = local authorities that responded to the consultation document.
b = local authorities that did not respond to the consultation document.
c = a + b = all local authorities.
d = all local authorities in column (a) that cited peripherality as a factor.
e = column (d) as a % of column (a).

Table 9.2 Representations of peripherality by local authorities

Local authority locality type	a	b	c
London	–	18	–
Other large cities	18	46	39
Districts with new towns	4	6	67
Resort/retirement areas	2	8	25
Coastal areas	31	55	56
Urban and mixed urban/rural areas	30	69	44
Industrial districts	8	34	24
Remoter rural areas	15	33	46
County/regional authorities	29	48	60
All	137	317	43

Key:
a = number of local authority submissions citing peripherality.
b = local authorities responding to the consultation paper.
c = column (a) as a percentage of column (b).

other, the emphasis or otherwise of peripherality in the review responses of local authorities (and indeed of others). As shown in Table 9.3, there are some apparent contrasts.

Generally, where peripherality is high, authorities tend to cite it in their representations. Where it is low, they tend to stress other factors. However, we should note the occurrence of 15 claims of peripherality problems by authorities located in the most accessible group of areas, and a failure on the part of some authorities to use the peripherality factor in their representations. Examples of the former include places such as Bradford, Wigan, Bristol, Nottingham and the Wirral. Examples of the latter include authorities such as those in Cornwall, Alnwick, South Pembrokeshire, Angus, and Dumfries and Galloway. The inference is that, in these areas, the representational base of the local authority, perhaps a more reactive style of involvement, generates a desire to move away from a peripherality tag. Against all this, we find, as reported below, a small number of really vigorous representations of peripherality.

Table 9.3 Objective peripherality and the claim of peripheral status

HGV peripherality* type by accessibility score and level of peripherality		Claim of peripheral status**		
		Yes	No	Total
0–999	high	7	1	8
1000–1999	fairly high	27	14	41
2000–2999	intermediate	54	29	83
3000–4249	fairly low	34	59	93
4250–20000	low	15	77	92
Total		137	180	317

Notes:
*Based on calculations used by the DTI (see Linneker and Spence, 1992).
**Authorities citing 'peripherality' or otherwise in response to the review.

9.4 How Was Peripherality Used?

The second question relates to the concept of 'peripherality' used by authorities and it is here that we find wide variations. This again allows us to introduce and apply the ideas of the representational base and of representational detail and method (Chapter 2, section 2.2.3). To what extent are representations of peripherality connected to local economic attitudes and approaches, and to the willingness overtly to promote what some may view as economic weaknesses in an attempt to secure outside funding? It is quite likely that peripherality is somewhat less charged than unemployment, so that the representational base is of less significance. Probably more important is the question of what resources and expertise are available to construct or generate particular images in a quest to 'win' in the funding stakes by getting across a particular message? Again, potentially, flexibility permits a variety of constructions.

Clearly, agencies mean – perhaps we should say, intend to project and infer – rather different things when they speak of 'peripherality'. Therein lies one of the more interesting aspects of this part of the review investigation. What do local authorities mean when they cite peripherality as a problem in need of attention? What are the consequences of such different interpretations and uses of the factor?

The representations of peripherality used by local authorities in the review fall into two broad categories; first, those submissions projecting an image of 'peripherality' as reflected in conventional measures and as an important problem issue; second, alternative, less conventional viewpoints about the notion of 'peripherality'. Such representations hold implications for attitudes to development constraints.

9.4.1 Conventional representations

The conventional view of peripherality is represented by the accessibility-based measurements in Table 9.3. This uses a standardised access cost model built around measurements for heavy goods vehicles (HGVs) and is indicative of a conventional approach that relies on the gravity model type elements of population size and distance. The further away from places and the smaller those accessible places are, the lower the overall accessibility grading achieved. This type of research views peripheral locations as disadvantaged in terms of high transport and communication costs coupled with production dislocation, poor quality transport links and large administrative costs (what has been labelled the 'hassle' of managing a plant at some distance from its parent, Fothergill and Guy, 1990, p. 146), staff movement costs, poor information flows between producers and customers, limited accessibility to large urban centres, and distance from market information and customer contact (Department of Trade and Industry, 1983; Keeble, Offord and Walker, 1986). Many of the commentaries have focused on peripheral regions such as Northern Ireland (Fothergill and Guy, 1990) or Scotland (Randall, 1987), although some work completed by CURDS at Newcastle in the early 1980s or more recently by Linneker and Spence (1992) has sought to classify localities in terms of their level of peripherality.

The local authority representations covered in this paper often reflect such conventional concepts of peripherality. They argue that peripherality essentially refers to remoteness from markets and the business disadvantages confronting some places. These are reflected in and measured by features such as rail journey times and impending rail closures, distance from the motorway system, and lack of airport access. Of course, linking through to representational detail and method, the various submissions can be differentiated on the bases of the perspectives emphasised and the line of argument followed, the use of graphical representations, and, to a degree, the involvement of the private sector viewpoint.

Authorities such as Allerdale and Copeland in West Cumbria emphasised the general transport and travel disadvantages of their localities. These are illustrated with information on journey times by car (Figure 9.1a), with a clear indication that the area is notably disadvantaged in accessibility terms, or by distances and times for rail and rail/air travel that again emphasise the poor accessibility of the area (Figure 9.1b).

Similarly, and not surprisingly, many of the Scottish authorities quoted the transport access and cost disadvantages of a peripheral northern location in their responses. For example, the Caithness and Sutherland submission (Table 9.4) stressed the great inaccessibility of the area in terms of air travel times/costs and road haulage costs. As shown in Table 9.4, Wick, the principal town, is remote and costly in its air access, compared even to other parts of Scotland. Moreover, in terms of road haulage costs, the area has a major relative disadvantage in its access to European access ports, and even to main ports in Scotland. This offers a conventional view of peripherality in terms of travel times and costs as they implicate individuals and businesses.

In a similar vein, the submission by Suffolk County Council, focusing on the Lowestoft TTWA, attempts to emphasise the remoteness of the Suffolk coastal settlements from major urban centres (Figure 9.2). In order to demonstrate the inaccessibility of Lowestoft (which is 128 miles from London, its nearest large conurbation), this portrays areas in Great Britain that are further than 128 miles from principal cities. Such a device reveals that only a few distant coastal areas are so marginal. This is a rather crude, basic representation, but it does reflect the self-image of the authorities involved. In that alone, it is significant.

Elsewhere, a conventional view of peripherality is represented in precisely calculated road or rail times. For example, the submission by Dorset County Council, focused on Weymouth and Portland, deliberately projects an image of relative inaccessibility for the area (Figure 9.3).

Other representations emphasise peripherality in terms of the Single European Market, the reduction of trade barriers and the tendency for industry to locate where it optimises its economic advantage (Lothian Regional Council). Although this may be an overexaggeration, there is evidence produced by local authority sponsored research (for example, East of Scotland European Consortium, 1992) that businesses in areas such as East Scotland will be disadvantaged in both competing in European markets and in attempting to attract inward investment. Such arguments make a strong case for regional policy support.

In the context of the Assisted Areas review, an excellent example of an authority really 'pushing' the conventional 'peripherality' argument is the Isle of Wight. In this submission, peripherality, referred to as 'insularity' – in the form of the costly barrier of the Solent (the so-called 'Solent factor') – is given great prominence (Figure 9.4). According to this conventional representation, the cost of crossing the water between the Hampshire coast and the island is a substantial

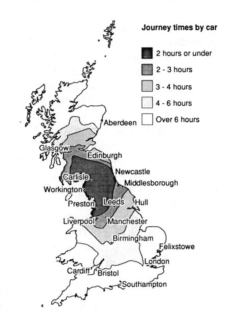

(a)

TRAVELLING TIMES FROM COPELAND

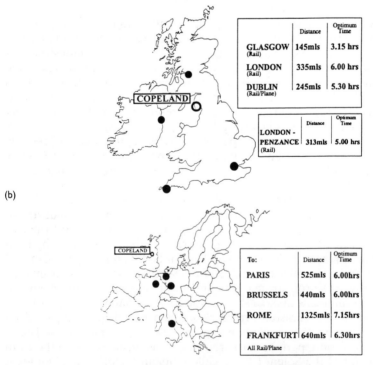

(b)

Figure 9.1 Journey times from (a) Allerdale and (b) Copeland in West Cumbria as submitted to the review by Allerdale and Copeland District Councils.

Table 9.4 Air and road haulage travel constraints as submitted to the review by Caithness and Sutherland Enterprise

(a) Air

	Travel time (hours)	Economy single fare (£)
Wick–London (Heathrow)	3.25	165
Wick–Manchester	2.75	151
Wick–Edinburgh	1.25	101
Edinburgh–London (Heathrow)	1.25	83–106
Edinburgh–Manchester	1.03	82

(b) Road haulage (£*)

From	To London	Birmingham	Leith Docks	Felixstowe
Wick–Thurso	720	580	340	725
Inverness	585	445	180	550
Swindon	175	155	na	250

Note: *Road haulage costs for a typical load carried on a fully laden 38 tonne articulated lorry.
Source: Caithness and Sutherland Enterprise, 1992.

imposition on local firms and a real constraint both on inward investment and on the survival or expansion of existing island firms.[1] A crude, somewhat surreal mapping of access costs, building in the impact of the Solent crossing, reveals the disadvantage (Figure 9.5).

Several authorities are distinct in their involvement of private sector interests in the projection of peripherality and its disadvantages. For example, in the preparation of a response to the consultation document, the Isle of Wight Development Board completed a survey of sixty local businesses to obtain information on the effects of insularity, focusing on the three key (self-perceived) problems of transport costs and time lost, skill shortages, and the effects of isolation from markets. Virtually all surveyed businesses claimed that the Solent factor seriously restricts their operations; some even suggested that they were considering shifting to the mainland (Isle of Wight Development Board, Appendix 9).

Great Yarmouth also used the tactic of building local private sector viewpoints into the representation of peripherality. As part of a wider survey of 'local' factors constraining local businesses, the question of relative accessibility was raised. The argument, backed by quotations from local food processing and transport firms, was that efforts to attract investment are often thwarted by poor road and rail links to other parts of the UK.

Added to all these familiar notions of peripherality are some variants that reflect fresh concerns. Central amongst these is what we might refer to as 'Channel Tunnelability'. Although it may be as much a psychological as an access-cost matter (see similar issues discussed by Anderson, 1994 in the case of Northern Ireland), authorities often voice a real concern over their lack of access to this important new infrastructural element. Authorities citing relative inaccessibility

Figure 9.2 Lowestoft representation: areas further than 128 miles from Great Britain's principal cities.

from the tunnel as a fear, substantial enough to be seen as a part of the rationale for Assisted Area designation, include not only geographically distant localities such as North Grampian or Newcastle-upon-Tyne, but also places like Chester, Bradford and even parts of Kent (such as Swale) that are geographically much nearer to the south coast of England. Clearly, the objective view of peripherality set out in Table 9.3 is somewhat different from the perceived view, or at least the representations, of many local authorities.

In general, there tends to be a stress on relative peripherality (peripherality within a core region) and also on connected peripherality – for example, linking remoteness to sectoral structure. The areas portraying themselves as peripheral in these various ways tend to be those which, in the objective sense represented

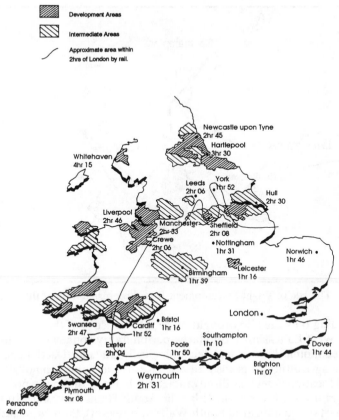

Figure 9.3 Rail accessibility from Weymouth as submitted in the Dorset County Council response.

in Table 9.3, are generally in the least accessible categories. However, that is only part of the picture.

9.4.2 Less conventional representations

Throughout the book, we have argued that representations of problems must be viewed as constructions, representations for a purpose. The focus on peripherality is no exception.

A number of authorities have developed arguments of need around rather less conventional representations or variants of peripherality, some of them connected to conventional ideas, but others attempting to develop a less tangible conception. Some, but not necessarily all, of these are authorities which have, against objective (conventional) assessment, still sought to develop the argument that they have some of the traits of some notion of 'peripherality' (Table 9.3).

Peripherality within the decision-making structures of local companies is one approach, with a claim that by giving firms the opportunity to bid for regional

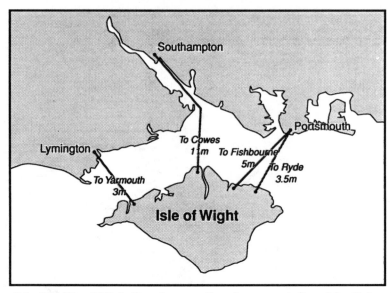

Figure 9.4 The Isle of Wight Development Board representation of the 'Solent factor'.

policy funding they may be brought more into the core of their parent company activities (West Lancashire). Similarly, peripherality connected to the nature of the local economic base – less technologically advanced activities, and more aligned to agriculture – is also raised (Restormel). For some authorities, a peripheral location is seen as disadvantageous because, linked to poor accessibility, it deters inward investment (Llanelli; South Hams (Totnes)). In the case of Llanelli (part of the industrial South Wales sub-region), there is an added dimension in their self-perceived position. This amounts to a kind of peripherality of confusion. On the western edge of the sub-region, and in a different administrative county (Dyfed) from the rest of the area, there is, claims Llanelli, a tendency for civil servants and non-local politicians to be unsure of its location when it comes to the assignment of aid programmes.

This view of peripherality brings us to another concept – that of adjacency. At least two authorities interpret, or at least project an image of, peripherality in this way. In Lancaster, the highly self-contained nature of the local labour market (Figure 9.6) is viewed as a form of peripherality. The area tends not to benefit from developments and work opportunities in adjacent areas, and suffers particularly from local closures (Lancaster and Morecambe). In a related sense, another authority (Arfon) argues that the collection of Assisted Areas to the east (North East Wales, Cheshire and Merseyside) effectively produce an 'investment barrier' (Figure 9.7) when it comes to a business decision regarding location along the North Wales coast corridor – a growth zone in the North Wales region.

9.5 Summary of Issues and Implications

In this chapter we have offered a rather different slant on the issue of peripherality from that usually discussed. Using the representations made by

Figure 9.5 The Isle of Wight Development Board representation of the impact of container lorry travel costs.

local authorities during the 1992/1993 review of the Assisted Areas map, we have assessed the use of the peripherality argument. A comparative analysis of such representations has not been attempted before and in this respect we are breaking more fresh ground. For example, we have been able to document which areas claimed peripherality, what kinds of peripherality they claimed, how they compared in their representations to some more objective measure, and what methods they used to project the required image.

The findings are both interesting and significant. There are conventional and non-conventional conceptions of peripherality. In the former, authorities have argued that they are disadvantaged and in need of assistance on grounds of inaccessibility through distance, limited transport networks, and market reach, with costs imposed as a consequence. In the latter, a more contrived, but interesting, set of conceptualisations have ranged from the notion of peripherality as a functional constraint, to that of it as adjacency, or as inaccess to assistance itself.

These different approaches reflect attitudes to development – whether local authorities are keen to open up their local economies. In most cases, they are. They also indicate local economic policy attitudes through the ways in which authorities perceive and represent themselves to be disadvantaged by

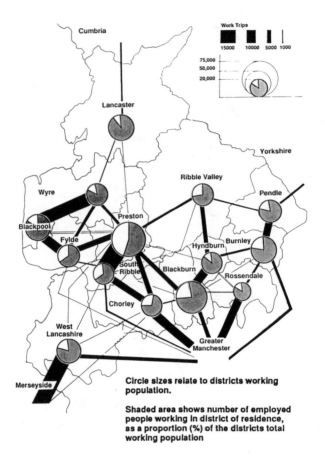

Figure 9.6 Lancaster's isolation as represented in the Lancaster City Council submission.

peripherality. The representational base is clearly significant here, although in less controversial terms than over unemployment representations. Some authorities, however, although inaccessible according to the official, conventional measurements, did not mention peripherality in their submissions. They appear to have been deterred by the fear of being seen as 'remote' – a stigma of the kind that Assisted status may be seen, by some, to impose. Of course, peripherality is a less sensitive issue and most did use it in their submissions where appropriate.

Perhaps more interesting is the question of representational detail and method. The images of peripherality constructed by authorities in their submissions varied widely. This can be interpreted as a reflection of local ideas about how most appropriately to represent peripherality, if at all. The locally generated ideas stretch to the drawing in of local business attitudes to access costs (in the Isle of Wight case for example) or to the flexible and varied ways in which the concept of peripherality is interpreted. The use of graphics, and the quality of the documents reflect local expertise and, above all, resources. Once again, flexibility (or imprecision in setting down definitions) facilitates a wide range of constructed images.

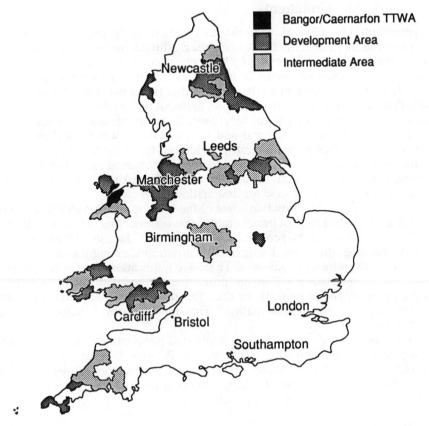

Figure 9.7 The Arfon submission – the disadvantages of the North Wales investment barrier.

In terms of who made representations on the basis of peripherality, it is interesting to note the particularly strong representation from some regions and some types of locality (Tables 9.1 and 9.2). This reflects a kind of North–South divide – the division of the UK into a 'distant' North and West, and a composite North West, Midlands and South (Table 9.1). However, the notion of and sensitivity to peripherality transcends North and South, to a degree. It is a problem that many authorities, North and South, perceive as confronting them, and in those places that, at first, would seem 'well-connected'.

The more vigorous representations tend to be from two types of locality; first, from those areas that perceive themselves to be seen from the outside as accessible but which believe themselves to be peripheral on some criteria; second, from those areas that do turn out to be objectively and unequivocally 'peripheral' on some criteria. More interesting – at least from a uniqueness perspective – is that seemingly accessible places claiming peripherality as a constraint that warrants recognition in Assisted Area designation (Table 9.3) takes us into the realm, potentially at least, of less conventional notions of 'peripherality'.

9.6 Concluding Comments

As represented by submissions to the review exercise, the issue of peripherality has provided another basis for investigating attitudes to local economic problems. Peripherality has never really been given great attention by researchers. The implicit assumption seems to have been that it is a rather matter-of-fact issue. However, the present analysis shows that this is not quite the case. For a start, there is clearly a perceived tension between the condition of peripherality and the desire for development. Moreover, there are variations in the ways in which the 'local' feels peripheral and in the ways in which local authorities represent themselves as peripheral. In addition, following our notions of representational detail and method as essentially stemming from local resource factors, it is also clear that authorities have adopted particular strategies to project and promote their case for designation.

It is something of an irony that some of the UK's least accessible places work hard at allaying the image of peripherality (see, for example, the work of Burgess (1982) on local authority promotional activity) but that, in seeking access to regional funding, they reveal a distinct duality, representing themselves in different ways for different audiences. There are implications here. Once again, is there a tension between self-image projection for promotion and that for regional resource acquisition? If so, does the tension translate itself into other aspects of policy and representation? That must remain a matter for future investigation.

From a policy angle, there is little doubt that peripherality may be alleviated by the development of quality infrastructure. Perhaps, it is the opportunity for such development that motivates some authorities into representing themselves as peripheral, despite constant attempts in other areas of image construction to put across precisely the opposite picture.

Note

1. By highlighting the differential implications of peripherality for individual industries, these submissions suggest, probably without any deliberate intent, that any policy decision which uses a general accessibility model, such as in the DTI appraisal, will effectively militate against some industrial groups. As Randall argues, industries producing low value, bulky goods are most likely to face difficulties as regards poor accessibility locations, while those with a high value-added component based on inputs of highly skilled labour seem best placed (Randall, 1987, pp. 229–31).

10

LOCAL AUTHORITIES AND THE PROCESS OF POLICY CHANGE

Many complex issues have been considered in this review. Our decisions were arrived at in a rational and structured way. The new map responds to the current position in the country and gives help where it is needed to enable areas to take full advantage of the recovery from recession. Assisted Area status will give all designated areas the opportunity to attract new investment and to provide new jobs.

(Tim Sainsbury, Minister for Industry, House of Commons, 26 July 1993)

Inward investment . . . is the lowest of any West Yorkshire District . . . as a result of the paucity of development land . . . The key attraction in the past was Regional Selective Assistance. The loss of this grant will make the promotion of inward investment even more difficult.

(Bradford City Council, Statistical analysis of the new Assisted Area list, July 1993, p. 6)

Our present problems are precisely those that have been addressed in the past by regional policy, which has allowed the north, north east, Scotland, Wales and most of the Midlands to have the industrial infrastructure required to ensure that businesses can succeed . . . with the awarding of Assisted Area status, we shall be able to build that infrastructure . . . Assisted Area status has already had some success in Hastings.

(Jacqui Lait, MP Hastings and Rye, House of Commons, 27 October 1993)

Although in financial terms it is currently a shadow of its former self, regional policy, as this book has confirmed, is always an emotive subject for all sorts of groups and for all sorts of reasons. For local authorities in Britain it offers a potential source of central government financial aid and perhaps a (perceived) pathway to European assistance; for businesses it provides a source of finance; and for politicians and governments it provides, in its 1990s form, a fairly cheap way of 'demonstrating' a concern about problem areas. The latter probably at least partly accounts for the fact that regional policy is still on the statute books after over 60 years of activity, roller coaster changes in government philosophies about intervention, and even the coming, going and threatened revival of Keynesianism.

In July 1993, following the review around which the analysis in this book has been based, the DTI announced some major changes to the Assisted Areas map. The immediate reactions – from politicians in both central and local government – revealed the real sensitivities linked to the ramifications of this policy change as it confronts those at the local level. In fact, the initial political debate brought to mind at least three apparent facts; first, the perceived importance of area policy at the 'sharp end' – in the local economy; second, the competitiveness with which local authorities enter the fray when there is a hint of cash in the air; and third, the fact that whatever local authorities say about their area economic problems, the government makes its own assessment and its own decision in the end.

That may be a somewhat depressing and overexaggerated view – and a matter that we will return to later in the chapter. Nevertheless, in this book we have been able to make use of local authority representations on the issue of the Assisted Areas and from that to draw out a range of aspects for investigation.

In this concluding chapter, we complete three basic tasks. First, in section 10.1 we conclude our evaluation of the 1992/1993 review of the Assisted Areas map itself in discussing the outcome and some of the ensuing reactions. Second, in section 10.2 we summarise the key achievements in the book, in particular drawing out some conclusions on the central themes of local authority engagement, attitude and representation that have been worked up as central organising features. Third, in section 10.3 we reflect on the material presented in the book, in particular exploring themes linked to the development of regional policy and the Assisted Areas, and the relationships of local authorities and other local interests within spatial economic policy.

10.1 The Outcome and Local Reactions

Once-rich South moves up the queue for aid handout.

(*Guardian*, 24 July 1993)

Reactions to the revised map may well not be the most important aspect of the review process. We have certainly argued that the representations have a significance that extends well beyond the confines of the Assisted Areas review exercise. However, the Assisted Areas map is a significant part of the spatial economic policy profile and thus reactions and responses to the changes are important and warrant discussion. In focusing on the reactions, we can draw out some more interesting – and unexplored – dimensions of the local–central connection.

In this section, the various levels of reaction – local media, local government and political debate – are investigated. In addition, there is a critical evaluation of the outcome and the effectiveness or otherwise of the engagement of local authorities in the review process, together with a consideration of the ensuing implications for the areas involved. First, we analyse the Assisted Area changes introduced in August 1993.

10.1.1 The 1993 revision of the Assisted Areas map

The new map represents the Government's assessment of those areas which now face structural unemployment problems. There are some major differences from the previous map. This is not surprising. Unemployment patterns have changed significantly.
(Tim Sainsbury, Minister for Industry, House of Commons, 26 July 1993)

Although factors such as the impact of major closures and the strength of local economies were claimed to have been included, the 1993 revisions to the Assisted Areas map were dominated by unemployment criteria. That, of course, makes our assessment in Chapter 8 all the more relevant. The new map covered some 33.8 per cent of the working population – approximately the figure set by the European Commission under its Competition Policy. Prior to the review, some 35 per cent of the population had been included, although the coverage of Development Areas – at 15 per cent – was slightly higher.

Perhaps the major change was the shift of attention towards London and the South (Figure 10.1). This was partly facilitated by the decision to accept the criticism that, in certain circumstances, the tendency to delimit entire TTWAs disadvantaged some areas. Jettisoning this suited the DTI on this occasion, as it facilitated a desired shift in the policy emphasis towards greater selectivity and control.

The review process generated thirty-one brand new Assisted Areas – two Development Areas (DAs) and twenty-nine Intermediate Areas (IAs); sixteen areas were downgraded to 'non-Assisted Area' (NAA) status, and twelve were moved from DA to IA. Conspicuously, and despite government rhetoric, most of the 'defence-sensitive' local areas were not among the most successful localities (Chapter 6), the only exceptions being the Weymouth and Portland part of the Dorchester and Weymouth TTWA, Barrow-in-Furness, and Plymouth. The pleas of Bristol, Portsmouth and others were not successful, simply because the TTWAs involved did not meet the, predominantly labour market, criteria required. The greatest 'success' came in the swathe of coastal resort and port areas (Chapter 7), particularly in southern and eastern England and in the small number of mining communities granted support (Table 10.1). Even here, there were some surprises at what appears to have been an unexpected success (Ball, 1994b).

As we have noted, many coastal economies – represented by resorts and ports – were successful in either gaining status (fifteen formerly non-Assisted Areas areas were successful – nearly half of the national total of thirty-one) or retaining

Table 10.1   The outcome of the 1992/1993 review of the Assisted Areas map: status changes by locality type

AA status condition	Industrial districts	Resorts and ports	Remoter rural areas	Major urban centres	Total
Retentions	35	20	5	8	68
DA	18	7	1	4	30
IA	17	13	4	4	38
Upgradings	17	17	6	3	43
NAA to IA	10	14	3	2	29
IA to DA	6	2	3	1	12
NAA to DA	1	1	–	–	2
Downgradings	20	2	4	2	28
DA to IA	9	2	1	–	12
DA to NAA	4	–	1	–	5
IA to NAA	7	–	2	2	11
Total	72	39	15	13	139

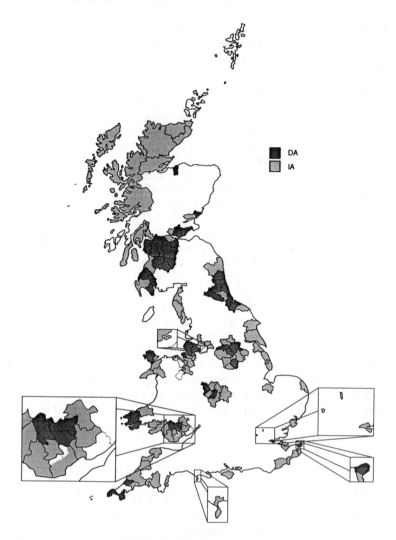

Figure 10.1   The outcome: UK Assisted Areas map.

it. Only two coastal areas were downgraded (from Development Area to Intermediate Area status). In total, the process generated thirty-nine coastal Assisted Areas in Great Britain, and seventeen of these as newly designated or upgraded (Figure 10.1).

The detailed pattern of change – important in its impact on local economic potential – is revealed in Figures 10.2–10.4. In addition to the defence-laden areas, the 'winners' in the process (Figure 10.3) are clearly revealed as the newly emerging 'problem localities' – those such as Mansfield suffering from coal-mine closures, ports and resorts such as Dover, Torbay, Clacton and Bridlington feeling the effects of a declining 'sea sector', and some parts of major urban centres, e.g. areas of East London, that had shown some tenacity as problem

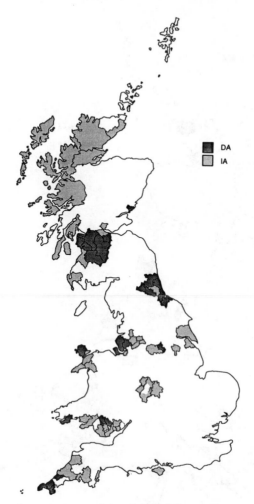

DA
IA

Figure 10.2   The survivors: areas retaining Assisted Area status.

locations over the previous few years but which government, via regional policy at least, had until 1993 been reluctant to confront. The 'losers' are also clearly shown (Figure 10.4) as some of the industrial districts such as Bradford and Corby that were baled out by regional policy in the 1980s.

Amendments to the map (Table 10.1; Figures 10.3–10.4) – a loss of status here and a gain there – unleashed the expected sensitivities (see section 10.1.2), including elements of a North–South controversy. The 'problems' of the South appear to have been recognised as requiring support, while there are many Northern 'losers'. The outcome was bound to have wide political ramifications.

The results for the cameo areas discussed in Chapter 5 are of interest. The long-term aspirant, Stoke-on-Trent, failed to acquire status, but was later to be awarded Objective 2 status under the European Structural Funds. As we have already noted, Bradford lost its Assisted Area status altogether. The Wirral/

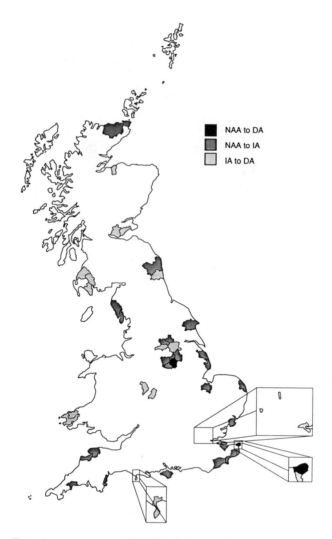

Figure 10.3 The winners: upgraded TTWAs (all or part).

Chester TTWA was downgraded from Development Area to Intermediate Area status. Alyn and Deeside lost Assisted status in part of its area, but retained it at a lower level in its major industrial districts. Hackney, classed by the DTI as the 'London end of the East Thames corridor', gained status, as did much of the East Kent coastal strip (Dover and Deal; Folkestone; Sittingbourne and Sheerness; and Thanet), with the latter being granted Development Area status.

    These outcomes clearly reflect the criteria adopted by the DTI in assessing the various cases. The statistical data used focused in particular on contemporary labour market problems (Chapter 4) and not those likely to occur in the future. In that sense, the apparent failure of some areas, such as Portsmouth, to secure Assisted Area status should be seen in a longer-term context. Representation

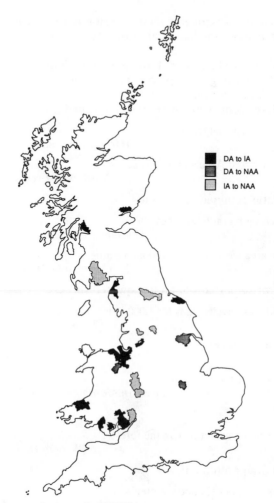

Figure 10.4   The losers: downgraded TTWAs.

certainly set before the government the potential problems of such areas and this is one advantage of making representations. Indeed, Department of Trade and Industry applications to the European Commission structural funds in October 1993 included Portsmouth and Bristol (see Wintour, *Guardian*, 12 October 1993). Perhaps the foundations for inclusion were established in the initial response to the Assisted Area review process?

10.1.2 Expectations and outcomes

The forces of sensitivity – local pride, local political ramifications, and inter-area competition – and the perceived opportunities that we have charted in earlier parts of the book and that produced a response from the 'local' at the time of the 1992 consultation paper, are, of course, no less evident in the wake of the review process and outcome. We can gain an impression of the reactions by drawing on local and national news media; local authority reactions; and formal political debates.

Although it tended to be a short-term news item, local media reactions reflect the sensitivity of according some places special status and omitting other places. A selection of local newspaper headlines from affected areas reveals such reactions. Thus, we can identify expressions of unbridled joy:

> Town celebrates its special status
> > (*Grimsby Evening Telegraph*, 24 July 1993)

> We've got it – Assisted Area status for Furness
> > (*North West Evening Mail*, 23 July 1993)

or of relief at status retained or regained:

> Tyneside survives job grants switches
> > (*Evening Chronicle* (Newcastle), 24 July 1993)

> Major boost as area wins back assisted area status
> > (*Northumberland Gazette*, 30 July 1993)

or a sense of surprise perhaps at an unexpected success:

> Resort wins aid and unveils plans for 1,000 jobs
> > (*Western Morning News*, 27 July 1993)

> Delight as town gets aid boost
> > (*Fenland Citizen*, 24 July 1993)

> Cash help on way for the South West
> > (*Western Morning News* (Plymouth), 24 July 1993)

or mixed feelings:

> Life-line for Navy towns but fury in the forest
> > (*Western Daily Press*, 24 July 1993)

or disbelief and disappointment:

> Town reeling as cash boost hopes shatter
> > (*Southend Evening Echo*, 26 July 1993)

> Cash blow as Forest loses 'special' status
> > (*The Citizen* (Gloucester), 24 July 1993)

> We were robbed!
> > (*Lancashire Evening Telegraph*, 24 July 1993)

Local sensitivities to change have already been highlighted in the book, when we touched on this issue in the cameos (Chapter 5). For example, in Stoke-on-Trent, the enduring quest for regional aid on the part of the local authority has been picked up from time to time by local media (see Figure 5.1).

The reactions to the review decisions are significant in themselves. For a short period, the news of status, gained, retained or lost, grabbed local headlines (see Ball, 1994b). In 'successful' defence localities, for example, there were emotive, charged headlines – comments such as 'operation fightback' (*North West Evening Mail* (Furness and West Cumbria), 24 July 1993), and a 'lifeline for Navy towns' (*Western Daily Press*, 24 July 1993) reflect the reaction to the news of

Assisted Area status. These offer valuable insights into the 'local' because, essentially, they are reporting a range of local authority and local business reactions. Sometimes these are 'off the record' and can be illuminating. Of course, in many cases, local news agencies, not having a real understanding of the policy package, misrepresent the changes involved. There were many misconceptions, with, for example, local newspapers confusing national with European Union regional policy. Nevertheless, local news media were important in that they 'whipped up' the debate, latching on to the resources and needs issue and thus generating and aggravating political sensitivities.

Local authority reactions are, of course, predictable. We have already mentioned the reactions of major 'losers' such as Bradford. Elsewhere, there was registered concern about the changes. In Newport (Gwent) for example, there was consternation over the marketability of some of the area's key investment sites which, following the review, were left a little 'stranded', outside the newly designated area (personal communication). In Carmarthen there was disappointment at the decision to downgrade both Lampeter and Aberaeron and Cardigan TTWAs since the financial incentives associated with status were seen as fundamental to the regeneration of the area that suffers from poor communications, defence industry cuts and the shake out in agriculture (personal communication). The reaction from 'winners', such as East Kent, was similarly predictable (Dawe, 1993).

At a formal political level, two debates in the House of Commons revealed the sensitivities – the bitterness in some cases – that surround decisions like those involved in the review (Hansard, 26 July 1993; 27 October 1993). At the level of political rhetoric and media attention, the issue was projected as a battle between the demand for regional policy assistance from an old industrial, coal-closure-hit North and a 'creaking' but high-potential South hit by defence cuts (Tighe, 1993a). As one writer described the situation, there was an 'affluent image problem' confronting the South (Evans, 1993). Without doubt, the political debate carried with it the 'baggage' of historical differences and traditional allegiances between political parties, with Labour MPs often seen to be supporting the declining industrial environments of the North and remaining sceptical of the plight of the South, and Tory MPs adopting a stance that, while sceptical of regional policy in general, favoured the extension of policy assistance into the Southern domain. Of course, it is difficult to separate the rhetoric of the political debate or the newspaper viewpoint from more objective and calmer assessments. Yet, it is certain that 'new' local economic problems such as those linked to the 'defence dividend' acted as a catalyst for new demands and new controversies.

10.1.3 Implications for the effectiveness of representations

In Appendix 2 we attempt to set out some ideas on 'playing the bidding game'. In general though, it is important to address the question of effectiveness – what was the impact of the representations in terms of the review of the Assisted Areas? How many successful places did not submit? To what extent is successful designation linked to response? If there is no clear link between response and result there are important implications for the use of resources in this particular bidding process.

There is pressure on local authorities and their partner agencies to be good at seeking out resource opportunities. The cost-effectiveness of all this is extremely important (see Oatley, 1994). So, what were the costs involved and were they effective? The submissions varied from the basic letter through to the expensively produced glossy pamphlet/booklet and with equivalently varying costs. A crude estimate of costs would put the average figure at around £1,100, with many submissions involving a much greater input of resources. This would include staff time in assembling and collating data and designing a response, the physical production of the material, and so on. If the document went through Committee then that would add additional costs, and there would be costs involved in assimilating the views at the DTI/Scottish Office/Welsh Office. A conservative estimate would put the cost to local authorities alone at around £0.5 million or more.

Against the costs, we must try to assess the benefits. These are difficult to identify. The general feeling from discussions with the DTI and others, is that the submissions had little direct bearing on the decisions made. They were supplementary in that sense, because the decisions were made on the basis of an objective analysis completed by the DTI in house. Flexibility in the presentations to a certain extent inevitably marginalised their contribution. However, we have argued that the impact of the representations extends beyond the immediacy of the policy review and into the realms of longer-term images and potential support (as well as into the implications that such representations generate outside the local–central connection, through, for example, the signals that are transmitted to outside agencies).

10.2 A Summary of Key Findings

While we can typify local areas as either 'winners' or 'losers', perhaps more interesting and revealing are the wider applications that the review process offers. As we stated at an early stage in the book, we have not simply been telling the story of a one-off event in the chequered history of regional policy, local economic development and central–local connections in the spatial economic policy arena. We have been able to draw out a wide range of insights into, for example, the processes of policy formation, attitudes to policy, and strategies (and effects) of representation. It is appropriate therefore briefly to recap and review the contents of the book.

In Part 1 we established the context for the Assisted Areas review. The review was interpreted against a background of shifts in the character and functioning of the spatial economic policy arena. The contemporary character of the regional policy package has led to the drive towards a more competitive policy environment (Chapter 1). This has placed a premium on a level of local expertise that is not always available. It has become increasingly important for local authorities to harness their skills in order to make effective, credible bids for resources. These radical changes in central–local relations resonate with debates about local autonomy, place marketing, and the ways in which the 'local' increasingly is interpreted as a coalition of internal and external elements. Significantly for the book, these issues can all be linked in to the review responses and we have approached this in terms of regional 'benefits' and local 'needs', with the latter conditioned by a range of influences (Chapter 2). Knowledge of the connections between central and local is limited in this policy area, and therefore trends in, for example, place marketing can themselves be used to inform the understanding and interpretation of the relationships.

A number of useful bases for interpreting and understanding the local end of local–central connections were established in Chapter 2. First, the argument was that representations are motivated by a range of potential objectives and not solely connected to bids for resources. Second, there are a variety of factors influencing the activities of local authorities in their relationships with central government over spatial economic policy. In Chapter 2 we teased these out – factors such as local problems and needs, approaches to policy reflective of local attitudes, traditions and ideologies, experiences of relationships with the centre, personnel factors and local authority credibilities, historical policy status, and local process factors linked to coalitions, local business attitudes and so on.

In Chapter 2, we also explored the detailed underpinnings to any local representation. We developed ideas on this that involved questions of mediating representational tension, and understanding formation via the notions of representational base, detail and method that help to comprehend the ways in which images are constructed for local authority objectives.

Finally, in setting up the later parts of the book, we went on to explore the strengths and weaknesses of submissions analysis, arguing that this is very much an under-used resource in policy analysis, but one that, subject to an acceptance of its limitations, can be of immense value.

Part 2 explored the detail of local authority engagement in the review exercise. The approach was to investigate variations in local involvement and to draw insights from that. The act of local authority engagement was shown to be a function of the factors established in Part 1 – there were wide variations and these connected to local needs, policy complexions and so on (Chapter 4; Appendix 1). The actual style and quality of engagement was also investigated, with submissions analysis focusing on coalitions, local business involvement, strategies and the packaging of arguments, and image projections. This provided a potential basis for assessing participation in 'the bidding game'.

The detail of engagement was explored in Chapter 5 using a range of material on the local policy and strategy process that was generated from the supplementary survey. The richness of the review event was reflected in the insights that could be gained by focusing on five areas. The cameos each investigated reactions to the review exercise in terms of local economic problems; response motives, formulation and elements; and managing the representation. This allowed an entry into the arena of lobbying, an important element of central–local interactions. The approach to policy response formation was discussed in detail, using the various survey material, thus offering insights into consensus, coalition, key officer involvement, and lobbying/managing activities.

Part 3 investigated local authority attitudes to regional policy as revealed in the submission documents. This provided some fascinating information on perceived policy potential. In general, and aside from any policy rhetoric, there was widespread support for some notion of regional policy. The analysis was also able to delve into the detailed arguments put forward by authorities and their partner agencies on the merits (and the limits) of access to the regional policy package (Chapter 6). That provided an opportunity to report on some of the findings from localised research on the policy impact. We also pulled out the responses and reactions of authorities shown to be prominent by the extent of their engagement – defence-laden areas and coastal areas. Finally, given the importance of the 'Southern question' in the mid-1990s, Chapter 7 focused on attitudes to policy on the part of authorities in London and the South East. This allowed us to identify and assess the lines of argument put forward by the 'South' in the competition for policy access.

In Part 4, we developed ideas about the ways in which the 'local' represents its economic problems to the outside world. Using the examples of unemployment (Chapter 8) and peripherality (Chapter 9) we were able to draw out ideas on the importance of representation and, most significantly, on the ways in which images of these factors are constructed in the quest to 'get a message across', whether for access to resources or for other purposes. The notions of representational base, detail and method were deployed to assist an interpretation of the various approaches. Representations were found to correspond closely to the image that a place projects. They reveal the complexion of a local authority, and point to a particular attitude to local labour market development, or geographical location. They also condition the image of a place, influencing local populations and potential developers and businesses.

10.3 Reflections on the Policy Process

In this book we have focused on the nature and the strength of the connections between local authorities and regional policy, investigating engagement levels and styles, attitudes to policy, and representations of local economic problems. These are issues that have been neglected by writers but which are important parts of the spatial economic policy arena. Their exploration has been made possible by weaving together material from submissions to the review exercise, available research findings and supplementary survey data. In this final section we reflect on some of the central elements of the book, setting up issues and, in some cases, in the spirit of any fresh approach, exploring what we do not know as much as what we do know.

10.3.1 Local–central relations – engagement and non-engagement

Local–central relations are a key part of the spatial economic policy arena. In Chapters 4 and 5 we charted and discussed variations in the engagement of authorities in the Assisted Areas review exercise and, in the process, drew out a range of implications. Even if the commitment to the policy on the part of the (local authority) applicant may not be 100 per cent, the lure of available resources attracts applications. We find a series of competitive battles taking place over the resources available. Some of these occur in the local scene, others are more widely framed. There are broader implications to be drawn from such findings.

The backcloth is local–central tension. Central government controls the purse strings of regional policy and, of course, wields discretionary power over which areas receive support. That renders the process a politically sensitive, charged and, potentially, manipulable entity. It also resonates directly and forcefully with the local autonomy–dependency debate discussed in Chapter 2. The irony is that authorities are led into a quest for dependency, when autonomy is so often an avid goal. As Cox argued, the process becomes dominated by the drive for effectiveness in local economic development (Cox, 1993) and local autonomy is confirmed as an unattainable short-term goal.

Aside from political intricacies at national–local level, there are local economic and political pressures on authorities to engage in the battle. The need to be seen to be defending the local territory is a sensitive and compelling issue. However, for some authorities there is no established culture of bidding and there must be a rapid learning process (see 10.1.3 and Appendix 2). Alternatively, or more likely additionally, authorities seem to have tailored strategies to overcome such weaknesses. For example, there has been a deliberate policy to encourage and support coalition (see 10.3.5) or, in whatever ways possible, either to teach themselves to connect with central government, or to hire (even headhunt) staff who have the requisite experience. Of course, local–central relationships develop further from bids in what amounts to an iterative process. In this way, the review exercise itself has functioned as a learning device for authorities.

The wide range of local authority abilities (termed as 'representational detail' in the book) extends from a culture of bidding to a culture of local authority parochialism. That will be significant in any future success in the acquisition of spatial economic policy resources.

The culture of assistance – a game to be played amongst those with experience plus a few aspirants – revealed itself in the detail of the review response (see Chapter 4, section 4.5). Quite clearly, past policy status was an important factor. Some authorities were clearly 'defenders' – those areas such as Bradford, the Rhondda, Sunderland, Newcastle-upon-Tyne, Manchester and Wrexham which were looking to retain their Assisted Area status. Others were 'seekers' – parts of East London, Wakefield and Dewsbury, Lancaster, and East Kent which were seeking inclusion on the map, either to recover status lost in the mid-1980s or to get on it for the first time. Some of the places that were likely to suffer from defence cutbacks were amongst this group, with places like Portsmouth, Plymouth, Barrow and Bristol putting in well-produced and strongly argued documents. Finally, there were authorities which, for a variety of reasons, deliberately did not respond to the review. Thus, for around 20 per cent of local authorities, places such as Oxfordshire, Surrey, Swindon, Salisbury and Harrogate, regional policy appeared to be of little concern as a local issue. They did not respond to the government consultation exercise and were, in effect, 'non-combatants'. Some, such as Chester-le-Street and East Cambridgeshire, left it to the county authority to present a response; a large number (including Hertfordshire, Somerset, Bournemouth, Ipswich and the Derbyshire Dales) saw no hope and did not respond; others (Kettering; East Devon), reflecting an old fear about being designated a 'problem region', viewed regional policy as a disadvantageous element that could stigmatise their areas.

Although evidence cannot be marshalled, the impression is that attitudes to involvement have changed, and that more authorities are engaging in ever more sophisticated representations. A greater degree of external projection seems to be under way. The catalysts for engagement have been the pressures exerted by a static or declining economy and a more competitive policy environment.

10.3.2 Place marketing and inter-area competition

Place marketing and inter-area competition, always present in local authority interrelations, have come to the fore in recent years. We have confronted some of the ensuing issues and assessed the styles of competition. Not only is the policy process confronted by overt place competition, there are also covert, clandestine forms. We have identified forms of lobbying and coalition formation as, to a degree, competitive devices. This involves the drive for more effective ways of influencing decisions, and the formation of coalitions for purposes of competing for resources.

In terms of the more familiar forms of image production, the book has also revealed some interesting features. Like any other institution, local authorities are avid image-makers. They construct promotional images to meet particular coalition objectives. However, as we have argued, the internal images presented for different purposes may be starkly contrasting. For example, the review process 'unleashed' local competition (Tighe, 1993b) and a need to make representations on economic problems. The images presented, and the strategies behind them, are both fascinating and informative on attitudes to development in the 'local' scene. However, the image of 'need' differs from the more familiar image of 'attraction', and the two are potentially in tension as 'images of confusion'. It is interesting to consider how these are resolved, if they are resolved at all. The latter may well be the most likely scenario, although in the book we have cited what appear to be strategies for resolution – for example, authorities putting the stress on problems as potentials (Chapter 4, sections 4.4.4 and especially 4.4.5).

The irony in this is that although a reputation for prosperity may be disadvantageous, an immediate use of the outcome in place marketing was evident. Discounting why it was awarded, promotions cited the potential availability of Assisted Area benefits (East Thames corridor – Assisted Area, *Regional Development International*, Vol. 17, no. 3, 1993), even though they may be modest and even inaccessible. Such is the importance of the chance for 'special treatment' – in this case, the regional policy bait.

10.3.3 A different perspective on the North–South divide

The question of North–South division in UK economic development is a familiar issue for social scientists (Townroe and Martin, 1992). Debates revolve around whether the 'divide' is real or contrived, and whether there is convergence or divergence (Martin, 1993b). However, the present book has established some new perspectives on the issue. For a start, it has confirmed that locally, there is no clearly articulated view of the North–South divide. That might have been suspected, but it has not been demonstrated across such a range of authorities before. We have been able to determine viewpoints on regional problems as seen from the perspective of authorities in different regional settings. In effect, regional problems are themselves representations from a position, and the review exercise has involved competing representations being played out in a political arena.

Competing representations have extended to competition on broad North–South lines for the potential resources that Assisted Area status offers. Such geographical issues emerged and were revealed during the review process with the advent of Southern competition involving London and the South versus the rest, and the protestations of some Northern authorities over extending the Assisted Areas to the South.

10.3.4 The significance of local views on regional policy?

It is quite possible that the local attitudes to regional policy reported in this book (Chapter 6) differ from what might have been anticipated. It seems that, although regional policy is much maligned on resource, quality and strategic grounds as an element of spatial economic policy, and is viewed as almost a token gesture, it is seen as significant and valuable by many working 'in the field'. They certainly do not appear to support a total indictment. In the places where it has been applied, policy benefits have been substantial, although it must be said that local authorities rarely take a wide evaluative approach, viewing the policy solely in 'local' terms.

There is another dimension to this. Regional policy is, it seems, rather more important than the level of resources committed to it would indicate. It has a significance that transcends the purely economic and social welfare domain, and which connects with the politics of place and competition. Even a small resource base for regional policy serves to differentiate, and unleashes forces linked to local status, local economic and political success, and so on.

To what extent, however, do local authority views about policy have significance? Have they actually influenced decisions? The answer is that, probably, the direct and immediate influence has been modest. Of course, there are other longer-term influences. Even more important, local authority views condition the acceptability of policy. Local perceptions of what policy can do are important as they condition attitudes to it, support for it and, in essence, its workability. The success of regional policy depends to a significant extent on the role of local authorities as channels of connection between national–regional 'benefit' and local applicant 'need'.

10.3.5 Coalitions and the policy process

As we have argued at various points, coalitions feature heavily in the processes of policy formation. There is a tendency in the literature to focus on growth coalitions almost as a generic group. However, there are many, varied forms of coalition. These may be permanent, semi-permanent or temporary, and formalised or less formalised. The most common experience is for less formal structures and for formal, but less permanent coalitions. For example, the review exercise itself functioned as a catalyst for coalition formation, sometimes breaking down long-standing political barriers to co-operation (Chapter 5). Elsewhere, it functioned as a force for the consolidation of existing coalition activities, internally within authorities and in their external relations. Thus, it was not just a vehicle for a one-off bid, but for a process of consolidation and change that goes well beyond the short-term issues.

Our argument has been that coalitions are wide-ranging. Some aspects need to be looked at more deeply – the notion of the local authority as a coalition is important. Consensus has reigned (Eisenschitz and Gough, 1993) but not universally and the whole area needs fuller exploration. We have been able to make some inroads into this topic. The functioning of coalitions has been addressed. For example, in Chapter 5 we were able to delve into the detail of the formation of policy position, to evaluate the role of coalition elements, and so on. The conclusion was that there are key individuals and key events that condition policy position. Some coalition elements emerge as dominant and others as compliant, almost in an observer role. Local authorities appear as notable facilitators in the formation of external coalitions and the role of 'lead' elements – individuals, events, or whatever – is something to be explored. It is clear that the review process was a catalyst for change and that coalitions appear as distinctly dynamic entities.

10.3.6 The representation of local economic problems

Local (authority) representation of specific economic problems is far from a simple matter. There is much flexibility inherent in any system of local economic assessment and that opens up the opportunity for differentiation via styles of representation. Submissions are constructed images, representations to suit a need, and they can be illuminating in such an interpretation.

We have established that there is wide variation in the use of unemployment and peripherality as key representations in the local economy; and some variations across most other key factors. This reflects different perceptions of problems across regions (10.3.3).

This implies that the representation of problems makes comparability very difficult. Because of their very nature, representations are inevitably marginal in any objective assessment. Amendments to the Assisted Areas map were mainly based on in-house (DTI) analysis. Submission is, therefore, on the surface, of questionable value. This generates a tension for the participants – not least, in terms of requests to submit views and the costs of submission. However, authorities will always suspect that what they say just might have a resonance in government offices. Moreover, there is probably scope for representations to have some influence – to raise matters that are not reflected in the bland statistics, or to question their accuracy and relevance, to stress problems 'in the pipeline' and so on. In addition, submissions made for the Assisted Areas review may be viewed as practice for a 'bidding game' where representations about problems and project potential are a much more decisive factor in success or failure. The principal point for reflection, however, is that there is an inherent flexibility that simultaneously allows images to be constructed (by authorities) and rejected (by central government) on similarly flexible and perhaps imprecise political grounds.

Of course, the limitations on the value of representations in their primary role are countered, for this book at least, by their considerable usefulness as vehicles for obtaining a fix on local policy attitudes and approaches.

10.3.7 From analysis to prescription

Much of our work in the book has been analysis-focused. However, looking at practitioner interest in particular, we have been keen to draw out some implications both for 'playing the bidding game' in the changed policy environment of the 1990s (see section 10.1.3 above and Appendix 2), and for the more general character and effectiveness of representations on local economic problems – particularly in Part 4 of the book.

What conclusions can be drawn on the quality of the submissions? In an earlier section, we noted that bids function as integrating forces through coalition consolidation and formation (10.3.5). Strong coalitions involving authorities and external partner agencies (chambers of commerce, local businesses, etc.) – often consensual by need – offer a strength of resource base in submissions: they bolster the 'representational detail'. In addition, forms of bidding behaviour are interesting, and it is important to assess the value of constructing submissions that generate what amount to 'threats', that fit circumstances to make a case, and that mobilise local business and other strengths along the way.

These questions were explored to a certain extent in earlier parts of the book. Some local authorities – mostly those with only a faint expectation of any success – submitted short, unadventurous and unappealing statements. They simply went through the motions. Others, however, produced elaborate, expensive, glossy and well-researched documentation. Problems of 'peripherality' were claimed by all those who could possibly claim it (Chapter 9), actualities and/or expectations of high unemployment were cited where possible (Chapter 8), and, in general, authorities set their store by signalling the problems of their economies. Declining core industry, unsatisfactory infrastructure, past successes of regional policy if they had it before were all stressed. Of course, prudent authorities were careful to look to the positive angle – they emphasised the many and varied successes that would be expected if they could 'offer' financial incentives to investors, tap in to European funding and so on, and set out their detailed local strategies for medium-term regeneration. Some managed to get private firms and associated agencies (chambers of commerce, etc.) to join with them in setting out a desire for designation.

Images, appeals and representations were central to the responses. For example, Portsmouth and Weymouth both created images connecting defence cutbacks to unemployment and the need to diversify. For some – arguably the best – the recipe seemed to be a combination of a plea, threats and despair. For example, the Lancaster City submission, representing a place that was an Assisted Area up to 1984 but which had been almost ten years without it, fitted this model. It made a plea on its cover: 'Lancaster – no doubt that the loss of Assisted Area status has disadvantaged the area' (Lancaster Chamber of Commerce, Trade and Industry); threw in a bit of despair, especially from a private firm: 'lack of Assisted Area status will mean that our major expansion plans will almost certainly be lost to Lancaster' (Celtech Ltd.); and followed that up with some hard-hitting evidence on local unemployment, economic isolation and various other problems.

Of course, as we have ascertained, the quality and depth of the submissions held little direct sway with the government. Some of the (arguably) 'best' presentations from a visual and documentary perspective (Lancaster; Bradford; Portsmouth; Stoke-on-Trent) failed to secure designation. The government's formula – placing a heavy, if not total, reliance on unemployment as an element – appears to have been maintained to the exclusion of elaborate local submissions. Some 6,000 pages of representations and many hours of local authority labour produced some excellent, incisive analyses of local economic and social problems and potentials. It 'flagged up' local problems but did it do anything more than that? There is some evidence of a correlation between submission quality and outcome, but it necessarily relies on inference (see Appendix 2; Table A.2.1). More than that of course, submissions may just have raised the government's consciousness of such problems and of the local potentials that places contain, as well as signifying the local political sensitivities attached to aid decisions. The announcement, soon after the decision on the revised Assisted Areas map, that European Commission structural support would be sought for some places that missed out (e.g. Portsmouth; Bristol), is testimony to that feeling.

10.4 Conclusions

The popular view of UK regional policy in the mid-1990s is that it is a contentious issue for a minority of interests. However, following the analysis of the review exercise we cannot accept such a viewpoint. Regional policy may be modest in resources and weak in policy weapons, but it still operates as a force for economic change and a catalyst for inter-area competition.

On reflection, it seems that the review process had the effect of reinforcing a rather reactive mode of policy response. Given the rigid criteria adopted, in the consultation phase, local authorities were led into reactive thinking and hence reactive representations – addressing central issues such as unemployment as problems for policy to counter. Some local authorities even developed strategies to get by this narrow focus, by going beyond the criteria and into the realms of potential, past success and so on.

The outcome of the review exercise has clearly been important at the local scale. According to some commentators, the decision about the changing map will be one of the more significant events for the next few years in the arena of central–local economic policy relationships and local economic futures (Economic Development Panel, Royal Town Planning Institute, 1993). Without doubt, how these relationships play themselves out in the future will be something that draws the attention of academics, politicians and many others in society.

Changing patterns of advantage are at the core of many reactions – whether of projected fear or jubilation. The uniformity of local policies is potentially unbalanced. As Eisenschitz and Gough argue, much local economic development has taken place under stressful conditions. Local authorities, under pressure for consensus and with a tendency for defence of the local economy at a time of low growth, have tended to produce local policies that have ended up looking much the same, and with the same extremely limited chances of success (Eisenschitz and Gough, 1993). Within such a situation, success is bred from small differences – key officers, key firms and so on. Success in 'winning' regional policy support could be the vital factor in the difference between 'success' and 'failure' at local economic development. Or such is the perception of local authorities.

Of course, the impact and relevance of the review event may be as much in the ways that images of the 'local' were projected into the outside world, and the degree to which new or enhanced local coalitions were developed, as it is in the tangible economic effects of the preferential treatment on offer. It is on that salutary note that we complete our discussion.

REFERENCES

Anderson, J. (1994) Problems of inter-state economic integration: Northern Ireland and the Irish Republic in the European Community, *Political Geography*, Vol. 13, no. 1, pp. 53–72.

Armstrong, H.W. and Taylor, J. (1983) Unemployment stocks and flows in the Travel-to-Work Areas of the North West, *Urban Studies*, Vol. 20, no. 3, pp. 311–25.

Armstrong, H.W. and Taylor, J. (1987) *Regional Policy: the Way Forward*, Employment Institute, London.

Armstrong, H.W. and Twomey, J. (1993) Industrial development initiatives of District Councils in England and Wales, in R.T. Harrison and M. Hart (eds.), op. cit.

Association of District Councils (1991) *Creating a Climate for Growth: the Views of the Association of District Councils on Regional Policy*, ADC, London, December.

Axford, N. and Pinch, S. (1994) Growth coalitions and local economic development strategy in southern England: a case study of the Hampshire Development Association, *Political Geography*, Vol. 13, no. 4, pp. 344–60.

Balchin, P.N. and Bull, G.H. (1987) *Regional and Urban Economics*, Harper & Row, London.

Ball, R.M. (1985) Regional industrial policy: no change for The Potteries, *Town and Country Planning*, Vol. 54, no. 2, pp. 74–5.

Ball, R.M. (1989) *Seasonality in the UK Labour Market*, Avebury, Aldershot.

Ball, R.M. (1994a) Playing the defence card: local authority responses to the 1992 regional policy consultation paper, *Local Economy*, Vol. 9, no. 1, pp. 31–47.

Ball, R.M. (1994b) The changing Assisted Areas map – local reactions and sensitivities, *Town and Country Planning*, Vol. 63, no. 1, January, pp. 23–5.

Barnes, C. (1992) The end of the North–South divide? *The Planner*, 2 October, pp. 13–14.

Barrow-in-Furness Borough Council (1991) *Reliance on Defence Work Survey*.

Bassett, K. (1986) Economic restructuring, spatial coalitions and local economic development strategies: a case study of Bristol, *Political Geography Quarterly*, Vol. 5, ss. 163–78.

Bateman, M. (1986) Economic and social change in a defence economy: the case of Portsmouth, in P. Cooke (ed.) op. cit.

Begg, H.M. (1993) The impact of regional policy regrading in Scotland, in R.T. Harrison and M. Hart (eds.), op cit.

Bennett, R.J. and McCoshan, A. (1993) Enterprise and Human Resource Development, Paul Chapman Publishing, London.

Beynon, H. and Hudson, R. (1993) Place and space in contemporary Europe: some lessons and reflections, *Antipode*, Vol. 25, no. 3, pp. 177–90.

Bishop, P. and Gripaios, P. (1992) Defence in a peripheral region: the case of Devon and Cornwall, *Local Economy*, pp. 43–56.

Boddy, M., Lovering, J. and Bassett, K. (1986) *Sunbelt City? A Study of Economic Change in Britain's M4 Growth Corridor*, Oxford University Press.

Bovaird, A. (1993) Local economic development and the city, in R. Paddison, W. Lever, and J. Money (eds.) *International Perspectives in Urban Studies 1*, Jessica Kingsley, London.

Brindle, D. (1993) Flotsam-on-Sea, *Guardian*, 26 July.

Bruce, A. (1993) Prospects for local economic development: a practitioner's view, *Local Government Studies*, Vol. 19, no. 3, pp. 319–40.

Buck, N., Gordon, I., Pickvance, C. and Taylor-Gooby, P. (1989) The Isle of Thanet: municipal conservatism, in P. Cooke (ed.) *Localities*, Unwin Hyman, London.

Burden, W. (1986) Economic and social change in the Medway towns, in P. Cooke (ed.) op. cit.

Burgess, J. (1982) Selling places: environmental images for the executive, *Regional Studies*, Vol. 16, pp. 1–17.

Campbell, M. (ed.) (1990) *Local Economic Policy*, Cassell, London.

Campbell, M. (1992) A strategic approach to the local labour market, in M. Campbell and K. Duffy, op. cit.

Campbell, M. and Duffy, K. (eds.) (1992) *Local Labour Markets: Problems and Policies*, Longman, Harlow.

Champion, A. G. and Green, A. (1990) *The Spread of Prosperity and the North–South Divide: a Report on Local Economic Performance in Britain during the Late Eighties*, Booming Towns, Gosforth and Kenilworth.

Champion, A.G. and Townsend, A.R. (1990) *Contemporary Britain: a Geographical Perspective*, Edward Arnold, London.

Chandler, J. and Lawless, P. (1985) *Local Authorities and the Creation of Employment*, Gower, Aldershot.

Chisholm, M. (1990) *Regions in Recession and Resurgence*, Unwin Hyman, London.

Cochrane, A. (1990) Recent developments in local authority economic policy, in M. Campbell (ed.), op. cit.

Cochrane, A. (1995) Global worlds and worlds of difference, in J. Anderson, C. Brook, and A. Cochrane (eds.) *A Fragmented World*, Oxford University Press.

Cooke, P. (ed.) (1986) *Global Restructuring, Local Response*, ESRC, London.

Coombes, M. (1994) The regional policy maps – plus ça change, plus la même chose? *Town and Country Planning*, Vol. 63, no. 1, pp. 20–2.

Coopers and Lybrand (1992) *Assisted Areas Review: the Case for Coastal Resort Travel-to-Work Areas*, report prepared on behalf of the English Tourist Board, September.

Copus, A.K. (1992) An assessment of the peripherality of the Scottish Islands. Consultancy report commissioned by Shetland, Orkney and Western Isles Island Councils, Scottish Agricultural College, August.

Cox, K. (1993) The local and the global in the new urban politics: a critical view, *Environment and Planning D*, Vol. 11, pp. 433–48.

Cox, K. and Mair, A. (1991) From localised social structures to localities as agents, *Environment and Planning A*, Vol. 23, no. 2, pp. 155–208.

Dabinett, G. (1992) *Local Authorities Role in Defence Readjustment*, Centre for Regional Economic and Social Research, Sheffield City Polytechnic.

Damesick, P.J. and Wood, P.A. (1987) *Regional Problems, Problem Regions and Public Policy in the UK*, Oxford University Press.

Dawe, T. (1993) Kentish claimants toast new found lowly status, *The Times*, 24 July.

Department of Trade and Industry (1983) *Regional Industrial Policy*, HMSO, London.

Department of Trade and Industry (1994) Reference to Trade and Industry Committee review.

Department of Trade and Industry, Scottish Office and Welsh Office (1992) *Regional Policy: Review of the Assisted Areas of Great Britain*, London.

Department of Trade and Industry, Scottish Office and Welsh Office (1993) *Regional Policy: Review of the Assisted Areas of Great Britain: Background Document on the New Assisted Areas Map*, London.

Duncan, S. and Goodwin, M. (1988) *The Local State and Uneven Development*, Polity Press, Cambridge.

East of Scotland European Consortium (1992) *Transport Links to Europe*. Consultancy report cited in the Lothian Regional Council submission.

Economic Development Panel (Royal Town Planning Institute) (1993) Economic development news, *The Planner*, July, p. 22.

Eisenschitz, A. and Gough, J. (1993) *The Politics of Local Economic Policy*, Macmillan, London.

English Tourist Board (1992) *Responses to DTI Consultation Paper on the Review of the Assisted Areas of Great Britain*, September.

Evans, R. (1993) Survey of UK relocation: an affluent image problem – profile of East Kent, *Financial Times*, 28 May.

Fenton, M. (1992) Economic development strategies: preparation in a time of retrenchment, *Local Government Policy Making*, Vol. 18, no. 5, pp. 21–2.

Fife Regional Council/Fife Enterprise (1991) *A Study of the Fife Defence Industry*, October.

Finch, J. (1992) Company-led strategies in defence sector restructuring: implications for local economic development, *Local Economy*, pp. 334–46.

Fothergill, S. (1992) The new alliance of mining areas, in M. Geddes and J. Benington (eds.) *Restructuring the Local Economy*, Longman, London.

Fothergill, S. and Guy, N. (1990) *Retreat from the Regions: Corporate Change and the Closure of Factories*, Jessica Kingsley, London.

Fretter, A.D. (1993) Place marketing: a local authority perspective, in G. Kearns and C. Philo (eds) op. cit.

Goldring, H. (1993) Ports sail out of the doldrums, *Planning Week*, 23 September, pp. 14–15.

Goodwin, M. (1993) The city as commodity: the contested spaces of urban development, in G. Kearns and C. Philo (eds.), op. cit.

Gordon, I. (1988) Unstable jobs, unstable people and unstable places: the case of resort labour markets. Paper presented to the Regional Science Association/Institute of British Geographers Conference on the Geography of Labour Markets, Birkbeck College, London, July.

Greater London Council (1984) *Regional Industrial Development: Council Response to the White Paper Presented by the Secretary of State for Trade and Industry*, Industry and Employment Committee Report, IEC 1593, 14 June, London.

Harloe, M., Pickvance, C. and Urry, J. (eds.) (1990) *Place, Policy and Politics*, Unwin Hyman, London.

Harrison, R.T. and Hart, M. (eds.) (1993) *Spatial Policy in a Divided Nation*, Jessica Kingsley/Regional Studies Association, London.

Harvey, D. (1989) *The Condition of Post-Modernity: an Enquiry into the Origins of Cultural Change*, Blackwell, Oxford.

Hasluck, C. (1987) *Urban Unemployment, Local Labour Markets and Employment Initiatives*, Longman, London.

Hasluck, C. and Duffy, K. (1992) Explaining the operation of local labour markets, in M. Campbell and K. Duffy, op. cit.

Healey, M.J. (ed) (1991) *Economic Activity and Land Use: the Changing Information Base for Local and Regional Studies*, Longman, Harlow.

House of Commons (1993) Assisted Areas debate, 26 July, Hansard, CD36, pp. 751–69.

Hudson, R. and Townsend, A. (1992) Tourism employment and policy choices for local government, in P. Johnson and B. Thomas (eds.) *Perspectives on Tourism Policy*, Mansell, London.

Johannisson, B. (1990) The Nordic perspective: self-reliant local development in four Scandinavian countries, in W.B. Stohr (ed.), op. cit.

Johnson, N. and Cochrane, A. (1981) *Economic Policy Making by Local Authorities in Great Britain and West Germany*, Allen and Unwin, London.

Johnston, B. (1993) Paying the peace dividend, *Planning*, no. 1004, 5 February, pp. 12–13.

Kearns, G. and Philo, C. (eds.) (1993) *Selling Places: the City as Cultural Capital, Past and Present*, Pergamon, Oxford.

Keeble, D., Offord, J. and Walker, S. (1986) *Peripheral Regions in a Community of Twelve Member States, Final Report*, Department of Geography, University of Oxford, October.

Krippendorf, K. (1980) *Content Analysis: an Introduction to its Methodology*, Sage, London.

Lawless, P. (1994) Partnership in urban regeneration in the UK: the Sheffield Central Area Study, *Urban Studies*, Vol. 31, no. 8, pp. 1303–24.

Linneker, B.J. and Spence, N.A. (1992) An accessibility analysis of the impact of the M25 London Orbital Motorway on Britain, *Regional Studies*, Vol. 26, no. 1, pp. 31–47.

London Boroughs Association, London Training and Enterprise Councils and the Association of London Authorities (1992) *Regional Policy: Review of the Assisted Areas of Great Britain*, London Boroughs Association, London.

Lovering, J. (1993) Restructuring the British defence industrial base after the Cold War: institutional and geographical perspectives, *Defence Economics*, Vol. 4, pp. 123–39.

McCrone, G. (1969) *Regional Policy in Britain*, Unwin, London.

Martin, R. (1993a) Reviewing the economic case for regional policy, in R.T. Harrison and M. Hart (eds.) op. cit.

Martin, R. (1993b) Remapping British regional policy: the end of the north–south divide? *Regional Studies*, Vol. 27, no. 8, pp. 797–805.

Martin, R. and Townroe, P. (1992) Changing trends and pressures in regional development, in P. Townroe and R. Martin (eds.) op. cit.

Mayho, B. (1993) Restructuring in the defence industry: a local authority associations seminar, *European Information Service*, no. 136, January, pp. 28–32.

Miller, B. (1994) Political empowerment, local–central state relations, and geographically shifting political opportunity structures: strategies of the Cambridge, Massachusetts, Peace Movement, *Political Geography*, Vol. 13, no. 5, pp. 393–406.

Miller, D. (1990) The future of local economic policy: a public and private sector function, in M. Campbell (ed.), op. cit.

Murphy, L. and Sutherland, J. (1992) Unemployment, in M. Campbell and K. Duffy (eds.) op. cit.

Novy, A. (1990) Learning experiences from OECD and EC reviews of local employment initiatives, in W.B. Stohr (ed.), op. cit.

Oatley, N. (1994) Winners and losers in the regeneration game, *Planning*, 13 May, pp. 24–5.

Parsons, W. (1988) *The Political Economy of British Regional Policy*, Routledge, London.

Pattinson, M. (1993) Seaside towns cry for help, *Planning*, no. 1032, 20 August, pp. 24–5.

Phillips, A.D.M. (ed.) (1993) *The Potteries: Continuity and Change in a Staffordshire Conurbation*, Alan Sutton, Stroud.

Pickvance, C.G. (1985) Spatial policy as territorial politics: the role of spatial coalitions in the articulation of 'spatial' interests and in the demand for spatial policy, in G. Rees, J. Bujra, P. Littlewood, H. Newby and T.L. Rees (eds.) *Political Action and Social Identity: Class, Locality and Ideology*, Macmillan, London.

Pickvance, C.G. (1990a) Introduction: the institutional context of local economic development: central controls, spatial policies and local economic policies, in M. Harloe, C. Pickvance and J. Urry (eds.) op. cit.

Pickvance, C.G. (1990b) Council economic intervention and political conflict in a declining resort: Isle of Thanet, in M. Harloe, C. Pickvance and J. Urry (eds.) op. cit.

Pickvance, C.G. (1991) The difficulty of control and the ease of structural reform: British local government in the 1980s, in C.G. Pickvance and E. Preteceulle (eds.) *State Restructuring and Local Power*, Pinter, London.

Prestwich, R. and Taylor, P. (1990) *Introduction to Regional and Urban Policy in the UK*, Longman, London.

Randall, J.N. (1987) Scotland, in P.J. Damesick and P.A. Wood (eds.) op. cit.

Reed, J. (1993) Lines of defence, *Local Government Chronicle*, 9 July, pp. 10–11.

Roberts, P, Collis, C. and Noon, D. (1990) Local economic development in England and Wales: successful adaptation of old industrial areas in Sedgefield, Nottingham and Swansea, in W.B. Stohr (ed.) op. cit.

Sadler, D. (1993) Place marketing, competitive places and the construction of hegemony in Britain in the 1980s, in G. Kearns and C. Philo (eds.) op. cit.

Sheehan, M. (1993) Government financial assistance and manufacturing investment in Northern Ireland, *Regional Studies*, Vol. 27, no. 8, pp. 527–40.

Staffordshire County Council (1992) Sector study: the defence industry and armed forces, *Staffordshire Economic Monitor*, Spring, pp. 11–16.

Stewart, M. (1994) Between Whitehall and town hall: the realignment of urban regeneration policy in England, *Policy and Politics*, Vol. 22, no. 2, pp. 133–45.

Stohr, W.B. (ed) (1990) *Global Challenge and Local Response*, Mansell, London.

Syrett, S. (1994) Local power and economic policy: local authority economic initiatives in Portugal, *Regional Studies*, Vol. 28, no. 1, pp. 53–67.

Taylor, J. (1992) Regional problems and policies: an overview, in P. Townroe and R. Martin (eds.) op. cit.

Tighe, C. (1993a) Assisted status 'sought for areas hit by defence cuts', *Financial Times*, 16 July.

Tighe, C. (1993b) Sedgefield battles with surprise rivals, *Financial Times*, 22 July.

Townroe, P. and Martin, R. (eds.) (1992) *Regional Development in the 1990s: the British Isles in Transition*, Jessica Kingsley/Regional Studies Association, London.

Tye, R. and Williams, G. (1994) Urban regeneration and central–local government relations: the case of East Manchester, *Progress in Planning*, Vol. 42, pp. 1–97.

Urry, J. (1990) Conclusion: places and politics, in M. Harloe, C. Pickvance and J. Urry (eds.) op. cit.

Watson, S. (1991) Gilding the smokestacks: the new symbolic representations of deindustrialised regions, *Environment and Planning D, Society and Space*, Vol. 9, pp. 59–71.

Woodward, R. (1993) One place, two stories: two interpretations of Spitalfields in the debate over its redevelopment, in G. Kearns and C. Philo (eds.) op. cit.

Appendix 1

RESPONSES TO THE 1992/1993 ASSISTED AREAS MAP REVIEW EXERCISE

Table A.1.1   Responses to the Assisted Areas review consultation paper

Type	E	EM	SE	NE	NW	SW	WM	Y&H	Wa	Sc	N	Total
1	14	45	83	28	49	26	47	38	42	66	–	438
2	–	–	4	1	7	–	1	1	1	–	1	15
3	3	2	13	2	6	4	14	13	5	5	–	67
4	1	1	3	–	5	1	2	2	1	–	–	16
5	4	2	3	1	2	5	4	–	2	6	–	29
6	2	5	19	7	2	4	8	10	4	–	–	61
7	–	5	10	6	11	3	9	11	11	25	3	94
8	–	–	4	–	–	–	–	1	–	–	–	5
9	–	–	–	–	–	–	1	–	–	–	–	1
10	4	–	85	24	49	56	4	9	17	9	–	257
11	1	1	2	1	1	1	–	5	2	1	1	16
12	1	–	9	1	3	–	–	–	3	2	–	19
13	–	–	4	–	–	786	–	–	–	–	–	790
14	4	21	35	12	19	6	26	18	6	6	–	153
15	4	–	7	–	2	3	3	–	1	5	–	25
16	1	2	–	–	–	–	1	1	–	–	–	5
17	–	1	5	–	3	9	4	3	–	1	–	26
Total	39	85	286	83	159	904	124	112	94	127	4	2017

Key to type of respondents:
  1 = Local authorities
  2 = Local authority associations
  3 = Chambers of Commerce
  4 = Local business or small firms clubs
  5 = Trade associations
  6 = Regional development bodies (non-statutory)
  7 = Statutory agencies
  8 = Academic institutions
  9 = Academic individuals
 10 = Private sector business
 11 = Political parties
 12 = Trade unions or staff associations
 13 = Members of the public
 14 = MPs
 15 = MEPs
 16 = Members of the House of Lords
 17 = Others (local newspapers, public industry, etc.)
  N = national level submission

Table A.1.2 The regional distribution of all responses to the Assisted Areas consultation document by TTWA

Region	(a)	(b)	(c)
South East	17	32	53
West Midlands	11	21	52
East Midlands	14	27	52
East Anglia	8	28	19
South West	22	50	44
North West	22	27	82
North	15	15	100
Yorkshire and Humberside	19	28	68
Scotland	57	60	95
Wales	29	34	85
Total	214	322	67

Key:
(a) = Number of TTWAs in each region for which representations were made.
(b) = Total number of TTWAs in each region.
(c) = Column (a) as a percentage of column (b).
Source: adapted from data provided by the Department of Trade and Industry.

Table A.1.3 Local authority responses to the Assisted Areas review by locality type

Local authority locality type	(a)	(b)	(c)
London	18	33	55
Other large cities	46	48	96
Non-metropolitan districts	–	8	–
Districts with new towns	6	12	50
Resort/retirement areas	8	13	62
Coastal areas	55	74	74
Urban and mixed urban/rural areas	69	159	43
Industrial districts	34	44	77
Remoter rural areas	33	63	52
County/regional authorities	48	59	81
All	317	513	62

Key:
(a) = Local authorities that responded to the consultation document.
(b) = Total number of local authorities by locality type.
(c) = Column (a) as a percentage of column (b).
Note: Locality type is classified following the work of Champion and Townsend (1990).

Table A.1.4   Local authority responses to the Assisted Areas review by region

Region	(a)	(b)	(c)	(d)
East Anglia	7	16	23	30
Scotland	51	14	65	79
North	28	4	32	88
Wales	43	2	45	96
South West	27	25	52	52
Yorkshire and Humberside	24	4	28	86
North West	34	4	38	90
South East	45	98	143	32
East Midlands	25	20	45	56
West Midlands	33	9	42	79
All	317	196	513	62

Key:
(a) = Local authorities that responded to the consultation document.
(b) = Local authorities that did not respond to the consultation document.
(c) = (a) + (b) = all local authorities.
(d) = (a) as a percentage of (c).

Table A.1.5   Levels of direct liaison in the submissions

Region	Percentage of submissions involving some overt collusion
South East	71
Yorkshire and Humberside	67
South West	59
East Anglia	57
East Midlands	56
West Midlands	54
North West	53
North	48
Wales	26
Scotland	19
All	46

Appendix 2

SUCCESS IN THE 'BIDDING GAME'

A.2.1 Submissions as 'Bids' – Some Pointers

As we argued in Chapter 1, centrally administered spatial economic policy has moved firmly into an era of competitive bidding where available support resources are disbursed and distributed to agencies whose 'bids' are deemed, on whatever criteria may be used, to be the most pressing and effective.

With the Assisted Areas review – and notwithstanding the fact that local authorities were not required to submit and certainly did not necessarily default by not responding – we have an early example of the 'bidding game'. In other words, the review response data base allows us to evaluate the submissions as 'bids' and to make observations. It is particularly valuable to be able to draw evidence from across the full range of local authorities.

Increasingly, local authorities are attuning themselves to this 'bidding' process and much can and undoubtedly will already have been learned from the experiences of recent events such as the Assisted Areas review and, of course, City Challenge, the Objective 2 review, the Single Regeneration Budget, and the UK National Lottery processes. This is not in any way a surprise. Again, we have already noted that the escalating scale and diversity of public intervention schemes has placed an ever-greater premium on the knowledge and capacity of local authorities and others to pursue resources, either through the attempt actually to influence the creation of schemes or acquisition of powers; or through the quest to acquire special area statuses (Pickvance, 1990a, pp. 34–5).

The Assisted Areas review, and the various submissions made, offers an excellent opportunity to delve into at least some aspects of the 'bidding game'. This is important; as we have argued elsewhere in the book, the growing requirement for bidding to secure external resources is in itself creating tensions between the expected return and the outlay of resources necessary to generate a quality bid with a chance of success. This whole area raises increasing problems (see section 10.1.3).

A.2.2 Assessing the Quality of Submissions

Parts 2 and 4 of the book have generated a wide range of analyses on the quality of the submissions. However, in reality, the judgement on any individual case requires unique local analysis. Nevertheless, some generalities can be established and these may assist those 'bidding' under similar future circumstances. Our assessment falls into three stages.

Stage 1: Evidence of success as a result of the submission and any accompanying activities

A judgement on the level of success of submissions in the review outcomes is difficult to make. We know little of the internal procedures used as these have remained – understandably – confidential. Decisions were made on 'rational and logical bases' and we must assume that a full and thorough evaluation of the case for any particular area was made. Moreover, who can say what the longer-term impact of a good, well-constructed and well-produced submission might be in terms of 'getting noticed'. Of course, some places did manage to jump the queue and there may well be submission quality factors at play. However, detection, and an unequivocal statement of impact, is not possible.

What is needed is an index of changed status which can be correlated with submission quality, and level of economic problems. This has been attempted using the review response data base, and the results are set out in a complex, but nevertheless revealing tabulation (Table A.2.1).

Table A.2.1 Searching for an 'effect': submission quality, post-review status and unemployment level

Status condition of affected local authorities and unemployment level	Submission quality							
	Modest		Average		High		All	
	%	*no.	%	*no.	%	*no.	%	*no.
Non-Assisted Area status retained	19	15 4 –	68	45 21 2	13	8 5 –	100	68 30 2
Assisted Area status retained	20	8 10 7	70	21 47 19	10	– 13 –	100	29 70 26
Assisted Area status gained – the 'winners'	2	– 1 –	73	15 24 4	25	3 10 2	100	18 35 6
Assisted Area status lost – the 'losers'	15	4 – –	73	20 5 –	12	2 2 –	100	26 7 –
All affected local authorities	16	27 15 7	70	101 97 25	14	13 30 2	100	141 142 34

Note: The three absolute figures refer to different unemployment status: the top figure to low unemployment, the second figure to mid-level unemployment; and the third figure to high unemployment.

As with Table 4.3 in the main text, each submission was, although fairly crudely, classified by its quality – modest (a letter or brief document with limited production quality); average (a document setting out detailed aspects of a case but with little more than a basic assessment); high (a more sophisticated submission that sets out information on the established criteria and adds fresh perspectives and analysis, and/or offers a higher quality of overall production). In addition, each of four status conditions are included, with an additional subclassification by the level of local unemployment in July 1992 (low = 5.0–10.0 per cent; mid = 10.1–12.5 per cent; high = more than 12.5 per cent).

This tabulation allows us to assess status changes, for example, 'winners' – places that gained Assisted Area status, in the context of submission quality and unemployment level. 'Success' might be implied from some circumstances, although in most cases the figures suggest more about the motives of the authorities than about the outcomes. Taking each status condition in turn:

Non-Assisted Area status retained. Although there were some high quality submissions (bids) there were relatively few areas with high unemployment. The implication is that motives other than access to regional policy support may have guided the submission, or that impending local economic problems were highlighted. Obviously, given the retained non-Assisted status, little can be inferred about the impact of the submissions.

Assisted Area status retained. This is where the status prior to the 1992 review was retained. Unsurprisingly, there were more high unemployment authorities in this category. Only 10 per cent were high quality bids, but most of these were by authorities with mid-range unemployment levels. This implies that they were investing in quality submissions in an attempt to retain status despite improved unemployment profiles. Some success is implied.

Winners (Figure 10.3). Those authorities winning Assisted Area status at the 1992 review virtually all submitted average to high quality representations. Some had relatively low unemployment levels and the implication is therefore that other factors were significant – looming economic problems, for example. It is not possible to disentangle the various factors but, given that 25 per cent of submissions were high quality, and that around 50 per cent of these were low–mid unemployment level authorities, it is possible that submission quality had some bearing on the outcomes.

Losers (Figure 10.4). Authorities that lost their Assisted Area status at the 1992 review tended, of course, to be those with low unemployment. They were likely to have perceived themselves to be under pressure to lose status. This is reflected in the high proportion of average to high quality bids from low unemployment authorities, where status was being defended with well-resourced submissions (for example, in Bradford). The relatively high level of modest quality submissions from authorities with low to average unemployment implies that they may have missed an opportunity to 'make a mark'. Of course, some potential losers managed to retain status (as argued above).

From this tabulation we find some evidence to support a submission effect. However, it is only possible to infer an impact – other factors may well have been significant. Submissions probably were influential to a degree. It is just that, given the complex combinations of factors that may contribute to success (lobbying, etc.), or indeed failure, we cannot easily isolate the effects.

Stage 2: Submission evaluation

Evaluating the submissions is possible and likely to be productive. By comparing approaches we can generate an evaluative benchmark – in terms of scale, approach, presentation and so on. This has been completed for the key factors of unemployment (Chapter 8) and peripherality (Chapter 9) and the analysis is not repeated here. However, it is useful to make some summary comments. From the analysis of the submissions, a number of key issues emerge.

- *The cost and the benefit* – the resources invested in a submission are likely to have some bearing on the impression that it gives. There is therefore a clear implication that local authorities should explore resource opportunities, perhaps liaising with TECs or other local interests to produce a document.

- *Finding a way to get the message across* – the content is important; if a particular slant can be developed then that may assist a line of argument.

- *Myths and realities* – too much content may well be anti-productive: it is unlikely to be read.

- *The accompaniments are important* – making effective use of news media may be valuable (for example, as in Alyn and Deeside in Chapter 5), although it probably will not influence outcomes. A lobbying strategy will be worthwhile if a serious effort for a positive outcome is to be made; a submission may well be enhanced by good management of its impact (see the Thanet case in Chapter 5). However, as with the case of Bradford in Chapter 5, it may not influence the outcome.

Stage 3: Specification of best practice

Using the deliberations set out in Stage 2, we arrive at what appears to be 'best practice'.

The likelihood of a submission influencing a 'special treatment' decision is uncertain. However, if any impact is to be made the submission needs to be carefully constructed. There is a real benefit in joint submissions – they show a congruence and consensus and may carry more weight. Certainly, some of the successful bids for Assisted Area status, e.g. Furness Enterprise; Dorchester and Weymouth; Torbay; and the East Kent coastal strip, were sophisticated, quality documents that delved into the detail of the case with some vigour. Thus, best practice may involve finding a partner or partners who can supply or fund a good quality of technical expertise and add weight to a bid. A local business involvement is likely to be useful, although a simple letter of support really adds little. Submissions should be in early; and the documentation should be concisely argued in order to increase the chances of catching the attention. The documentation probably has relatively little direct, short-term influence, although it may catch the attention and it may well project and promote an image that itself has a resonance at some future stage. In other words, it may sow the seeds of success in any future bids for resources, or at least mould the impression and image that central government and others have of a particular locality.

A.2.3 Conclusions

Getting on the map is a very inexact matter. If the 1992/1993 Assisted Areas review is in any way typical, 'success' follows from a combination of fortuitious occurrences – the emergence of a local economic problem (e.g. a threatened closure of a major employer) at the 'right' time, a population level that does not bring the total included within the Assisted Areas over the limit (Southend was taken off the list of recommended areas and Wisbech, the next in line, put on, simply because the former took the population level over the limit and the latter did not). In addition, it is clear that decisions are made on what is quite flawed data – registered claimants as a surrogate for unemployment and so on. As such, a carefully constructed representation may have some value in assisting an area to get on to the map. Of course, it is difficult to judge the impact of submissions. They are all relative to each other – and, in addition, other congruent agencies may make submissions. For example, many coastal authorities submitted 'bids', but these were supplemented by submissions from groups such as the English Tourist Board (Chapter 6). Add to that the level of submission management that takes place – much of it in a clandestine form – and the chances of judging effectiveness are even more difficult.

Appendix 3
SUGGESTED LEARNING ACTIVITIES

It was argued in the book that local authorities need to learn how to confront government agencies in the quest to bid successfully for resources such as those available through spatial economic policy. Appendix 2 should provide a range of ideas about engaging with the learning process. In addition, we set out below some short training/learning activities that might be of use.

A.3.1 Submission Evaluation and Investigation

Each individual in a group should be provided with a local authority Assisted Areas review (or alternative bid document) submission. The task is to complete the following:

- Summarise the document in terms of its approach, content and quality.
- Isolate and assess the key indicators used/not used in the submission.
- Assess the position taken by the local authority in question.
- Offer an explanation for the apparent strategy used.
- Consider the implications that follow from the submission.
- Suggest a basis upon which we might assess, compare and contrast the submission with others.
- Consider the extent to which the submission might have influenced the Assisted Areas (or other alternative) decision-making process.

When these tasks have been completed, it would be useful to run a plenary session on the theme of 'local authority sensitivities to regional policy change'.

An alternative format – in the absence of submission documents – would be to set individuals the task of producing a submission/bid document. The analysis in Part 2 of the book provides a range of useful ideas.

A.3.2 Evaluating the 'Success' of Representations

In the book it has only been possible to infer a modicum of 'success' in the assessment of the review submissions (Appendix 2). A student or employee evaluation activity could be used to generate a recipient-based assessment.

The procedure would be to select some of the representations of unemployment or peripherality in Chapters 8 and 9 and to complete the following tasks:

- Identify the 'messages' that each diagram or table is seeking to transmit.
- Review the impact that such representations are likely to have.
- Consider how the effectiveness of these constructions might be most appropriately assessed.
- Generate alternative methods for presenting a similar line of argument.

The activity linked to this exercise could take the form of listing identifiable 'messages', scoring various alternatives on the basis of some pre-specified objective criteria, and in general, building similar representations in a group discussion context.

Appendix 4

SUBMISSION REFERENCES

This list includes only submissions that have been considered in detail or referenced in the book.

Allerdale Borough Council: *The Case for Workington TTWA* (and Appendices).

Alyn and Deeside District Council: Letter.

Arfon Borough Council: *Development Area Status: the Case for Arfon.*

Avon County Council; Bristol City Council; Kingswood Borough Council; North-avon District Council; Wansdyke District Council; Woodspring District Council; Avon Training and Enterprise Council: *Bristol TTWA: Case for Assisted Area Status.*

Barking and Dagenham; Hackney; Haringey; Newham; Tower Hamlets; and Waltham Forest (London Boroughs of): *The Case for the East London Area.*

Bradford (City of) Metropolitan Borough Council: *The Case for the Bradford TTWA.*

Bradford (City of) Metropolitan Borough Council: *The Case for the Keighley TTWA.*

Bradford (City of) Metropolitan Borough Council: Briefing for meeting with Minister for Industry, 29 October 1992.

Brighton Borough Council; Hove Borough Council; East Sussex County Council; The Federation of Sussex Industries and Chamber of Commerce; and Sussex Training and Enterprise Council: *The Case for Regional Assistance for Brighton and Hove.*

Calderdale Metropolitan Borough Council: *Assisted Area Status for Calderdale TTWA.*

Central Regional Council; Clackmannan District Council; Falkirk District; Stirling District Council: *Central Region – the Case for Development Area Status.*

Cheshire County Council: *Review of the Assisted Areas of Great Britain – the Case for (1) Retaining Assisted Area Status for Wirral and Chester and (2) Extending the Assisted Area Boundary to Include Crewe and Northwich TTWA.*

Chester City Council: *Retaining Assisted Area Status for Wirral and Chester TTWA.*

Clwyd County Council: *Re-building the Economy of Clwyd: a Task Unfinished.*
Touche Ross Management Consultants Assisted Areas Review: the Case for Clwyd's TTWAs.

Copeland Borough Council: *Whitehaven TTWA Submission for Development Area Status.*

Coventry City Council; Warwickshire County Council; Nuneaton and Bedworth District Council; North Warwickshire Borough Council; Rugby Borough Council; Warwick District Council; Stratford-on-Avon District Council; Coventry and Warwick TEC; and Coventry and Warwickshire Chambers of Commerce and Industry: *Rebuilding the Local Economy: the Continuing Challenge.*

Darlington Borough Council: *Darlington – the Case for Continued Assisted Area Status.*

Doncaster Metropolitan Borough Council: *Review of the Assisted Areas of Great Britain – a Submission to the Secretary of State, Trade and Industry, in Respect of Development Area Status for the Doncaster and Rotherham-Mexborough TTWA.*

Dorset County Council; West Dorset District Council; Weymouth and Portland Borough Council; and Dorset Training and Enterprise Council: *Dorchester and Weymouth TTWA: the Case for Assisted Area Status.*

Dorset County Council; West Dorset District Council; Weymouth and Portland Borough Council; and Dorset Training and Enterprise Council: *The Case for Assisted Area Status: Supplement to the Submission Relating to the Dorchester and Weymouth TTWA.*

East Kent Initiative (Kent County Council; Ashford Borough Council; Canterbury City Council; Dover District Council; Shepway District Council; Swale District Council; and Thanet District Council): *Review of Assisted Areas in Great Britain: the Case for East Kent.*

Forest of Dean District Council, Gloucester Chamber of Commerce, Gloucester County Council and Gloucestershire Training and Enterprise Council: *Submission to the Regional Director for the DTI (Southwest) for the Retention of Intermediate Development Area Status for the Cinderford and Ross-on-Wye TTWA.*

Furness Enterprise: *Development Area Status Submission: the Catalyst for an Economic Regeneration of the Barrow TTWA.*

Great Grimsby Borough Council; and Cleethorpes Borough Council: *Assisted Areas Review – the Case for the Grimsby TTWA.*

Great Yarmouth Borough Council: *A Submission for Regional Aid for the Great Yarmouth TTWA.*

Hackney (London Borough of): *Assisted Area Status for Hackney* (London Borough of Hackney).

Partnership in East London – *a Bid for Assisted Area Status* (London Boroughs of Hackney, Newham and Tower Hamlets).

The Case for East London (London Boroughs of Barking and Dagenham, Hackney, Haringey, Newham, Tower Hamlets and Waltham Forest).

Hastings Borough Council; and Rother District Council: *Hastings TTWA: Bid for Assisted Area Status.*

Isle of Wight Development Board (on behalf of the Economic Forum): *The Isle of Wight's Case for Designation as an Assisted Area.*

Lancaster City Council: *Lancaster and Morecambe TTWA: the Case for Assisted Area Status.*

Mansfield District Council: *Mansfield TTWA – a Case for Assisted Area Status.*

Nottinghamshire County Council: *Regional Assistance for Nottinghamshire.*

Portsmouth City Council; Gosport Borough Council; Fareham Borough Council; Havant Borough Council; Hampshire Training and Enterprise Council; and South East Hampshire Chamber of Commerce and Industry: *Rising to the Challenge: a Bid for Assisted Area Status*; update report, November 1992; and supplementary document – South East Hampshire Chamber of Commerce and Industry: *Rising to the Challenge: the Argument for Assisted Area Status*.

Restormel Borough Council: *The St Austell TTWA – a Submission for Assisted Area Status*.

Rotherham Metropolitan Borough Council: *Review of Assisted Areas of Great Britain: the Case for Rotherham*.

Sedgefield District Council: *Continuing the Progress – the Case for Retention of Assisted Area Status*.

Sheffield City Council; Sheffield Training and Enterprise Council; Sheffield Chamber of Commerce and Industry; and Sheffield Development Corporation: *Sheffield's Case for Development Area Status*.

Stoke-on-Trent TTWA Partners Group (Stoke-on-Trent City Council; Newcastle-under-Lyme Borough Council; North Staffordshire Chamber of Commerce and Industry; Staffordshire Moorlands District Council; Staffordshire Training and Enterprise Council): *Representations by the Partners Group for the Stoke-on-Trent TTWA*.

Strathclyde Regional Council: *Review of the Government's Regional Policy Map*.

Sunderland Metropolitan Borough Council: *DTI Assisted Area Review – City of Sunderland Response*.

Weymouth and Portland Borough Council; Purbeck District Council; Dorset County Council; and West Dorset District Council: *The Case for Assisted Area Status: Dorchester and Weymouth TTWA*, and Supplement – Weymouth and Portland.

Wigan Metropolitan Borough Council; St Helens Metropolitan Borough Council; West Lancashire District Council: *St Helens/Wigan TTWA – the Need for Continued Assisted Area Status*.

INDEX